Mediation Theory and Practice

Create scenario.

due : Tuesday : typed.

info med. has.

disputents

Mediation Theory and Practice

Suzanne McCorkle

Boise State University

Melanie J. Reese

Boise State University

Boston ■ New York ■ San Francisco
Mexico City ■ Montreal ■ Toronto ■ London ■ Madrid ■ Munich ■ Paris
Hong Kong ■ Singapore ■ Tokyo ■ Cape Town ■ Sydney

Series Editor: *Brian Wheel*
Executive Editor: *Karen Bowers*
Editorial Assistant: *Jennifer Trebby*
Marketing Manager: *Mandee Eckersley*
Editorial Production Service: *Tom Conville Publishing Services, LLC*
Manufacturing Buyer: *JoAnne Sweeney*
Cover Administrator: *Kristina Mose-Libon*
Electronic Composition: *Omegatype Typography, Inc.*

For related titles and support materials, visit our online catalog at www.ablongman.com

Between the time Website information is gathered and then published, it is not unusual for some sites to have closed. Also, the transcription of URLs can result in typographical errors. The publisher would appreciate notification where these errors occur so that they may be corrected in subsequent editions.

Library of Congress Cataloging-in-Publication Data
McCorkle, Suzanne.
    Mediation theory and practice / Suzanne McCorkle, Melanie J. Reese.
       p.   cm.
    Includes bibliographical references and index.
    ISBN 0-205-36108-0
    1. Conflict management.   2. Mediation.   I. Reese, Melanie J.   II. Title.
HM1126.M395 2005
303.6'9—dc22   2003069696

Printed in the United States of America
  10 9 8 7 6 5 4 3 2 1   09 08 07 06 05 04

BRIEF CONTENTS

CONTENTS

PREFACE

The field of mediation is growing. Likewise, the theory and research that explores mediation is expanding. This book offers both the student and practitioner an overview of the basic tenets of mediation in a variety of contexts. It provides an outline of the essential steps of mediation and a guide to explore the process through case examples. Each chapter provides discussion questions for instructors and students to explore the intricacies of the theoretical discussions and to draw insights about the mediation process. The book also serves as a useful review for individuals currently practicing as mediators as they refine their craft.

Mediation Theory and Practice provides a thorough curriculum for the undergraduate mediation course and supplemental information for graduate and conflict management courses. By blending theory with practical application, this book introduces the process of mediation while grounding the learner in informative research and theory. While no single book or class can prepare one adequately for mediation practice, this book provides a solid introduction to the ever-expanding world of mediation.

Chapter 1 explains how mediation has evolved historically and how people find their way to mediation today. Comparing mediation to other forms of dispute resolution, the reader can discern the primary benefits and disadvantages of choosing mediation. This first chapter introduces the student to the book's interest-based philosophy of conflict management.

Chapter 2 distinguishes between two approaches in mediation, the conciliation approach and the problem-solving approach. The balanced mediation model is presented as an integration of the two approaches and serves as the philosophical approach and mediation model in this book. Variables that can make a difference in mediation, such as communication interactions and structural differences, are explored.

Chapter 3 focuses on the primary skills required for mediators; for example, listening skills are essential. A variety of tactics are presented to aid mediators in validating and moving parties through the mediation process.

Intake coordination, involving interviews with the parties prior to the mediation sessions, is the subject of Chapter 4. Getting parties to the mediation table requires skills in education, information gathering, and assessment.

Chapter 5 overviews the mediator's mental preparation steps and discusses the ethical considerations that face mediators in the roles they play, their neutrality and impartiality responsibilities, and their competence for mediating in differing contexts. Additionally, Chapter 5 shows how a mediation plan is made prior to mediating based on information gathered during intake. The chapter has an additional focus of exploring the nature of conflict and exploring various causes and assessment strategies for mediators, such as mapping and metaphor analysis.

Chapters 6 through 10 explore the balanced model of mediation. Chapter 6 outlines the mediator's opening statement where the mediator sets the tone and informs the parties of important information prior to their participation in mediation. This chapter provides a sample opening statement for the reader, as well as items for consideration in creating a mediator's opening statement.

Chapter 7 introduces the readers to the storytelling and issue-identification phase of the mediation process. Symbolic interaction and attribution theories are introduced as informative about disputants' perspectives during storytelling. This chapter identifies specific mediator strategies and common pitfalls experienced by mediators.

Chapter 8 lays out the agenda phase, providing tools such as the two-way commonality statement and the general commonality statement. Readers will examine how best to formulate and communicate the agenda, as well as see how framing the agenda in neutral terms enhances the process.

The negotiation and problem-solving phase of mediation is discussed in Chapter 9. Agreements need to come from the parties, and so the negotiation phase involves fostering a cooperative environment for the parties. This chapter provides the beginning mediator techniques for fostering cooperative negotiation and informs the reader about traditional, competitive tactics used by parties. Strategies, such as fractionating apparent differences, creating contingency agreements, and using caucusing to respond to difficulties, are discussed.

Chapter 10 is a comprehensive guide to closing mediations with or without agreements. The details of agreement writing are presented, with the primary goal being able to make expectations clear, avoid confusion, reality test agreements, and make agreements behaviorally focused.

Chapter 11 explores the ever-expanding world of the mediator. It presents different models of mediation, such as the panel model and co-mediation. The chapter covers the standards of mediation practice adopted by most states, as well as areas of mediation practice and the benefits of mediation training in everyday life.

Acknowledgments

Bringing any book to completion involves many people. We thank Gwen Smith, Randall Reese, and Bayard Gregory for their insights as instructors of the basic mediation course. We are grateful to the students in the Boise State University dispute resolution program and in our mediation courses for their feedback as students on the early drafts of the book.

We are grateful for the discerning critique provided by our reviewers: Amy Bippus, California State University–Long Beach; Alice Crume, State University of New York–Brockport; Cornelia Glenn, Owensboro Community College; Rosanne Hartman, State University of New York–Geneseo; Chris Kennedy, Western Wyoming Community College; Christina Granato Yoshimura, University of Montana; and Sheryl Youngblood, Marywood University. We appreciate the work of the editors and staff at Allyn and Bacon, specifically Karon Bowers and Jennifer Trebby, who ensured that the project was successful. We thank Tom Conville for providing the copy editing and grammatical standards for the book.

Finally, we thank our family and friends for their support and tolerance as we labored on the manuscript: Heide Finnegan and Stuart King. Melanie thanks her boys, Braden and Taylor, for providing quiet (and distractions) when needed.

Mediation Theory and Practice

CHAPTER

1

Introduction to Mediation

*W*elcome to the world of mediation! You are about to engage in the study of an activity that spans many cultures and many thousands of years. Mediation, one form of alternative dispute resolution (ADR), is a process where a third party helps others manage their problems—a worthwhile activity in itself. However, mediation is more than just another alternative to the court system or an offshoot of community problem solving. For many practitioners, mediation is a philosophy of human nature, or as Kritek argues, "…the resolution of human conflicts is a moral enterprise that is the responsibility of every human" (1994, p. 17).

Individuals trained as mediators find that the skills they learn are applicable to daily communication in their personal and professional lives. People from all walks of life have become mediators—attorneys, counselors, teachers, police officers, human resource professionals, homemakers, college students, and even young children. Some who are trained have found a calling in mediation—an outlet for their lifelong goal of helping people. Others use mediation in their career path or integrate the skills into their existing vocations.

What is it about mediation that appeals to so many different kinds of people and is useful in so many different contexts? The study of mediation is about empowering people in conflict to make informed decisions that affect them, rather than having a third party (such as a judge) make a decision for them. Mediation is grounded in the belief that conflict offers an opportunity to build stronger individuals, stronger relationships, and stronger communities. As a student of mediation, you will learn the philosophies and theories that underlie mediation, as well as introductory skills any mediator must possess.

We live in a society replete with conflict. We also live in a litigious society. Every day we hear stories about someone's being sued for serving coffee that is too hot, having icy sidewalks, or failing to fulfill a promise. Although litigation has a respectable and important place in society, few argue against whether there is a better, cheaper, and quicker way to resolve some of these conflicts. As we hear about neighbors who sue each other about where they put their trash on garbage collection day and other strange tales, we wonder: "Why didn't these folks just talk it out?" In a nutshell, that is what mediation offers disputants: a chance to "talk it out" in a safe and controlled environment. In Case 1.1 we introduce you to the world of mediation through a case mediated by one of the authors.

Why Mediate?

The situation in Case 1.1 with Dana and the Klimes seems like a simple misunderstanding. However, each party is seeing only his or her own picture of reality, and in each person's view, the other is acting inappropriately. Dana has legal rights to protection from harassment from her neighbors and their dog. She has the right to involve the police and to press for justice. When the case appeared in court, the judge, who was a mediation advocate, referred the case to the community mediation program. The judge wanted to see whether they could resolve the issues together before assigning time in her already overloaded court calendar. In short, the parties in this case were ordered to mediation to work out their dispute, if possible.

Furthermore, the judge moved the case out of adjudication because she believed that the parties' interests would be served best in a place where they could explore not only the legal issues of the case, but the issues surrounding how they experienced the event. In court, the judge realized, only the legal issues would be resolved. If a judge decided the case, a neighborhood would be left in turmoil and the neighbors might be enemies forever.

*W*HAT ISSUES *in Case 1.1 fall outside the scope of the legal system? What would happen to these issues if the neighborhood misunderstanding case were to be settled in court?*

Mediation is better equipped to explore the relational and emotional issues of a dispute than usually can occur in court. Mediation is particularly appropriate when the parties will have a continued relationship, such as in the case of the Klimes and Dana. The parties met one afternoon with a mediator in what began as

CASE 1.1

A Neighborhood Misunderstanding

Dana moved from urban Chicago to a small town to be nearer to her grandmother. Prior to moving, Dana lived for 27 years in an apartment with her mom in a rather rough metropolitan neighborhood. Dana was raised to "mind your own business" and not to engage the neighbors in conflict. As she put it, "You never know who is living next to you—they could be dangerous!"

Across the street in her new neighborhood, on a cul-de-sac in a quiet subdivision of older homes, live Tommy and Mary Klimes. The older couple was retired, with a grown son who lived elsewhere in town and an elderly Boston terrier named Button. The couple didn't have a fence, but Button didn't wander much. Besides, all the neighbors knew to whom the dog belonged.

Button didn't like Dana from the first moment they saw each other, and anytime both were outside Button would bark at the new neighbor. Dana felt threatened by the dog. She also felt apprehensive about talking to the neighbors directly. So, she called the police instead. The police came, stopping first at Dana's house to get her statement and then going across the street to speak to the Klimes. The Klimes were not given the name of the person who complained about the dog, but later another neighbor told them that the police had first stopped at the "new neighbor lady's" house. Tommy, noticing Dana's car in the driveway, promptly walked across the street to introduce himself and apologize for the dog. He rang the bell and knocked, but there was no answer.

Several days later, Button barked at Dana again and came into the street as she got into her car. Again, Dana summoned the police. This time, the Klimes were issued a citation. When Dana returned home from work, the neighbors' son was outside of his parents' home and yelled obscenities at her as she walked into her house. Mr. Klimes heard the comments, came outside and admonished his son, then walked across the street to apologize to his neighbor.

However, Dana, feeling threatened, didn't answer the door. Tommy knew she was in there and peeked in the front window to see if she just didn't hear the bell. Finally giving up, he went home. A few minutes later, the police arrived for the second time that day. Dana had called reporting that her male neighbor was peeping in her windows.

---

a very tense session. The Klimes were offended at their treatment by Dana, and Dana was adamant about the righteousness of her complaints.

Through the process of mediation, Dana was able to express her beliefs and concerns about neighbors in general and, subsequently, created a way for the Klimes to understand her actions. The Klimes, not having the opportunity in the past to apologize for the dog and for their son, were allowed to express themselves and assert their desire for a friendly relationship with their new neighbor. The result of this real-world mediation was Dana's agreeing to come over to the Klimes for coffee and to get to know Button, the dog. Dana agreed—but only if she could bring some of the chocolate chip cookies that she made that morning. With a mediated agreement in hand, the court case was dismissed.

How Do People Find Their Way to Mediation?

There are many paths to mediation. Mediation can be sought by disputants, recommended by an outsider to the dispute, or mandated by a third party such as the courts. Families, communities, organizations, courts, and schools are common contexts for mediation to occur.

Family Mediation

Family mediation takes a variety of forms. For example, a mediator may facilitate negotiations with a teenage son and his mother over family rules. Family members who cannot work out the details on an estate settlement after the death of a parent can hire a mediator to assist them. Divorcing parents in most states are required or advised to use mediation to work out the parenting plan for their children prior to facing a judge in a divorce settlement.

Community Mediation

One of the early applications of mediation was in promoting community peace. Community mediation programs can be found in every state. Police who are called for neighbor disputes may refer the neighbors to a community mediation center. Neighbors who do not get along well, but would like to, may attend mediation as a way to open communication between them. Mediation can bring out concerns of citizens with police departments, transportation services, and other agencies.

Victim-Offender Mediation

A highly specialized form of mediation, victim-offender mediation, holds offenders accountable for their actions and offers a means for bringing closure for victims. Judges may refer juvenile or adult criminals to victim-offender mediation so the affected individuals can determine a restitution plan rather than simply fining or sentencing the offender—a procedure that leaves victims out of the process.

School-Based Peer Mediation

From the early grades to universities, schools have instituted mediation programs where students are trained to mediate cases involving peers. Teachers refer students who fight in the halls to a student-run peer mediation program. Dormitory roommates may be referred to a campus mediation center to work through competing study habits and social time conflicts.

Organizational Mediation

Mediation can be included as part of the normal conflict management processes in an organization. Bosses refer employees who cannot work well together to the human resources department for mediation or, if trained, conduct their own mediation interventions. A business threatened with a lawsuit by a dissatisfied customer may suggest mediation as a way to work through the difficulty. When a real estate purchase falls through, the buyer and seller can elect to mediate a fair distribution of the earnest money deposit. Government officials negotiate the creation and enforcement of rules in a process called *negotiated rule-making (neg-reg)*, where businesses, individuals, or other government entities who violate regulations meet to create a plan for future compliance (Stephenson & Pops, 1991; Van Winkle, 1997).

Other Roads to Mediation

Groups find their way to mediation in a variety of ways. Some situations involve several constituent groups who share a common decision, such as whether or not to build a nuclear power plant in their community (Susskind & Field, 1996) or how to manage the declining population of a particular species of sage grouse on public lands. Other types of mediation specialists work with faith congregations who are in conflict over management, personnel, or doctrinal issues. In the western United States, the water rights of entire river drainage systems are being negotiated through mediation and adjudication processes to determine who has first rights to scarce water resources. Internationally, mediators meet with cultural and political rivals to negotiate innumerable issues—including matters of war and peace.

Mediation offers an alternative to other forms of conflict resolution. Instead of filing a case in the courts or attempting to strong-arm an opponent into complying, mediation brings the parties together to consider their mutual options. Mediation can be seen as an alternative to systems that focus primarily on the rights of individuals and systems that rely on power to determine outcomes.

Resolving Disputes: Power, Rights, and Interests

In 1988 Ury, Brett, and Goldberg argued that conflict management approaches can be viewed from three perspectives: power, rights, and interests.

Resolving through Power

Power-based approaches to conflict can be summed up with the adage, "might makes right." Power is the ability to influence another person or a situation. In the scenario earlier in this chapter, Dana could kick the dog and thus exert her superior physical power to put the dog in his place. However, other affected parties could also exert their power. The couple's son may be stronger than Dana and have a physical power advantage. Conversely, Dana's grandmother might be quite wealthy—giving Dana monetary power to obtain a better attorney than the Klimes could afford. If Mary Klimes were the former prosecuting attorney for the city, her power resources could trump the others, as networking and influence are very powerful resources.

The power approach to conflict resolution is used widely. War, violence, and revenge are extreme examples of the power system of resolving conflicts. The consequences of the use of power may be highly detrimental to relationships (between individuals, businesses, or countries). Reliance on power to "win" leads to distrust and what Galtung (1969) referred to as negative peace: peace resulting out of forced submission, not a change of heart. As illustrated in international conflicts, such negative peace rarely is long lasting. There is some evidence that people who "lose" in disputes may resort to punitive actions of their own, often manifested on college campuses through vandalism or theft (Hebein, 1999). In Chapter 7, we will discuss how power comes into play during a mediation session and what a mediator can do to "balance" power for the disputants.

Power, however, can be appropriate in some circumstances. As a parent, it may be necessary to use physical power to control a two-year-old bent on running into a busy street. The act of forcing, or in this case grabbing the child and removing him or her from danger, is an act of power. However, reliance on power as a sole source for resolving conflicts would create a tumultuous society, one with people of low power being trampled by those in high power. Fortunately, humans have created other alternatives.

WHAT ARE the benefits of resolving disputes with power? What are the possible harms? What might be the consequence of the power approach in the neighborhood misunderstanding case?

Resolving through Rights

The second major approach to conflict resolution is derived from the science of rights, a finely tuned system developed throughout European history and adapted into the U.S. legal arena. In this approach, the rights of individuals (as laid forth in the law) are upheld as keys to fair and just resolution to conflict. In the U.S. Justice System, the rights of the individuals are outlined in the Constitution, modified by lawmakers, and interpreted by judges. The legal system offers a highly ritualized process for resolving issues that have legal merit (and for dismissing those that do not). In theory, the legal system offers access to justice for everyone. All who appear before a judge are governed by the same rules of evidence and legal criteria—regardless of race, creed, or social status. The legal system promises disputants a structured means of resolving their disputes.

However, few would argue that power is not wielded in the halls of justice. Money buys better legal representation. Those who are lacking in resources may find going to court not worth the effort, time, or expense. In one case, a couple had divorced, and then a few months later reconciled and resumed their married life (without the formality of remarrying). For six years, they lived together, sharing all expenses. They separated again and created their own custody agreement without the courts. Five years after their second separation, the ex-wife sued for back child support from the date of the original divorce eleven years earlier. The amount of money in dispute was $17,000. The cost to each party for attorneys was approximately $8,000. The case was heard over a year later, and the ex-husband prevailed; the ex-wife didn't receive any additional support. The children were the ones who suffered, however, since $16,000 was used for attorney fees that year instead of for their household. Litigation was an expensive way to resolve this dispute for the two single parents living under the poverty level.

Some disputes are inappropriate for the courts because they lack technical legal merit. A court is not the place to settle hurt feelings. Furthermore, when cases are settled in court, relationships may suffer due to the very adversarial nature of the rights-based process.

Consider the relationship of Dana and the Klimes. In the rights-based system, each would take an adversarial position to the other and attempt to convince a judge and/or jury to rule in her or his favor. While individuals may represent themselves in some courts, more often they are represented by attorneys—further removing those who have the conflict from the decision-making process. At best, one side would be deemed the "winner" while the other would be the "loser," leaving at least one party feeling unsatisfied with the outcome. At worst, the individuals will spend enormous time waiting for their day in court, spend considerable money on attorneys and fees, and the judge will make a ruling that satisfies neither party. Their future relationship would be marred by the escalation of the scenario to the courts and tainted by mistrust and anger. Possible consequences for their neighborhood include other neighbors choosing sides, continued confrontations, and creating a chasm in the neighborhood.

WHY DO you think our society requires a rights-based approach to resolving legal conflicts? What kind of conflicts would be best served through a rights-based approach? What type of cases would not be served well through a rights-based approach? Explain why.

Resolving through Interests

The third approach to conflict provides a forum for issues that do not require resolution in a legal setting. Interest-based resolution was popularized by Fisher and Ury from the Harvard Negotiation Project in their book, *Getting to Yes*. Stemming in part from their attention to basic human needs as identified by Maslow in his famous hierarchy of human needs, <u>interest-based conflict management</u> can be viewed as any process that places the interests and underlying needs of the parties in a primary role in the framing of the resolution process and permits their feelings, concerns, and needs to gain a foothold in the negotiations. The interests of the parties may include issues of power or rights, but also include the less tangible issues of respect, esteem, and feelings. Wilmot and Hocker (2001) assert that power and self-esteem are the two most prominent interests in all conflicts.

Moore (2003) divides interests into substantive, procedural, and psychological interests. *Substantive interests* relate to tangible or measurable things such as time, specific goods, money, or other resources. Two substantive issues for Dana from the case study are trespassing and the dog not being contained. *Procedural interests* arise from stylistic differences about how to communicate with each other, organize meetings, plan work, or structure rules and settlements. The Klimes wanted to meet informally with Dana and talk out the situation. However, through the process of trying to meet with her, Dana felt threatened and an informal interaction was not acceptable to her. Dana pursued legal means to resolve the dispute, but the judge had other procedural interests and sent the case to mediation. *Psychological interests* underlie all of the emotions and feelings that disputants bring to a session. The couple's confusion over Dana's behavior, their need to be seen as good and non-threatening neighbors, Dana's feelings of intimidation and her discomfort with the dog, and the desire of all parties to have a peaceful existence are psychological interests. While there are no guarantees that relationships will be improved through interest-based resolution, engaging in a process that explores the interest-driven motivations of disputants typically responds more directly to the disputants' concerns and is less damaging than adversarial approaches.

Kritek (1994) in *Negotiating at an Uneven Table* discusses how interest-based approaches may seem counter-intuitive to cultures that rely on "being right" to maintain their power. Humans, however, see the world from many vantage points and have different views of reality and what is "right." Each person's interests stem from his or her own perspective on reality. Through interest-based negotiations and the assistance of a mediator, each person has the opportunity to view the world as others see it.

When the neighborhood misunderstanding case was referred to mediation, an interest-based mediation process occurred. Through the promptings and guidance of a mediator, Dana shared her personal background, feelings of distrust, and genuine fear of the dog and strangers. The Klimes were able to have their apology heard, state their views of what it means to be good neighbors, and express their frustration that Dana would not talk to them when the conflict first occurred. Through interest-based negotiations, each party began to see the other as a partner in fixing the problem. The mediator was able to assist the neighbors in resolving the conflict. The neighbors shared phone numbers and worked out a plan for Dana to choose other alternatives than the police department when dealing with the dog.

WHAT TYPES of disputes would be inappropriate for interest-based resolution? What are the risks to the parties in this approach? What should parties consider before engaging in an interest-based approach?

The three approaches to conflict—power, rights, and interests—have their place in society. While the interest-based approach seems from the previous example to be an ideal choice for resolving disputes, each of the three approaches offers risks and advantages not met by the others. No one approach can be considered appropriate for all cases. Table 1.1 presents some advantages and disadvantages of each approach. The needs of the clients, the issues involved, the power resources of each side, as well as the concerns for the greater society should be considered in the determination of the most appropriate approach to conflict management.

TABLE 1.1 Three Perspectives on Resolving Disputes

Type of Approach	Benefits	Disadvantages
Power-based	Clear winner and loser Often expedient Violence can be avoided by threats Power resources usually easy to identify	Negative peace Lack of satisfaction by one party May lead to violence Little room for positive expression of concerns Power is tenuous and constantly under threat of being thwarted People with low power resources use what power resources they do have to be heard
Rights-based	Clear rules for engagement Specific requirements for evidence The law is the same for everyone People can be represented by attorneys Process is usually open to public scrutiny Precedents are set	Many emotional issues and interests are not allowed credence Usually expensive Usually very time consuming May require representation by attorneys Decisions are made by judges or juries Laws may prohibit creative solutions Decision making removed from the parties
Interest-based	Open to exploring emotions of parties Solutions can be unique to the parties Not limited to precedence or conventional approaches Structurally flexible as decision making stays with the parties May be more expedient than litigation May be less costly than litigation	May have little or no public scrutiny Private justice instead of public, therefore open to bias and malpractice by mediators Some may not be able to negotiate effectively and may be better served by representation No precedent set Lack of consistency in practice May deter the establishment of important precedents

The need to explore differences in safe and healthy ways while working together toward resolution is underscored by increasing diversity and the blurring of international lines as nations become more and more politically, economically, and socially globalized. As neighborhoods and businesses become more diverse in ethnicity, gender, nationalities, age, and lifestyle, it is imperative to develop channels to manage the normal differences in values, style, and goals that diversity brings. In fact, the modern mediation movement was born out of communities dealing with inner-city racial and social tensions during the turbulent 1960s. This tradition of offering skills, tools, and processes lives on in numerous community mediation programs across the United States.

Historical Roots of Alternative Dispute Resolution

The People's Court, a 1980s precursor to the now common courtroom-based television program, ended each broadcast with the announcer intoning, "Don't take the law into your own hands, take them to court!" The development of an increasingly over-burdened court system suggests the advice from *The People's Court* has been taken too much to heart. In 1999, the Administrative Office of the U.S. Courts (1999) indicated civil cases filed from 1994–1998 increased 9 percent from previous years and had a 20 percent increase in cases pending. Bankruptcy courts increased 71 percent. Part of the current explosion of mediation activity derives from the courts' search for alternatives within a litigious society and an overburdened justice system.

Alternative dispute resolution (ADR), however, is not a new concept. Alternatives to formal litigation have deep roots in many cultural traditions. In some tribal societies, community and spiritual leaders aided members to work through their problems, keeping the needs of the individuals and community in the forefront. Religious traditions (for example, Judeo-Christian, Islamic, Hindu, Buddhist, Native American, and many tribal religions) are rich with examples of mediation processes, both formal and informal, as part of the guiding principles for peaceful coexistence. Asian cultures are replete with historical practices of mediation. In the United States, mediation has a strong tradition from the early Christian peace churches (such as the Quakers and Mennonites), as well as from other cultural traditions (such as Japanese, Jewish, Native American, and Chinese). Authors such as Moore (2003) and Trachte-Huber and Huber (1996) offer a detailed summary of cultural traditions of mediation.

ADR approaches continued to weave their way into practice throughout recent history. Internationally, ADR is integral to the Permanent Court of Arbitration established at the turn of the twentieth century and was central to some of the work of the League of Nations established in 1918. According to the Permanent Court of Arbitration located in The Hague, their mission is "to meet the rapidly evolving dispute resolution needs of the international community.... The PCA administers arbitration, conciliation, and fact finding in disputes involving combinations of states, private parties and intergovernmental organizations" (Permanent Court of Arbitration, 2003).

Singer (1990) illustrates that ADR practices were part of early American commercial history, where "private channels" were set up to resolve differences between shippers, retailers, and trade associations. In 1887, the United States passed the Interstate Commerce Act advocating voluntary arbitration in resolving employee disputes with railroad companies. In 1926, Congress passed the Railway Labor Act to oversee conflicts in national transportation labor disputes and led to the 1934 National Mediation Board—giving rise to the practice of requiring mediation before airline employees are permitted to strike (Global Arbitration Mediation Association, 2000; Simkin & Fidandis, 1996). In 1947, the Federal Mediation and Conciliation Service was created to aid labor and management disputes. The Association of Family and Conciliation Courts was created in 1963 to promote court-connected family resolution options (Shailor, 1994). When the Civil Rights Act became law in 1964, the Community Relations Service was created to manage urban crises and racial disputes (Lovenheim, 1989). According to the National Center for State Courts (2003), a series of legislative acts passed by the U.S. Congress promoted ADR substantially. (See The Alternative Dispute Resolution Act of 1998 authorizing mediation in federal courts, Section 901 of Title IX authorizing mandatory and voluntary arbitration in ten district courts.) The Civil Justice Reform Act of 1990 expanded ADR into all 94 federal district (trial) courts and resulted in an increase of ADR in the court system (Stienstra, 2003).

The 1970s and 1980s brought about increased awareness and interest in ADR processes. The change in state laws to no-fault divorce catapulted family mediation into widespread national practice, with the first states adopting mandatory child-custody mediation in the 1980s (Beck, 1999). The victim-offender mediation movement began to prosper in the United States, being implemented in more than 1,200 communities by the year 2000 (Umbreit, Coates, & Roberts, 2000). Community mediation programs increased through efforts of groups like the Quakers in Philadelphia, the San Francisco Community Boards Project, and Neighborhood Justice Centers in Atlanta, Kansas City, and Los Angeles (Bailey, 2000).

Professional ADR organizations expanded or emerged during the last three decades of the twentieth century, such as the American Arbitration Association, Academy of Family Mediators, and the Society of Professionals in Dispute Resolution. The National Association for Mediation in Education was created in 1994 to serve a burgeoning number of school-based mediation programs (Girard & Koch, 1996). Today, several ADR organizations—the Academy of Family Mediators, Conflict Education Resource Network (CREnet), and the Society of Professionals in Dispute Resolutions—have merged to form one premier professional group called ACR—the Association for Conflict Resolution. Other ADR professional organizations include:

Justice Center of Atlanta (http://www.justicecenter.org/)
United States Institute of Peace (http://www.usip.org/)
Victim Offender Mediation Association (http://www.voma.org/)

National Agency for Community Mediation (http:///www.nafcm.org/)
Federal Mediation and Conciliation Service (http://www.fmcs.gov/)
American Arbitration Association (http://www.adr.org/index2.1.jsp)
Campus Mediation Clearinghouse (http://www.campus-adr.org/)
The Association for Conflict Resolution (http://acresolution.org/)

Bradley and Smith (2000) noted that a 1965 Presidential Commission on Law Enforcement and the Administration of Justice, and a similar report in 1976, highlighted the overburdened status of courts and called for reform and experimentation within the judicial system. ADR was one method used to divert cases from the courts. In the 1990s mediation continued its exponential growth. In 1990, college mediation programs existed at fewer than twenty campuses. By 2000, there were centers at over two hundred North American universities (Warters, B., 2000; Warters, W. C., 2000).

Today, mediation is practiced nationwide in an array of contexts, including family, divorce, community, business, labor, public schools, and government. To understand the mediation process, it is helpful to analyze how mediation is different from the rights-based litigation and arbitration systems.

The Dispute Resolution Continuum

Litigation

Litigation, also referred to as *adjudication*, is the process of resolving disputes through the formal court system. In litigation, disputants (either represented by attorneys or representing themselves) appear before a judge and/or jury to present their case. A case is evaluated based on legal merit and subjected to analysis via the well-defined science of rights. Litigation is a public forum (given the litigants are of legal age) and each case is weighed against existing precedent, constitutional rights, and interpretation of the law. In a jury trial, the case is presented and a judge instructs the jury of the applicable law(s) and their boundaries in making decisions. The jury returns a decision and the judge rules regarding the outcome. In the United States, disputants have the right to appeal the decision to a higher court and continue to appeal to even higher courts through several levels, finally culminating at the Supreme Court of the United States. The other approaches of dispute resolution discussed in this section are seen as alternatives to the adjudicative (or court) process.

Arbitration

In arbitration an expert third party knowledgeable in the arena of the dispute is empowered to make a decision for the disputing parties. The American Arbitration Association defines *arbitration* as "the submission of a dispute to one or more impartial persons for a final and binding decision." The parties can negotiate in advance of entering into arbitration which issues will be resolved, the type of outcome, and other procedural aspects of the process. Not unlike the judicial process, where the judge and jury hold the decision-making authority, arbitrators offer the final solution for the dispute. Arbitration requires the arbitrator to be neutral, yet informed enough to render opinions and decisions. Arbitrators typically are experts in their area of practice (such as real estate, labor, contracts, or wages). Arbitration usually is less expensive and more expedient than the traditional legal system, as well as offering more flexibility in decision making than the courts. Problems may arise from the lack of public disclosure allowed in some arbitrations.

Binding arbitration is a process where the decision rendered by the arbitrator is contractual—the parties agree in advance to accept the arbitrator's ruling. If you read the small print on common contracts for video rental or financing consumer products, you will find that you have agreed to binding arbitration of any disputes with the company when you signed the contract.

An example of binding arbitration occurred when a real estate agent had a new client walk through the door one afternoon with pictures of a house she wanted to see. The agent showed her the home and an offer was made and accepted by the seller that day. The problem was that another agent had been working for months with this client, and the pictures of the home came from the original agent. The question was, which agent should get the commission from the sale: the agent who had worked with the client the longest or the new one who closed the deal. The case was brought before a Realtor's Association Arbitration Panel to be decided. The panel, in a very formal setting, heard the case, asked questions and weighed the evidence, deciding that the agent who first showed the home would receive the commission. Once the panel had made its decision, the parties were required to abide by it. The only recourse was through appeal, and then an appeals board within the association would hear the case.

Another approach is *nonbinding arbitration*, where parties may use the ruling as a suggestion, a decision, or as information gathering in their pursuits of another resolution forum (such as proceeding to litigation). In the case of a farming dispute, a pilot of a crop-duster plane inadvertently sprayed the wrong fields and killed a half million dollar crop. Given the size of this case, the attorneys representing each side engaged in nonbinding arbitration. Hiring a retired judge, they each presented their case privately to him and asked him to make a decision on the legal merits of the case. This process enabled each side to weigh the strengths and weaknesses of their case and make a more informed decision about how to proceed in the courts. The judge in this case sided with the farmer who lost the crops. The result was an offer of settlement by the crop-dusting company to the farmer. The nonbinding arbitration succeeded in keeping the case out of a lengthy and expensive court hearing.

Med-Arb

Med-Arb (mediation-arbitration) is a hybrid process where parties agree to come together to mediate their dispute. However, they agree in advance that if they do not reach an agreement, the third party will move into an arbitrator's role and render a decision (either binding or non-binding). *Med-Arb* is defined as a process where disputants initially have control of the decision, but consent to an arbitrated settlement if an agreement is not reached during the mediation phase. In a community resolution program designed to improve relations between the community and the police department, cases are brought to an ombudsman who neither represents the city nor the community. The ombudsman may hear a complaint by a citizen alleging a police officer did not follow proper procedure in arresting her juvenile son. In a med-arb situation, the ombudsman would bring in the parties to see if a joint resolution could be reached. However, if the parties could not come to agreement during mediation, the ombudsman would render a decision. The right to appeal would be part of the process, but the ombudsman would be acting in a dual role of mediator and (binding) arbitrator. As Figure 1.1 illustrates, one primary distinction between mediation and arbitration is who controls the decision-making power.

Mediation

Mediation is a difficult term to "pin down" to a single definition. It is easier to say what mediation is not. Mediation is not any or all types of intervention by a third party. Mediation is not a third party giving advice on what to do, nor is it the forced decision making that characterizes binding arbitration.

For the purpose of this book, we define *mediation* as the process whereby a mutually acceptable third party, who is neutral and impartial, facilitates an interest-

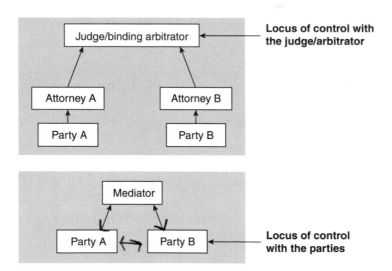

FIGURE 1.1   Locus of Decision-Making Control

based communicative process, enabling disputing parties to explore concerns and to create their own outcomes.

In the purest form of interest-based mediation, the following standards will be met:

Mutually acceptable: The mediator must be someone whom both parties agree is appropriate for the mediator role.

Neutral: The mediator must be someone who is invested in the well-being of both individuals, but does not have a preference or liking for one party over the other.

Impartial: The mediator has no stake in the outcome of the mediation and will not be affected by the decision. The mediator is free from bias toward outcomes or the parties.

Interest-based: The mediator aids disputants in identifying concerns that affect them and exploring the specific needs that must be addressed in any outcome. —needs —desires —concerns —fears

Communicative process: The mediator facilitates the discussion so parties may understand one another, explore ideas in a safe environment, and approach their problem solving as empowered participants. The mediator strategically uses his or her skills to keep the communication process balanced, fair, and productive.

Parties create their own outcome: The mediator does not suggest, lead, or persuade parties of possible outcomes to their concerns. Ideas for possible solutions arise from the parties, and the mediator helps parties to explore the usefulness of their suggestions based on their expressed interests.

Each element of the definition of mediation is necessary to create the mediation process. What would happen to the mediation if one standard was missing or changed? For each of the standards, explain how removing it would change the nature of the mediation.

Culture Clash and Mediation

The approach to mediation described in this book is a European American model. Each culture brings its own assumptions to mediation. Beer and Stief (1997) suggest that cultural differences can be detected by asking the question: "How should conflict be mediated?" Most European Americans would answer that a mediator should be an impartial and neutral stranger. Some Native American tribes and traditional Asians would prefer someone known to both parties, who cares about both of them and understands their background and values. The use of intermediaries to negotiate conflicts has a long tradition in Hawaii where an extended family member fulfills the mediator or *haku* role. Chinese culture similarly embraces elderly or known intermediaries as a means of saving face while working on conflicts. In many cultures, neutrality is not as important as a familiar person who can maintain impartiality to the outcome (Ma, 1992).

Mediators should be aware of cultural expectations and preferences, even if they are operating from a different cultural model. Although this book presents a European American approach to mediation, understanding and being open to modifying the model to embrace other cultural dynamics is important. Suggested readings in mediation and culture appear in Appendix A.

A Disclaimer about Mediation Training

The saying "a little knowledge is a dangerous thing" applies to mediation. This book will present basic theory and skills essential to any competent mediator. No single publication or training program, however, can provide all of the information, skill, and practical experience needed to be a competent practitioner. Most states or territories have standards of practice for mediators, and the information in this book covers only one portion of those standards. We encourage readers to explore the standards of practice in their own state or territory and to engage in supervised practice before striking out on their own as mediators.

How similar or different is the definition of mediation provided on the Web pages of the organizations listed in on pages 11 and 12 to the definition of mediation in this book?

MEDIATOR NOTEBOOK 1.1
Starting Your Mediator Notebook

The mediator notebook is a customized set of information, tools, and worksheets. These assignments will be items that you should keep in a notebook. Initially, a binder with removable pages is the best format for your mediator notebook materials.

The mediator notebook, when completed, will have useful information for training and actual mediation practice. Bring the mediator notebook with you each time you attend training or class.

The first assignment is to secure a three ring binder and tabs appropriate to create at least four sections within the notebook.

Summary

The process of mediation is not new. In fact, many cultures dating back thousands of years have utilized some form of mediation in maintaining the health of their societies. Mediation offers disputants opportunities to play an active part in the resolution of their own conflict, instead of relying on a third party to make a decision for them. Mediation offers an interest-based approach to resolving conflict. Other approaches to resolving disputes exist, such as rights-based approaches and power-based approaches. There are benefits and disadvantages to each type of resolution process, and all three have an important role in society. People from all walks of life practice mediation, either as a career or as part of another vocation.

Disputants come to mediation from many divergent paths. Some are referred, some are sent by other parties, and some find mediation on their own. All disputants are looking for resolution for their needs, which are categorized into substantive, procedural, and psychological interests.

Litigation, or the adjudication process, is a rights-based approach to resolving conflict. Alternative dispute resolution (ADR) offers alternatives to litigation. The three ADR approaches discussed are arbitration (binding and nonbinding), med-arb, and mediation, which differ primarily in where the locus of control lies for decision making. ADR is not a new phenomenon and has roots dating back to early civilizations. Most cultural traditions have some type of ADR process for handling conflicts. In the United States, the ADR movement was influenced by needs of business and government, as well as cultural and religious traditions. Subsequently, there are many different approaches to mediation—leading to much confusion about what mediation entails. This text covers a pure, interest-based mediation model, with roots in the European American traditions of neutrality and impartiality.

Mediators should be aware of cultural expectations of mediation and be open to adapting them into their own practice. Furthermore, people who are just beginning the study of mediation should be aware of the standards of practice in their jurisdiction. Becoming a practitioner requires much more than taking a class or reading a book.

2 The Basic Components of Mediation

Mediation is a term that encompasses a wide array of models, strategies, and outcomes. Therefore, we cannot simply offer a "mediation model" without first determining the philosophical underpinnings guiding the purpose of mediation. Before we can answer the question "How do we mediate?" we must first establish our reasons for mediating. In this chapter, we will discuss the assumptions that are embedded in choices mediators make, compare several models, and present the *balanced approach mediation model* used in this book.

The phases, steps, or processes that unfold during a mediation session typically are organized into what are termed *mediation models*. Different models of mediation are used throughout the world and vary according to their overall philosophical approach to conflict management, the emphasis given to specific

---

CASE **2.1**

The Disputed Deposit

LeMar and Tasha moved back to their home town after finishing graduate school in August. LeMar was starting a new job, Tasha was seven months pregnant, and they wanted to buy a house as soon as possible. When they rented an apartment, they signed a six-month lease, although Mishelle, the apartment manager, said it wouldn't be a problem if they moved out before the lease was up if another tenant was found to occupy the apartment. Two months into their lease, they found a home to buy in a nearby town. October was to be a busy month; the baby was due mid-month and they were closing on the house on the tenth. Tasha informed Mishelle that they had bought a home, and the apartment would be available on November 1. LeMar and Tasha stayed in the apartment until October 10, then moved to the new home. LeMar and his friends moved the belongings, although they didn't clean the apartment afterward. Tasha had the baby on the thirteenth. Two weeks later, Tasha, along with a group of her friends, went back to the apartment with the intent of cleaning it. However, they went in only to find that it had been cleaned thoroughly, top to bottom. Tasha went to the manager's office and was greeted by an angry Mishelle who said that she thought the apartment had been deserted. She said that she spent most of the last weekend cleaning it herself so that she could show the apartment. Tasha argued that she had paid rent until October 31, and since it was only now October 27, the manager shouldn't have assumed the apartment was deserted or cleaned it. Mishelle stated that she would be keeping the $400 deposit because the apartment was left in a mess. Although Tasha's first inclination was to sue for the deposit, she agreed to try mediation. Mishelle also agreed to mediate.

---

components, and the unique demands of specialized contexts. What mediation models share in common is that once a model is adopted, it becomes a prescription for what will and will not happen—what is essential and what is forbidden—during a mediation session.

Philosophical Assumptions

Every choice a mediator makes throughout the process alters the course of the mediation. Determining "why we mediate" provides a direction for those choices. There are two basic philosophical approaches to mediation: the conciliation approach and the problem-solving approach.

WHAT IS the purpose for mediating the dispute between LaMar/Tasha and Mishelle in Case 2.1?

Conciliation Approach

The goal of conciliatory mediation is to build healthy relationships, improve communication between parties, create understanding, and promote healthy communities. Bush and Folger, in their 1994 book *The Promise of Mediation*, capture the spirit of conciliation in their exploration of the goal of "transformation."

Transformation, according to Bush and Folger, is driven by the belief that every choice made by the mediator in framing the process or issues sets a stage biased by the mediator's worldview and past experiences. A major concern for Bush and Folger revolves around the mediator's "bias to settle," which they cite as a criticism to a problem-solving approach to mediation. Instead of focusing on the problems to be solved, the mediator should focus on the moral growth of the individuals.

Bush and Folger assert that with a transformation goal, mediators use skills to assist the parties in discovering their own values, empower the disputants' own inner strengths, and help each person to recognize and empathize with the other party. Mediators arrive with a mental map and list of questions to help the parties through a journey of self-discovery that may or may not lead to problem resolution. From this perspective, mediators assume that transforming and empowering individuals will lead to settlement as a natural byproduct.

WHAT MIGHT a conciliation mediation focus on in the case involving Mishelle and LaMar/Tasha? What would be a desired outcome from a conciliatory perspective?

Problem-Solving Approach

Problem-solving approaches generally assume that, regardless of the context or the people involved, mediation is about helping people resolve their substantive issues. In the process of helping people to resolve their issues, third parties who assume a problem-solving perspective *may or may not* delve into the emotional aspects that caused the conflict and *may or may not* help the individuals improve their relationship and communicative habits. A problem-solving mediator usually subscribes to a model of mediation that prescribes a more orderly and stately movement from one phase of the process to another, culminating in negotiation and settlement on the problem that brought the individuals to mediation.

WHAT SUBSTANTIVE issues exist in the case of Mishelle and LaMar/Tasha? What possible outcomes would a problem-solving approach have in this situation?

Overview of Mediation Models

Functional Models

Most mediation models are *functional*, meaning they focus on tasks that must be performed or results that must be achieved in a moderately sequential order for the mediation to be successful. At its most basic, a functional mediation model presents three or four steps with an assumption that each step requires different mediator skills and processes. For example, Domenici and Littlejohn (2001) posit a four-step model with subfunctions embedded within each step:

1. Introduction (of parties, words of encouragement, explanation of process, ask questions prior to beginning)
2. Storytelling (listening, summarizing, clarifying, reframing, reflecting, acknowledging)
3. Problem solving (defining the problem, agenda-setting, option generation)
4. Resolution (including closure) (pp. 63–98)

There are innumerable variations on the functional model of mediation. Some models are very prescriptive. Some require that a specific skill be applied at a particular point during the mediation session. For example, some models require a *caucus* where the mediator speaks with each individual separately. Other models may prohibit the mediator from bringing the parties together in the same room. Some models are designed for panels of two or three mediators. Community mediation models using volunteers with minimal training sometimes adopt a "trust the model" philosophy that involves lock-step phases proven to be effective with relatively simple cases involving neighbors. The therapeutic family mediation model includes an assessment step to detect and refer out families with violence or other issues that make child custody mediation problematic (Irving & Benjamin, 1995). Juvenile victim-offender models might include steps that change depending on the age of the offender. Public school or playground peer mediation models are simplified to fit the sophistication level of child mediators. One peer mediation model for grades 6 through 12 (Cohen, 1995) instructs the adult coordinator to select and screen the cases which are then mediated by students using a four-step model similar to Domenici's.

Adaptation of Functional Model for Cross-Cultural Mediation.   The United States Institute of Peace (2001) developed a document on conflict management training best practices in cross-cultural and international interventions. In that context, Moore identified several functions that typically occur in cross-cultural mediations:

1. Establish contact with each other directly, by written words or symbols, or through an intermediary
2. Create at least a minimally positive professional relationship
3. Identify topics to be addressed and determine how discussions will be conducted
4. Transmit both substantive information and messages about the type and strength of feelings
5. Communication about their desires, positions, or demands and possible needs and interests

6. Generate options and assess their viability
7. Seek to influence each other to obtain advantage or satisfaction
8. Create procedures and rituals for gaining final approval of agreements
9. Develop ways to implement, monitor, and ensure compliance with understandings that have been reached. (p. 14)

Functional Models in Legal Settings.   With the advent of the Internet, consultants, attorneys, training programs, and associations have weighed in with their own field-tested mediation models. Due to their accessibility, more people may read these materials than any of the previously discussed professional or scholarly models. *NoLo's Legal Encyclopedia* provides on-line information for individuals who might choose mediation over litigation in small claims or civil cases. NoLo's model includes six steps that emulate debate or courtroom practices:

1. Mediator opening statement
2. Disputant's opening statement
3. Joint discussion
4. Private caucuses
5. Joint negotiation
6. Closure

Most problem-solving models of mediation are similar in their progression from orienting the disputants to the process, getting their stories on the table, identifying the issues, and engaging in some form of negotiation.

Integrating Philosophies

Antes, Hudson, Jorgensen, and Moen (1999) concur with Bush and Folger's critique of purely problem-solving approaches, noting that mediation models that claim to have steps or stages in the process rarely have strict adherence to those stages. Many factors can affect the flow of the mediation process. For example, one party may balk at the very end of mediation, when an agreement is almost reached, because he or she has unresolved matters that were not discovered at the beginning. Other anomalies include: parties skipping stages, or approaching the "stages" or steps nonsequentially; reaching solutions without the aid of the mediator; and mediators affecting the substance of the mediation, not just the process. As Antes, Hudson, Jorgensen, and Moen contend, "good things happen even without reaching agreement" (pp. 288–291). A strict step model may prove too rigid for actual practice.

Antes, et al. (1999) suggest the *facets of mediation model* to embrace the conciliation philosophy and to correct the anomalies in a lock-step perspective. The mediator completes a set of nonsequential tasks that address several questions:

- What are we doing here?
- What is this about?
- What is important to self?
- What is important to other?
- What do we do? (p. 293)

The balanced approach mediation model we present in this book has an inherent problem-solving orientation, but one strongly influenced by the desire to engage in conciliation strategies where appropriate and one that acknowledges that mediation phases may progress in a nonlinear fashion. In order to balance both perspectives, a mediator must be aware of the many choices to be made throughout the course of a mediation and be aware of the possible consequences to the process for each choice.

Variables That Make a Difference in Mediation Models

Our analysis of the mediation models discussed above uncovered several variables that—when included or excluded—dramatically alter the flow of the mediated session and the experiences of the disputing parties. The variables and the skills introduced in this chapter will be discussed in later chapters in more depth.

Pre-Mediation or No Pre-Mediation

Some models depend on the mediator (or someone working on the mediator's behalf) establishing prior contact with the disputing parties to screen them and their issues for appropriateness to mediation and to fulfill other informational and relationship-building functions. In other models, pre-mediation or screening never occurs and the mediator starts the session cold—with no knowledge of the issues or the disputants. Pre-mediation is a standard procedure in victim-offender mediation where the comfort and safety of the victim is paramount. Some divorce and family mediators will use pre-mediation meetings to ascertain family dynamics and safety issues in high conflict situations. In the case of Mishelle and Tasha, in-depth pre-mediation probably would not be used, as the parties can be educated about the process during the initial mediation phases.

Interrupt and Process during Disputants' Opening Statements or Allow Uninterrupted Talk

Some models, such as Beer and Stief (1997) or the NoLo legal model, provide time for disputants to speak without interruption from the other party or the mediator—sometimes without limits to the length of time a person may speak! Other models assume the mediator will actively, but constructively, interrupt the disputants' speeches to validate emotions, clarify ambiguities, reduce negativity, summarize, focus on the immediate task, or divert attacks on the other party. In the case of Tasha and Mishelle, the mediator determined that Mishelle was very distrustful of Tasha and the mediation process. During the opening statement Mishelle said, "I feel like I'm being railroaded." The mediator interrupted to validate and explore that perception with Tasha. Tasha assured Mishelle that she just wanted to work out the money matters in a fair way. Once Mishelle was more comfortable, she was able to continue her opening statement without further interruption.

Allow, Require, or Forbid Private Meetings between the Mediator and the Parties

Models such as NoLo require a _caucus,_ or a private meeting, during the mediation session between the mediator and each disputant. A few models forbid a caucus. Most models present the caucus as an option that the mediator may employ strategically. Even then, how a caucus is conducted varies. Some models require that if a mediator meets with one party, then he or she must meet with the second party. Other approaches allow mediators to meet with only one party and then to return to the mediation. What is discussed in caucus in most models is considered confidential communication, although some models may allow the mediator to provide a "range of negotiated acceptability" to both parties that includes information garnered in caucus.

   In the mediation between Mishelle and Tasha, the parties reached a stalemate about the return of the deposit and the mediator acted to break the deadlock by speaking to each party in a private caucus. Tasha, without Mishelle in the room, admitted that she thought that Mishelle deserved something for her work cleaning the apartment, but believed it was wrong for her to keep the whole deposit. The mediator helped Tasha explore options without Mishelle and opened the door for Tasha to address those options when Mishelle returned.

Require an Agenda before Negotiating, Negotiate as You Go, or Slide Back and Forth from Issue Identification and Negotiation

Some models require a formal establishment of an agenda of specific issues that will be negotiated, usually after fairly lengthy information giving by each party and probing by the mediator. In these models, negotiation of issues is withheld until after the agenda is established, even if one or more of the parties make offers during opening remarks. Other models do not emphasize the establishment of a formal agenda and permit the mediator to either negotiate issues as they arise or to flow from issues identification to negotiation without an agenda.

When Tasha and Mishelle first started the mediation process, the issue was whether the deposit was to be returned or not. During discussion, Mishelle emphasized that she worked to clean the apartment for six hours, with no reimbursement from the apartment's owners. On hearing this, Tasha tossed out the comment that perhaps Mishelle should be reimbursed for her time. The mediator immediately moved to negotiate the new topic, "reimbursement," instead of continuing to focus on return of the deposit.

Consider the Parts of the Mediation as Functional Phases or as Chronological Steps

Most models present functional steps that emphasize what the mediator should accomplish during a particular portion or phase of the mediation, with an acknowledgment that the phases are not written in stone. A few models, particularly those intended for use by children or mediators with relatively little training, are extremely prescriptive in the presentation of chronological steps—even to the point of offering a manuscript of what the mediator should say at particular times during the mediation.

Approaching the mediation process as functional and not strictly chronological allows the mediator leeway in addressing concerns as they arise. For example, Mishelle and Tasha agreed that Tasha would pay Mishelle $12/hour for her work in cleaning the apartment if the full deposit was returned. During the agreement writing, Mishelle asserted that Tasha should not get the full deposit back because there were pet stains on the bedroom carpet. Tasha disagreed, so the mediator needed to step back to the storytelling phase and work through the process on this new issue before returning to agreement writing.

Focus on the Problem, the Emotions, or Balance Problems and Emotions

Some models focus almost exclusively on processes to find and negotiate the substantive issues such as, "How much is the car worth?" "What is the amount of the cleaning deposit to be returned, if any?" Conciliation models focus mostly on psychological or emotional causes of conflict, such as, "Who are the parties to each other?" "How did it feel when the neighbor ignored the request to quiet the dog?" "What affect did cheating have on the relationship?"

The relationship between Tasha and Mishelle was not ongoing, and chances are they would never see each other again. Tasha was hurt by Mishelle's withholding of the deposit. However, given that the relationship between the parties was over once this matter was resolved, the mediator chose not to spend much time addressing Tasha's hurt feelings and focused instead on the money issues. As will be addressed later, the mediator makes these strategic choices with consideration of the needs of the disputants.

Prescribe Automatic First Moves within Phases or Allow Mediator Choice

A few models contain specific opening moves within particular phases. For example, a few models say one must *brainstorm* (a problem-solving technique that will be discussed in Chapter 9) at the beginning of the negotiation or solution phase. Most models permit the mediator to select opening moves to fit the unique circumstances of each mediation. In the case of Mishelle and Tasha, the mediator chose to forego brainstorming or mutual-option generating and decided to caucus with each person privately before exploring options together.

Allowing or Prohibiting Parties to Speak to Each Other

In some models, even when the parties are in the same room, they are never allowed to speak directly to each other. In other contexts where extreme power imbalances exist, a history of violence is present, or other safety issues arise, mediators may place disputants in different rooms and shuttle back and forth between them or may conduct a mediation by phone. Most mediation models prefer face-to-face contact.

In Case 2.1, once the parties returned from the caucus, they began to talk directly to one another about what would be a fair resolution. The mediator, sensing that this was a productive conversation, chose not to redirect the parties back to her. Only when the discussion of the pet odors on the bedroom carpet became tense did the mediator enter the conversation and actively redirected the flow of discussion toward herself.

Writing and Signing or Not Signing Agreements

Agreement formats vary widely depending on the purpose of the mediation. Some agreements must follow specific formats, particularly when the agreements are to become legal documents. Other agreements serve as records of the mediated event and are for the disputants' eyes only. Agreements will be discussed in Chapter 10.

In the case of Mishelle and Tasha, the mediator wrote down the points of agreement, each party signed the agreement before closing the session, and the mediator made copies for each of the parties.

CONSIDER THE *benefits and drawbacks on Mishelle and Tasha's mediation for each of the following choices made by the mediator:*

1. Allowing uninterrupted talk from each party
2. Holding a private meeting with each party
3. Focusing mostly on the emotions of the parties
4. Not allowing parties to speak to one another during the mediation
5. Writing a formal agreement

Phases in the Balanced Mediation Model

This book presents the balanced mediation model as the best approach for beginning mediators. The balanced model contains functional phases that were selected to cover the necessary components and skills essential to entry-level mediation or for skill enhancement of practicing mediators. As the mediator enters a specific arena of mediation (victim-offender, community, business, environment, child custody, and so on), the actual model of mediation implemented may vary considerably from the balanced model presented in this book. However, the balanced model introduces the primary concepts and skills essential to most models of mediation. Chapter 3 discusses mediator competencies in more detail.

The balanced mediation model (Figure 2.1) is a *phased approach.* We assume, however, that the phases are moderately fluid and that the mediator will return in a cyclical fashion to previous phases as new information, issues, or emotional barriers emerge. In addition, the model offered is a *balanced approach,* focusing both on the emotional and on the content aspects of mediation, providing the mediator with a variety of skills and options to match the unfolding needs of each particular case. This chapter outlines the phases of the balanced model. Each aspect will be discussed in-depth in later chapters.

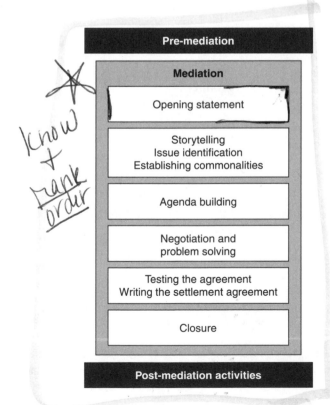

FIGURE 2.1   **Phases of the Balanced Mediation Model**

Pre-Mediation

Pre-mediation includes all activities that occur before the mediation session begins. Contact with the parties usually is desirable and often is necessary to persuade one or both parties that mediation is a good option for resolving their disagreement. While not all contexts of mediation allow for pre-mediation, mediators should be knowledgeable of, and competent in, pre-mediation activities when the need arises.

Pre-mediation serves three general purposes. First, if one party has contacted the mediator unilaterally, the mediator must approach the other party to determine her or his willingness to mediate. In other cases, an employer or a court refers both parties to mediation, and the mediator may need to contact both parties. Second, pre-mediation is a time to discover who is involved and should come to the mediation session, develop a preliminary sense of the issues, and determine the presence of power imbalances or other unique personal dynamics. Third, during pre-mediation, the mediator typically has an opportunity to educate the parties about the mediation process and to begin building his or her trustworthiness and credibility.

Activities during pre-mediation may include:

- An initial contact with one or both parties
- Intake of information about the parties and the conflict
- Gathering of documents about the conflict
- Creating a case file
- Distributing mediation forms and documents
- Screening for appropriateness of issues in comparison to the mediator's skill
- Selecting and arranging an appropriate venue for the session
- Negotiating the time and date for each session

Each aspect of pre-mediation and the skills essential to competence during pre-mediation will be discussed in Chapter 4.

CONSIDER THE benefits and drawbacks for the mediator if he or she conducted or did not conduct pre-mediation activities with Mishelle and Tasha.

Mediation Session

During the actual mediation, the mediator will lead the disputants through a series of phases. The phases are sequential in the sense that a majority of the functions of one phase must be accomplished to make success in the next phase more likely. However, it is incorrect to think of the phases as a linear, one-way, lock-step procedure. Mediators will often move back and forth across phases, as each unique mediation requires. This chapter highlights the types of functions that occur in each phase, with later chapters delving more deeply into their functions and skills.

Mediator Opening Statement.   The opening of a mediation is a time when the mediator presents information and sets the tone for the mediation. The opening statement, sometimes called the mediator monologue, fulfills several functions:

- Welcomes the parties to the mediation
- Introduces the mediator to the parties and the parties to each other
- Provides information about the mediator's credibility
- Establishes who should be at the mediation table
- Explains the nature and scope of mediation
- Explains the mediator's role
- Explains why the mediator might meet privately with each party during a mediation
- Explains neutrality and impartiality
- Explains confidentiality
- Discloses the purpose of the mediator's notes
- Establishes ground rules
- Discusses the potential time length of the mediation
- Establishes the role of outside experts
- Secures a commitment to begin
- Transitions to the storytelling and issue identification phase

The mediator's opening statement and skills for beginning a mediated session are presented in Chapter 6.

Storytelling and Issue Identification.   The name of this phase, storytelling and issue identification, is descriptive of the two simultaneous functions that occur once the disputants begin to speak. The mediator encourages disputants individually to tell their stories from their own perspective. As each disputant relates what brought her or him to mediation, the mediator will insert a series of skills (discussed in Chapters 3 and 7) to reduce any emotional barriers to settlement. At the same time, the mediator also listens to the stories for the relevant facts concerning the disputants' past relationship and the problems at hand, deducing from the facts a list of the parties' interests and issues to be negotiated. The mediator then can create a plan based on the type of issues that stand between the disputants and settlement and strategize on how to proceed during the negotiation phase.

In the case of Tasha and Mishelle, Mishelle might begin by saying, "I couldn't believe, after all I did for Tasha and LeMar, that they would treat me this way." In essence, Mishelle is pointing to the issue of respect as being more prominent (at that moment) than the money issue. A mediator would note this relational issue to explore later. If, however, both parties are disinterested in a future relationship and Tasha says, "I'm never going to see Mishelle again because I moved 50 miles away, and I just want my $400.00," then the mediator would explore the substantive issue of the deposit. Often, mediators are faced with a dual focus on both the substantive and emotional issues.

As the disputants tell their stories, the mediator also listens for what the two individuals have in common. At strategic points in the mediation, the mediator will reveal the commonalities to the disputants to create a common bond and common motivation to resolve the problem together. In the case of Tasha and Mishelle, both parties claimed that they wanted to treat each other fairly, but didn't want to be taken advantage of by the other. This commonality of purpose allowed the mediator to bring the parties to a place where they could problem solve what was "fair."

In this stage mediators also work to enable the disputants to hear each other's story and concerns and to create a level of understanding between the parties. By focusing on the interests of the disputants, mediators help parties to gain perspective from the other's point of view. Often in mediation, disputants are so caught up in their own emotions that they cannot hear the other person or even consider the other's ideas or feelings. A mediator may work to frame or present one party's story so that the other person can empathize with him or her (but always being cautious to avoid appearing to take sides). Chapter 7 details skills and mediator choices during storytelling, issue identification, and establishment of commonalities.

Agenda Building.   In the balanced mediation model we highlight setting an agenda as a separate function. While experienced mediators may be successful intermixing storytelling and issue identification with negotiation activities, novice mediators need to learn to distinguish between the skills of fact-finding and the skills of negotiation, as well as mastering how to set an agenda. Framing the goals of the session links the two disputants together as sharing the need to find a solution. For example, a mediator might say: "From what I have heard thus far, what the two of you need to find is a solution that enables Joe to have the privacy he needs at the same time that Mary, as a parent, has a way of knowing that Joe is safe and secure in the apartment at the university."

Setting the agenda entails a formal listing of the issues to be negotiated. For Tasha and Mishelle's case, the agenda could be framed: "The issues we need to address are: the process of returning deposits, the issue of giving up the apartment, the issue of landlord access to the apartment for showing it, and the issue of how the apartment was cleaned." At times, the order in which issues are negotiated becomes the first item on the negotiation list. The principles and skills in establishing an agenda are presented in Chapter 8.

Negotiating and Problem Solving.   During the negotiation and problem-solving phase, the mediator determines an order in which to address the issues, whether to treat each separately or combine them, and other strategic options. For each of the issues, communication techniques are applied to assist the parties in:

- Generating options for settlement
- Assessing options for settlement
- Making, modifying, rejecting, or accepting offers

The negotiation phase is a good example of how mediation phases are not linear. A return to storytelling and fact elaboration often is required during the negotiation phase as disputants reveal new information about the situation or hidden issues emerge. The tactical choices and skills necessary to assist disputants during negotiation are detailed in Chapter 9.

Testing and Writing Settlement Agreements or Agreeing to Disagree. If a tentative agreement is reached on each of the issues on the agenda, the mediator leads the disputants in a revision of each point in the agreement, testing for specificity and workability. Because this book presents the theory and skills of basic mediation, this essential aspect of mediation is highlighted with its own phase. Poorly written mediation agreements that disputants interpret differently can cause more damage than if mediation never occurred. For example, if roommates agree to "respect each other's time for studying," but do not determine what "respect" means for each of them, this term is open to interpretation. If Sarah wants to have a party on Friday night, Elli can say, "That isn't very respectful!" But Sarah could argue that having it on Friday instead of Sunday is very respectful. Only when the agreement is clear, unambiguous, and understood by both parties should a settlement agreement be solidified. If the disputants do not reach agreement, the mediator will move to closure without a settlement or schedule additional sessions.

A key point in the balanced approach, however, is that writing agreements is not the goal of a mediation, nor is it a measure of the mediation's success. Knowing how to assist in agreeing to disagree or in finding other avenues for resolution is as important as agreement writing. Chapter 10 presents the skills of agreement writing and closure.

Closure. Once the agreement is signed, the disputants reach an insurmountable deadlock, or the session must end for some other reason, the mediator transitions to close the session. In sessions ending in agreement, the mediator will praise the disputants for their work, make all parties a copy of the written agreement (if there is one), and inform the parties of any post-mediation actions. In mediations that do not result in settlement, the mediator will prepare the disputants for the other options that may be available to them.

Post-Mediation

After the mediation session, several actions may be required, including:

- Agreement management if the mediator or agency have responsibilities to monitor the adherence to the agreement
- Follow-up evaluation of the mediator's skillfulness or disputant satisfaction

- Typing final agreements
- Filing case files, as required by agencies or courts
- Destroying notes
- Billing the disputants for services, as appropriate
- Briefing the case with superiors or co-mediators

Summary

The theoretical assumptions a mediator holds affect how a mediation proceeds. Conciliation and problem-solving philosophies of mediation present the most striking differences. Conciliation mediation focuses primarily on building relationships and creating understanding between parties. Problem-solving mediation focuses on the process of issue resolution.

Determining "why we mediate" helps mediators make informed choices about the techniques and models they will use. An integrated model of mediation called the balanced mediation model incorporates both conciliation and a problem-solving approach. Unlike lock-step models that offer no room for adapting mediation to fit the specific situation, the phases in the balanced mediation model are more flexible. This model is the primary teaching tool to assist in mastering the key skills of mediation. The basic mediation model includes pre-mediation, mediation, and post-mediation. During the session, a mediator will proceed through an opening statement, storytelling and issue identification, establishing an agenda, negotiation and problem solving, agreement testing and writing, and closure. The next chapter presents the skills and knowledge deemed essential for entry-level mediators.

3 Essential Skills for Mediators

"What makes a good mediator?" is a question often posed by students pursuing mediation training. The mediator has many roles to play in the course of any mediation and must juggle all of the roles simultaneously. First and foremost, though, mediators are good communicators.

Mediators facilitate the process of a mediation. They ensure that the focus of the discussion stays on target and that the disputants move toward productive outcomes. Mediators listen to the disputants' stories, allow them to vent their frustrations, validate each person's worth and feelings, and provide appropriate feedback. Mediators are conduits of information. They allow parties to share information with each other and enable parties to understand each other's perspective. Mediators keep communication focused on important and relevant issues. They help disputants discover and express their own interests and goals. Mediators are links to additional expertise, data, or resources that may be required to settle a dispute. They know the services available in their community and assist the parties to determine if outside, objective data are required. Mediators are boundary keepers when they frame issues, moderate emotions, and contain the conflict within a productive range.

Mediators are adept at multitasking—simultaneously keeping an eye on the process, emotions, content, individuals, flow of information, power issues, verbal and nonverbal messages, and much more. Acquiring the fundamental tools that

CASE **3.1**

The Mistaken Grade

The dean of the College of Arts and Sciences referred a student grade appeal to the campus mediation center, hoping that the case could be resolved before it progressed to the formal grievance procedures. Both Valerie Smith, the student, and Mr. Roland Washington agreed to mediate. A student and a professor associated with the mediation center on campus co-mediated the case.

After the monologue, the mediators asked Valerie to start and to tell them what her feelings were about her grade. Valerie explained in very emotional terms that her work in the technical writing class was the same as the other students in the class, but she received a "C" when other students received an "A." She didn't want to say why she thought that was happening, but it wasn't fair. Mr. Washington, an adjunct professor from a local corporation brought in to teach the class, related that he liked Valerie and enjoyed having her in class, but she hadn't put in as much effort as the other students on the practical project and that even though her grades were good on individual projects, he didn't think she had earned an "A."

enable mediators to succeed is the first step in mastery of the art and practice of mediation. While the array of mediator skills may seem daunting, training and skill practice can build both confidence and competence.

An Overview of Mediator Skills

To some extent, the skills of entry-level, general practice mediation and advanced mediation are the same—the primary difference being the depth of accomplishment and competence in each skill area. In other ways, the skills of advanced mediators are quite different. Advanced mediators often specialize in a limited number of mediation contexts or types of client, for example: child custody, victim-offender, real estate, business, or environmental issues. Each client group and context requires specific knowledge or advanced skills that extend beyond those of entry-level, general practice mediation.

Singer (2001) describes the skills necessary for competent mediation as a blend of theory and practice. Among the general attributes mentioned by Singer are the abilities to:

- Analyze situations and alternatives
- Use persuasion
- Listen actively
- Gather information through open-ended questions
- Provide effective feedback

- Emphasize without a patronizing tone
- Create multiple options
- Master multiple strategies and techniques (p. 22)

While these are general skills that might apply to many human services professionals, mediators must adapt the skills to understand barriers to conflict management and to break through those barriers.

Picard (1998) emphasized mediators need skills and knowledge. The knowledge base of general mediators should include:

- What can and cannot be mediated
- How to obtain a commitment to mediate
- The difference between issues and interests
- The mediator's personal limitations
- The moral and legal issues in mediation
- The difference between mediation and other ADR processes
- Appropriate ground rules
- Knowledge of the topic of a case
- When and how to involve other available referral sources (p. 115)

Skill competencies noted by Picard include: listening, responding sensitively
and accurately to feelings, identifying issues, describing behavior nonjudgmen-
tally, effectively using questions, formatting the parties' agreements, managing
the mediation process, and managing power imbalances (p. 115).

*A*RE THERE *skills that can't be taught? What personal attitudes, philosophies, and
experience beneficial to mediation do you already possess? What must individuals
who want to become mediators do to learn new skills?*

Trusting and Controlling the Process

Trusting the Process

One key competency that a mediator must attend to is *process.* As discussed in
Chapter 2, the mediator must have a strong grasp of the philosophical differences
inherent in each approach to mediation. Each model or philosophical choice demands certain skill sets from the mediator. The mediation model offers the mediator direction and structure for orchestrating the session.

Trusting the process—the phases in a mediation model and its philosophical
guidelines—is imperative for mediators. Sometimes even experienced mediators
wonder if things are progressing as they should. There is a constant temptation to
jump to the end of the process by engaging in problem solving too early. Being
able to assess what stage you are in during the mediation and where it is likely to

go next helps the mediator determine if the process is on track. Trusting that parties can eventually create their own agreements without mediator input is easier to do when you know that the "process" works.

For example, in a divorce mediation where there were a significant number of issues to work through (child custody, alimony, child support, division of property, and so forth), the mediation finally was nearing completion, with only one more issue to work through—dividing up one party's 401(k) retirement plan. The mediator, growing weary of a long session, opted to voice an opinion about what the parties should do, saying that they could be done if they just split the retirement fund down the middle, 50/50. The parties said, "fine." The couple was scheduled to return the next day to pick up a draft of their agreement. Instead, both parties called to say they would not be coming as they decided they didn't like the agreement. Neither party had ownership over the agreement, thus canceling all of their hard work. In this case, the mediator lost focus on his impartiality toward the outcome and ultimately wasted the time of all parties involved. Even when you are tempted to abandon the process, remember that the process is your guide and it does work.

Sometimes, just initiating the process will resolve the problem. John and Jerome lived near each other off campus and were referred to a campus mediation center by the police, who were called because John's dog chased Jerome's daughter out of her own front yard. After the mediator presented the monologue and his understanding of the issue that brought the two students to the mediation center, John turned to Jerome and handed him a sheet of paper, saying: "Here's my phone number. The dog is supposed to be chained. It shouldn't happen again, but if it does, call me and I'll take care of it or get rid of the dog. I wouldn't want my kids threatened either." The neighbors, who had never met or spoken before, started a dialogue that improved their relationship without the mediator's assistance. While most cases are not this easy, the processes that comprise mediation are crafted carefully. Trust the process.

*M*EDIATION PURISTS *consider a mediator who offers solutions unskilled or unethical. What are the consequences to the mediation process if a mediator offers suggestions, solutions, or opinions?*

Controlling the Process

Control of the process is an instrumental skill in mediation. Control often has negative connotations, but for mediation to work, the mediator must exert control. The mediator controls the stage. The disputants retain autonomy over their own agreements.

Many experienced mediators can attest to the problems associated with having a disputant "gain control of the process" in the middle of the mediation. Once one party begins determining the direction of the mediation, the other party responds to the shift in power with defensiveness, withdrawal, or distrust of the process. The mediator is not acting as a dictator by controlling the process, but rather is like the captain who steers the "mediation" ship down a safe channel. The disputants may try to take the helm of the ship and steer it into narrow side channels, but it is the mediator's responsibility to resist and to maintain control.

Mediators also control the tone of the mediation. *Emotional contagion theory* serves to explain how a mood is established among the parties. One party's behavior influences the emotions of others, as if a mood is contagious. Hatfield, Cacioppo, and Rapson (1993) argue that understanding the nature of emotional contagion theory can aid professionals in shaping the emotional tone of a session. For mediators, recognizing the human propensity to mimic behaviors or adopt the emotional state of those around us can provide an impetus to the mediator's choices in the tone of the mediation and his or her own emotional expressiveness. It also offers a warning for mediators to be wary of unconsciously adopting the mood of disputing parties who are depressed, hopeless, or exhibiting other strong emotions. A mediator who creates a context and tone where genuine care is offered may foster similar responses in the parties.

Similar to emotional contagion theory, *communication accommodation theory* (CAT) examines how humans subconsciously regulate their own behavior to meet the communication patterns of another person. If a disputant has a slow rate of speech or uses dramatic gestures, the mediator might regulate his or her own rate of speech or size of gesture to be similar to the disputant—creating a feeling of kinship and comfort for the disputant.

Communication accommodation theory also provides a tool to analyze cultural communication among diverse groups. It is likely that a mediator will have cases where either the disputants have significant cultural differences or the mediator will have cultural differences from one or more of the disputants. Recognizing patterns of behavior when faced with cultural differences is an important skill for the mediator.

When people communicate, CAT posits that one individual's behaviors will converge, diverge, or overaccommodate to the other person. *Convergence* is a strategy where we adapt to each other's communication pattern. Our behaviors converge to a common volume, eye contact patterns, or rate of speech. When taken by both parties as sincere, convergence is perceived as thoughtful (West & Turner, 2000). *Divergence* occurs when communicators purposefully accentuate a difference in communication patterns in an effort to separate their own identity. Mediators should be aware of these patterns, especially as divergence can be a method of establishing power. Intentionally using a sophisticated vocabulary when in conflict with a person who had less opportunity for advanced education may be a divergence tactic that the mediator will need to address. Finally, *overaccommodation* occurs when one party overadapts to the other's communication style. Frequently, overaccommodation is a reaction to a perceived communicative inadequacy. People may speak more loudly when talking to an individual whose root language is different from their own, as if volume would aid in comprehension. Mediators should be alert to the CAT responses of disputants and their own communicative responses to ensure they do not overaccommodate.

Listening: A Bedrock Skill for Mediators

While mediators must master a series of skills to be successful, no skill is more essential than the ability to listen. North Americans commonly and mistakenly assume that listening is a natural activity requiring little effort or skill. *Hearing* is a physiological activity that occurs naturally when one's physical hearing organs function properly, but *listening* only occurs after the brain receives the message. Hence, people who are deaf and who can lip-read or understand American Sign Language cannot hear, but may listen well. Listening is a mental activity that requires attentiveness and energy. To be competent at listening one must understand the listening process itself, which is composed of reception of messages, attention to the message, concentration on processing the message, message interpretation, and memory (Ridge, 1993).

As Nichols observes, "listening is so basic that we take it for granted. Unfortunately, most of us think of ourselves as better listeners than we really are" (1995, p. 10). The assumption that we all are naturally good listeners simply is not true. We often tune out messages that are boring or not what we want to "hear." We are sidetracked from listening by our own thoughts or preoccupations, distractions, daydreams, or anxiety about what we will say when it is our turn to speak. We may attend only to the meaning of the words a person is saying and miss the body language that would help us interpret the full intention.

Listening is a mental process of attending and co-creating meaning from what another is saying. As Van Slyke (1999) notes, listening is not just about the words, "…*listening* can be defined as the process of becoming aware of all the cues that another party emits…. It is the act of attending to what another person is saying and what he or she is not saying" (pp. 98–99).

Types of Listening

Several types of listening are identified by communication scholars: *listening for comprehension* (to understand what is said), *empathic listening* (supporting and helping the speaker to talk through his or her own problem and feelings), *critical listening* (evaluating what is said), and *appreciative listening* (listening for enjoyment) (Wolvin & Coakley, 1993). A competent mediator is adept at empathic listening, listening for comprehension, and critical listening. Each phase of the mediation process requires more focus on one type of listening than on other types of listening. For example, empathic listening is essential to the initial storytelling phase, and critical listening is vital to the negotiation and settlement writing aspects of a case. In mediation, as in all listening contexts, a "skillful listener is one who comprehends the context of the listening instance, produces from his or her repertoire a plan or strategy for selection of the appropriate skills, and executes those chosen skills" (Ridge, 1993, p. 4).

İn case 2.1, the disputed rental deposit, what types of listening would the mediator use? Is the proportion of time spent on each type of listening different for conciliatory and problem-solving approaches? Are the same types of listening skills required in Case 3.1?

Variables That Affect Listening

Research in the 1980s indicated there might be a difference in the listening skills of North American men and women, with men less adept at listening and less attuned to the nonverbal nuances that enable one to interpret the complexities of human communication (see the discussion in Borisoff & Merrill, 1991). Another study found females adopting a people-oriented style of listening with a focus on emotions and personal stories and men a more action-oriented style of listening with attention to concise presentations of facts (Johnston, Weaver, Watson, & Barker, 2000). Johnson, et al. (2000) also found that individuals with a *communal cognitive structure* (featuring openness, caring, kindness, helpfulness, and similar characteristics) preferred people-oriented styles of listening, whereas persons with an *agency cognitive structure* (focused on *agency* and goal-orientation, assertiveness, self-protection, and mastery) preferred an action, content, or time-oriented listening style.

Whether or not biological sex or gender identity affects one's listening style, adeptness at listening *is* intricately involved in the mediation process in several ways. First, sometimes one or both disputants are poor listeners. The inability to listen beyond the surface message or to deduce the underlying connotative implications of messages can prevent individuals from managing their own conflicts. Second, emotional involvement or personal identification with an issue can prevent disputants from being able to work effectively with those who disagree with them. Finally, each mediator must discover his or her own listening weaknesses, styles, and preferences, and master a variety of listening skills.

Internal Listening Barriers

Internal Preoccupation: Using the gap between speaking (125–250 words per minute) and comprehending (500 words per minute) for topics other than the one at hand, such as thinking about your own personal difficulties instead of focusing entirely on the disputant.

Self-involvement: Focusing on one's own role and how one appears instead of focusing on the needs of the disputants.

Selective attention: Assuming we know what the disputant is going to say or assuming repetition of a topic or concern is not important.

Listening with an agenda: Listen for facts that will fit one's preconceived ideas about the case or its resolution.

External Listening Barriers

External distractions: Letting background noise, setting, or other distractions catch the mediator's or the other disputant's attention.

Communication style: Focusing on the accent, grammar, or other stylistic features of speech instead of the speaker's meaning and intentions.

Preconceptions: Past interactions with the disputant, including first impressions, contaminate how the mediator interprets messages, so the meaning is misinterpreted by the mediator.

Constituencies: Assuming the disputant will think or behave in particular ways because of groups he or she affiliates with. (Adapted in part from Van Slyke, 1999, pp. 114–119)

The mediator must be a highly skilled listener who uncovers the hidden issues important to the disputants, as well as a skilled communicator who creates an environment where disputants can begin to listen to each other. Barker, Johnson, and Watson (1991) comment, "Because of the stress associated with conflict, appropriate listening behavior may be especially difficult, but it is central to conflict management" (pp. 142–143). Van Slyke (1999) presents an excellent explanation of why listening is the preeminent variable to settlement of conflicts: "The problem in conflict, however, is not whether the other party listens to us, but rather whether we listen to and understand the other party's perspective. Only after we have listened to the other party will that party want to listen to us. Only after the other party feels understood will he or she want to understand and be influenced by us" (p. ix).

Often, the stress and emotion in a conflict situation seem to promote a defensive reaction. Conflict management scholars utilize Gibb's 1961 introduction of the concept of supportive and defensive communication to explain the destructive communication cycles and nonlistening behaviors that manifest during interpersonal conflicts. Gibb posited that certain types of communication behaviors create *supportive climates* where individuals feel trust, openness, and cooperation. Other communication behaviors lead to *defensive climates* where individuals feel threatened, wary, and combative. Compare the behaviors that invite supportiveness to those that encourage defensiveness:

Supportive Climate	*Defensive Climate*
Admitting one's own responsibilites	Blaming others
Stating issues clearly	Speaking vaguely or in generalities
Being sensitive to word choices that stereotype, offend, or trigger negative effect in the other person	Speaking only for oneself or to provoke the other
Avoiding threatening statements, hostile joking, hostile questions, and sarcasm	Using threats, hostile joking, hostile questions, and sarcasm
Acknowledging the opinions of both parties	Focusing on one's own solution
Identifying the problem in mutual terms	Identifying solution in one's own self-interest
Proposing solutions that meet both people's needs	Proposing solutions that are in one's own self-interest
Brainstorming or searching for new, mutual solutions	Sticking only to one's own preferred solution
Avoiding negative criticism of the other person or their ideas	Criticizing everything the other person wants
Trying to understand the other's perspective	Not caring about the other's perspective
Searching for ways to achieve equity or balance	Acting superior or trying to control the relationship or the negotiation
Being responsive to the other's ideas, even when one disagrees	Ignoring, trivializing, silencing, interrupting, blaming, or changing the topic when the other speaks
Being responsible for one's own portion of the conflict	Blaming, denying, or judging the other
Avoiding personal attacks and sarcasm	Attacking the other's integrity, values, or beliefs (Adapted from Borisoff and Victor [1989], pp. 29–57).

The inability of disputants to assume supportive postures keeps them from regulating their own difficulties and solving their own problems. It is the mediator's job to control the communicative interactions and, if possible, assist in transporting the disputants who arrive with a hostile and defensive cloud hovering over them to a better, interactive climate. Ideally, the mediator can assist in beginning changes that permit a more supportive communication pattern for the individuals and a climate conducive to mutual problem solving.

Whether disputants arrive in a defensive posture that must be moderated by the mediator or arrive in a conciliatory mood, mediators are required to listen to the disputants. Mediators also need the disputants to be able to listen to each other. Listening—either to the other party or to the mediator—is the only way disputants can understand what is driving the conflict. Listening is the only way for the mediator to understand and address what is keeping the parties from being able to settle their conflict. Listening is the most basic mediator skill and was mentioned as critical by virtually all of the practitioners interviewed in a study by Isenhart and Spangle (2000, p. 215).   *potential* T/F

CHANGING A climate from defensive to supportive takes more than just being a good listener. Discuss how each of the following variables can affect the climate of the mediation: environment, seating, clothing choices, timing, professionalism, level of formality, speaking tone, and topics of conversation. Offer other variables that may affect the climate of the mediation.

Skills for Listening to Emotion, Relationship, and Content

The mediator uses a variety of listening skills to cut through defensiveness and uncover the information that can lead to settlement. The mediator listens for three levels of meaning in the disputants' messages: What emotions are expressed? What is the implied relationship between the disputants? What is the factual content of the case? To manage the emotion, relationship, and content, the mediator applies a variety of listening skills. The dialogue between Sidney and Gino illustrates the three levels of meaning inherent in any message:

CONTENT: Sidney noticed a smelly odor coming from the cat box.

EMOTION: Sidney is frustrated and disappointed. Gino hasn't cleaned the cat box, and she is worried about being embarrassed when Gino's mother and father arrive for dinner that night.

RELATIONSHIP: Sidney doesn't feel she can tell Gino directly to clean the cat box. Their communication patterns with one another have defined direct requests as nagging. So, she hints about her discomfort in an effort to persuade him to clean the cat box.

Mediators listen to a message to determine which level must be considered as the most important. The mediator's listening responses are aimed to encourage speakers, validate, clarify, and make messages more palatable to the other party.

The mediator's toolbox contains different types of listening skills that can be used separately or together to achieve the desired outcomes. Among these skills are empathic listening, validation, paraphrasing feelings, reframing, and pure-content paraphrasing. This chapter introduces an array of listening skills for mediators and will integrate them into the phases of the balanced mediation model throughout the book.

Empathic Listening. Empathic listening is important to building trust and confidence. *Empathic listening* is listening for understanding with the goal of reflecting the perspective of the other party without evaluation. Binder, Bergman, and Price (1996) observe that individuals rarely have an opportunity to talk to someone who will not judge them or give advice—an apt description of a mediator. When empathic or nonjudgmental listening occurs, "most people are strongly motivated to continue communicating. Almost without realizing it, people will tend to provide an ever-increasing amount of information" (Binder, Bergman, & Price, 1996). In addition to building trust in the mediator, empathic listening elicits the disclosure of personal information that often is unknown to the other disputant.

In Case 3.1, a mediator might show empathy for both parties by listening intently, giving full attention to each person as he and she speaks, and providing appropriate, nonverbal feedback.

Validation. *Validation* is a general strategy of empathic listening accompanied by acknowledgment of the disputants' concerns or feelings. Disputants come into the mediation session with needs for validation. Parties may be frustrated because they believe that no one listens to them and that no one understands their concerns. They may feel ignored, disrespected, or victimized. Disputants may exhibit one emotion, such as anger, that is masking an underlying hurt or fear that is the real barrier to resolving the conflict.

A major role of the mediator is to create a place where parties can be heard and understood—to be validated. Ideally, the mediator would orchestrate each party's understanding of the other party. At the very least, parties must believe that the mediator has heard and understood their perspectives, emotions, and issues. In Case 3.1, Mr. Washington could be validated simply by repeating his statement, "So, you liked having Ms. Smith in your class." The mediator could show empathy to Ms. Smith by saying, "It must have been difficult for you, opening your grade report and seeing a grade you didn't expect." Validation also may be accomplished through the use of other listening skills, such as feeling paraphrasing.

Paraphrasing Feelings. *Paraphrasing feelings* is a subset of empathic listening. When listening empathically, one focuses on the feeling rather than on the content of what is being said. In fact, sometimes the feelings are, at that moment in time, the most important aspect of what a disputant is communicating. A disputant may angrily say: "I can't believe I had to learn from another customer that Joe was complaining all over the neighborhood about my business, but never talked to me!" The "heat" behind the statement begs for some empathic acknowledgment. A simple validation of the disputant's feelings ("So you were bothered by that") sometimes goes a long way to build trust and to identify a potential emotional blockage to settlement. Emotional paraphrases that validate the legitimacy of feelings also have a calming effect that functions to decrease the amount of time and energy that a disputant might otherwise put into reliving the same emotional outbursts. Conversely, when the disputants are not emotional or are not using emotional language, paraphrasing feelings will sound—and be—contrived.

ACTIVITY **3.1**

The Skill of Paraphrasing Feelings

Purpose: To validate the emotions while a disputant is venting and to uncover emotional blockages to settlement.

Useful When: The disputant is visibly emotional, upset, or using emotional language such as "I am angry." You may need to use an emotional paraphrase three to four times before a visible lessening of high emotion will occur.

Process:

1. Ignore all substantive content of the comment for the moment.
2. Focus on the emotional words or tone underlying the comment.
3. Interrupt and give the three- to six-word emotional paraphrase over the top of the disputant's comments.
4. Stop talking and listen. If the disputant says, "Yes," or nods and continues, the emotional paraphrase or validation was on target. If the disputant says, "No, I'm not _____, I'm _____," the validation was slightly off. In that case, simply repeat what the disputant just said, "Oh, so you're _____."
5. Stop talking and let the disputant continue relating her or his information.

Examples of Emotional Paraphrasing: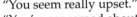

"You seem really upset."
"You're concerned about [the general issue]."
"It sounds like you were frustrated."
"You seem to really care about [a place, a principle, a value]."

While some sources (for example, Domenici, 1996, p. 54) give a list of words to describe emotions to use for validations, each mediator should develop a repertoire of descriptions that he or she can use comfortably while mastering the skill.

Emotionally paraphrase the following comments:

1. "I am so mad. I hate it when she uses the copy machine and then just leaves when it runs out of paper...."
2. "John is just a pit bull. He roars into the meeting and wants to have everything his own way. He just can't let go of his own ideas...."

How they feel ; what would they like to see

(EP) (R)

resaying in your words

Another benefit of emotional paraphrasing is that, along with validating the disputants and helping them identify the feelings behind their comments, feeling paraphrases "humanize" the parties to one another. In conflict, disputants see only their own emotional frustration and rarely consider the feelings and frustrations of the other party. Through feeling paraphrases, the mediator simultaneously validates one party while exposing the second party to the emotions and frustrations of the first party. The mediator's emotional paraphrasing fosters an opportunity for empathy to grow between the disputing parties.

Reframing. The term *reframing* encompasses a series of tools and an outcome. A mediator applies reframing to make information more usable in the mediation, while still affirming the general intent of the parties. For example, reframing is a listening skill that validates the general interest of one disputant without confirming his or her tone, position, or slanted perspectives of the facts. Reframing also can be used to identify a general content issue.

taking sting out

After listening to a complaint, the mediator generalizes the disputant's concern without validating any stated positions or proposed solutions. If the disputant says: "He has to clean up his trashy yard or move out of the neighborhood, or else I'm going to have my attorney file a suit," the mediator would offer a reframe of

---

MEDIATOR NOTEBOOK 3.1
Emotional Paraphrases

Every mediator needs a list of emotional paraphrases that she or he is comfortable saying. As you read the textbook, listen to sample mediations, or think about emotional paraphrasing, create a list of emotional paraphrases that will work for you. For example, some individuals could say, "Gosh, you seem really upset." Others might find "gosh" a silly word that won't work for them or their clients.

Start a page in your mediator notebook labeled: "Emotional Paraphrases I Can Use." In the top half of the page, create a section called "My Emotional Paraphrases" with space for ten different emotional paraphrase introductions. An emotional paraphrase introduction is a phrase that you could fill in with a word that describes an emotion or a feeling. For example, "You sound _____." By the end of your mediation training, or by the time you finish the book, record ten emotional paraphrase introductions.

Describe emotions

On the bottom half of the same page, create a section called "Emotion Words." Create space for ten words that describe emotional states that you could use. For example, some people could use the word "hurt," while others might prefer a more general word such as "concerned."

the general concern and delete the threat and the positional demand. For example, the mediator might respond: "You like a neat yard" or "You're concerned about how the neighborhood looks." After reframing a comment, be sure to listen for confirmation. If the disputant says "No," listen again to better understand the general interest and reframe again.

The theoretical concept behind reframing assumes that each disputant paints a canvas representing her or his own view of reality and favored outcome—in the example earlier in this section, cleaning up the yard or suing are one disputant's solutions. Communication scholars know that language is ambiguous. What is a "trashy yard" to one person may be a "work in progress" to another. Even if the appearance of the yard is less than desirable, there may be numerous other alternatives that would suit both neighbors than the two initially mentioned. For example, they may ultimately decide to build a tall, sturdy fence. By reframing the general concern rather than repeating any of the specific solutions or allegations, the mediator transforms the frame through which the disputants view the conflict.

ACTIVITY **3.2**

Reframe the following:

1. Role play the scenario in Case 3.1. How would you reframe the interests of Ms. Smith or Mr. Washington?
2. Role play the scenario in Case 1.1. The individual playing the mediator should reframe Dana and her neighbors' interests, rather than repeating their statements of frustration.

Reframing offers an important tool for the mediator to mitigate the harm that occurs when disputants engage in destructive or defensive communication. In conflict, disputants have a tendency to blame others, rely on stereotypes, make faulty attributions about the other party's behaviors or motivations, and say things that are not productive. Reframing allows the mediator to take what is valuable from a statement while reducing the "sting" of inflammatory words. For example, during a mediation with a middle-aged male landlord and a twenty-year-old female tenant, the landlord bluntly told the mediator, "Kids these days are so irresponsible, and this girl is no exception. She poured it on with honey on how good she'd be even though she didn't have any references. Then she trashed the apartment. You can't trust them!" Imagine being the young woman hearing those comments. Most likely, you would feel defensive or embarrassed. In response, she retorted, "If you weren't such a slumlord, you wouldn't have these problems."

Both parties are sharing valuable information about their perspectives, but not in a frame that the other party will be able to accept. She's hurt; he's angry. If the mediator does not intervene quickly to reframe the message, the process could deteriorate. In this case, the mediator combined the skills of validation, feeling paraphrasing, and reframing to meet the goal of directing the process back on track and moderating the emotional climate. The mediator said, "As a property owner, you're disappointed with the way the apartment was left and want to discuss the damages. Being respected is important to both of you, although neither of you are feeling respected right now." Then, the mediator refocused the session on the substantive issue by asking, "Could one of you tell me more about the agreement you had?"

Pure-Content Paraphrasing. Pure-content paraphrasing is a familiar skill for many people. In *pure-content paraphrasing,* the mediator summarizes in his or her own words the essence of the facts that a disputant relates. Pure-content paraphrasing is best applied when the disputants are calm and are relating the specific factual details surrounding an issue. Mediators often will paraphrase facts regarding what a typical day is like in someone's work routine, how houses are related spatially to one another, or the proposed schedule for repayment of a business debt.

Content paraphrasing can be particularly useful when keeping track of many details. For example, one disputant presented the following information: "I had several estimates done on the car. One guy said he could fix the fender for $200, but painting it would be another $250. The other guy said he could do it all for $500, and fix the busted taillight, too. The last guy was sky high and said it would take $900 to fix everything."

A content paraphrase summarizes the facts of the statement, highlighting important details without parroting every word. The mediator could say: "So the range of estimates to fix the car was between $450 and $900." Content paraphrasing is an important tool in verifying important information and clarifying facts.

Content paraphrasing can be destructive when applied to emotional statements or facts presented in one disputant's slanted self-interest. It is not productive to content paraphrase the statement, "I really hate Joe," by saying, "Oh, so you hate Joe." Content paraphrasing at the wrong time can validate one person's slanted view of reality, to the detriment of the other party. Generally, mediators avoid paraphrasing a disputant's *position.* Offering a paraphrase of the *underlying interest* reframes the position into something more open to negotiation.

How can we determine which level of a message (emotional, relational, or content) is most critical for mediators to validate (if validation is warranted)? What dangers are there to a mediator focusing on the "wrong" level?

Listening to Nonverbal Communication

The skilled mediator listens to more than just the words a disputant utters. Mediators also listen with their other senses to detect the underlying tone of the words, contradictions between words and body, and shifts in attitude toward the other party. A mediator may perceive that a person is hurt or angry not from the denotative meaning of the words, but from the tone of voice that utters the words. Looking at the other disputant directly and saying, "I've always enjoyed the music from your parties," conveys a message where the words and the nonverbal meaning match. Glaring at the other disputant and saying with a sarcastic tone, "I've always *enjoyed* the *music* from your parties," conveys quite a different meaning.

Mediators also "listen" with their eyes to the nonverbal communication of disputants to gauge when they are ready to begin negotiating in good faith. Disputants who are angry may sit with their bodies slightly turned away from each other. When they shift in their seats to a more direct orientation, it may mean they have shifted their perceptions and are now more open to negotiation.

Because nonverbal communication is ambiguous and open to many interpretations, mediators should check their perceptions through emotional paraphrasing or asking questions. If one party "looks" surprised at the information the other is relating, the mediator might say, "You seem surprised by that remark. Is this new information for you?"

Nonverbal communication is a separate area of research. Many institutions offer specialized classes in nonverbal communication and we encourage mediators to learn more about this important communication channel.

Listening Interculturally

In cases where one or more disputants or the mediator come from different cultural backgrounds, the mediator must adopt a heightened listening sensitivity to detect potential areas for miscommunication. For example, if one disputant's culture or faith believes that events are fated to occur and the other disputant believes in personal control over one's own destiny, statements such as "our car accident was fated to be" could be inaccurately perceived by one party as a ploy to avoid responsibility. In some cultures, it is impolite to say "no" and to save face, disputants will say "yes" to an agreement they have no intention of fulfilling. Not looking directly at a person of higher status, such as the mediator, could be perceived as avoidance or nonconstructive behavior by a mediator focused on his or her own cultural norms.

We encourage mediators to learn more about culture and intercultural communication and have included some sources in Appendix A to start the exploration. A culturally competent mediator must learn about the culture of the populations he or she works with and go beyond superficial self-knowledge to understand one's own culture and the cultures of others (Sockalingam & Williams, 2002).

The Mediator's Role as a Listener

In summary, mediators have a multitude of roles they must manage in the area of listening. Mediators must:

- Validate the emotions of the parties
- Help the parties explore, understand, and articulate their interests
- Clarify important information
- Determine what type of issue needs attention, such as the emotion, the relationship, or the content (or all three at once)
- Summarize without reducing the concerns of the parties
- Help parties create a common story that integrates their unique perspective
- Address power imbalances by encouraging the lower party's participation
- Make sure that both (or all) parties have access to problem solving and decision making
- Recognize messages sent nonverbally, as well as verbally, and respond to them effectively
- Gain the commitment of parties and keep that commitment until the closure of the mediation

Clarifying and Asking Questions: Bedrock Skills for Mediators

The simple question is not so simple in mediation. The mediator should understand the functions of different types of questions and develop a repertoire of question types to formulate the right strategic question at the right moment during the mediation process.

Open versus Closed Questions

Open questions do not have an exact answer. "What is your house like?" is an *open question* to elicit whatever information the disputant chooses to be important. "Does your house have a basement?" or "How many people live in your home?" are *closed questions* that require a specific piece of information as the answer. Open questions suggest a topic of response but do not require a specific item of information. The more "open" the question, the more choice the disputant has in answering.

Generally, open questions should be used *before* closed questions. Open questions elicit a broad sweep of information about the mediation context and the needs of the disputants. The broadest of open questions can be used to open the storytelling phase of a mediation, such as, "What brought you here today?" When a mediator uses too many closed questions early in the mediation process, the choice of questions by the mediator may "fix" the issues in the disputants' minds in a different way than might have emerged otherwise. Additionally, disputants may feel they are being interrogated, which might reduce trust and confidence in the mediator. Finally, closed questions may, in the words of Binder, Bergman, and Price (1996), cause the mediator to "miss both the trees and the forest" (p. 56). By focusing too soon on the details, the mediator may miss some of the issues that are important to the disputants. Closed questions are useful to verify the mediator's

> ## MEDIATOR NOTEBOOK 3.2
> ### What's the Question?
>
> Asking open-ended questions is a skill. As you read the text and listen to other mediators, be alert for good open-ended questions that apply to many types of mediations. Create a page in your mediator's notebook called "Open-Ended Questions." Create space for at least ten open-ended questions. Each time you hear a good example of an open-ended question, record it in your notebook.

understanding of a disputant's interests or issues, to probe for facts, or to test an agreement.

QUESTIONS THAT begin with "why" often lead to feelings of defensiveness in the party being queried. Offer possible reasons for this phenomenon.

Ethical Issues and Listening

While listening is an essential skill for mediators, the application of listening skills within a mediation does more than just guide the mediation. The skills discussed in this chapter function to alter the perception of the conflict in the minds of the disputants. In fact, some skills are intentionally designed to create perception changes because the conflict must be *transformed* if the disputants are to have the opportunity to alter their relationship or solve their problem. However, the application of active listening skills inherently includes more subtle transformations that may not be consciously intended by the mediator.

Phillips (1999) notes that "active listening plays an important role in building or sculpting meanings, ideas, insights, and solutions between people, none of which would have been generated individually" (p. 179). How a story unfolds during a mediation and how the individuals develop their narrative (jointly or individually) about the conflict is guided by the mediator's paraphrasing and reframing—by what the mediator chooses to select or ignore, by whether the mediator chooses to solicit elaboration statements or discourage elaboration, and by the words selected in the mediator's paraphrases, reframes, or other reformulations. In particular, Phillips (1999) discusses the inequities that can occur when a mediator uses listening and questioning skills differently with each disputant—perhaps as a result of some unconscious bias toward one of the disputants. For example, a mediator may encourage one disputant's perspective merely by using *open reformulations* that encourage more elaboration of a comment ("Oh, so you are saying you'd like more cooperation. Tell me more.") and minimize the other disputant's perspective through the use of *closed reformulations*—a paraphrase immediately followed by a topic shift or a shift to the other disputant ("Oh, so you are saying, you'd like more cooperation. I'd like to go back to another issue you raised earlier about..."). The result of the inequitable treatment could be a framing of the stories and issues that subtly advantage one disputant over the other. As the mediator masters listening and questioning skills, it is important also to learn consistent and fair application of the skills, as well as an awareness of the potential strengths and weaknesses of one's own preferred communicative style.

EXPLAIN HOW actively listening to disputants can affect the course of the mediation. What should mediators do to be ethical in their listening endeavors?

Summary

Mediators must acquire a variety of skills and assume numerous roles. All mediators must have both knowledge and skill competencies. Mediators must understand and trust the processes in the model they are implementing and learn to control the flow of a mediation. Emotional contagion theory and communication accommodation theory help explain disputant and mediator behaviors that may affect the session. Mediators should be aware of diversity issues and be vigilant to avoid overaccommodation.

Listening is foremost among mediator skills. Three types of listening are applied in mediation: comprehension, empathic, and critical. Mediator listening skills include empathic listening, validation, paraphrasing feelings, reframing, and pure-content paraphrasing. Mediators also "listen" to nonverbal messages and cultural context. Supportive and defensive climates deeply affect listening behaviors.

Asking appropriate questions is an important mediator skill. Mediators use closed and open questions to probe the emotional, relationship, and content aspects of the case.

Finally, mediators must be aware of the ethical implications of how they apply listening and other communicative techniques. Inequitable application of skills such as reformulation can create bias.

4 Pre-Mediation Activities

*T*he work of mediation begins before the disputants meet face-to-face with the mediator. Disputants come to mediation in many ways—they may initiate the process, be referred, or be mandated to attend by a third party. One way or another, disputants need to connect with the mediator. Contact between the mediator (or his or her staff) prior to the actual session is called *mediation casework* or *intake activities.*

In larger mediation programs, different people may fulfill the roles of "intake Coordinator" and "Mediator." However, it is typical for a mediator to take on the role of intake coordinator in small practices and not unusual in larger mediation companies or community centers. Having an intake coordinator who is not the mediator can be beneficial in four ways. First, if someone else manages the initial contacts, the dispute and the disputants are "fresh" to the mediator and preconceived views or biases may not have a chance to solidify. Second, the workload can be shared. Third, individuals who are not talented mediators can develop fulfilling roles as intake specialists. Fourth, the disputants may better understand what is pre-investigation work and what is their mediation session.

Separating the mediator and intake functions creates three potential disadvantages. First, having a mediator and an intake coordinator creates an additional level of complexity. For example, it creates an intermediary between the person doing the scheduling and the one being scheduled. Second, the cost of the service may in-

---

CASE **4.1**

Irreconcilable Differences

Roland and Janet have been married for twelve years, have two sons, and cited irreconcilable differences in their mutual decision to divorce. Complicating the dissolution of their marriage is a community house for helping runaways and teen mothers that they jointly manage. Both put their hearts into growing the community house into the successful program that it has become. Although they no longer will be married, their work relationship will continue (as well as the co-parenting of their sons). The tensions surrounding their separation are now affecting their work. There are major issues that need to be resolved, such as the division of property and financial obligations, as well as the distribution of labor in the agency. Janet has contacted an attorney to begin the divorce proceedings, but Roland decided to contact a mediator recommended by a friend. Roland makes the call to a mediator without consulting with Janet.

---

crease. Third, the mediator cannot begin the trust- and credibility-building functions during the early casework contacts. Whether the roles of intake coordinator and mediator are performed by one or two persons, knowing that the roles are separate is important.

Contacting Disputants

Disputant-Initiated Calls, Referrals, and Cold Calls

People in need of mediation services find their way to mediation in a variety of ways. Referrals from counselors or attornies are common paths to the mediator's door. The courts and other government agencies also send people to mediation—both voluntarily and involuntarily. Most commonly, mediation occurs when one party requests it. Whether by choice, referral, or mandate, disputants often find themselves calling mediators to procure services. Even though a disputant may make the first move, he or she may not know very much about mediation. For example, in Case 4.1, Roland called the recommended mediator, but did not really understand what the process was or if it was an appropriate venue for his difficulties. The intake coordinator explains the mediation process and screens the case for appropriateness.

A common job for intake coordinators is the initial contact with the second party. When the second party does not have any advance notice that mediation is being contemplated, the contact with the second party is termed a cold-call.

[handwritten margin note: 2nd party does not know they have been "called to medi.."]

When cold-calling the second party, the intake coordinator may need to over-come natural suspicions. For example, in Case 4.1, when called by the intake co-ordinator, Janet may assume that the mediator was working for Roland. Janet's view is that her attorney is her advocate; the mediator is Roland's advocate. Intake coordinators must explain the mediation process and work to alleviate fears, anxi-eties, suspicions, misassumptions, and other obstacles to persuade the second party to try mediation. In essence, intake coordinators are the salespeople for mediation.

Goals to Accomplish during Intake Coordination

As expressed in previous chapters, mediation is not a panacea for all disputes, nor are all mediation specialists well matched to all types of disputes. Because the public is generally uninformed about types of mediation, the intake coordinator has the multiple roles of educating disputants, gathering information from disputants, and assessing whether the dispute is a match for the mediator. Although we will discuss the functions of education, information gathering, and assessment separately, the intake coordinator fulfills the three roles simultaneously.

Education Role
- Educate about mediation
- Explain mediator's expertise and credibility
- Communicate mediator expectations (role and process)
- Communicate disputant expectations (behavior and success)
- Establishing boundaries
- Explore other resources (if necessary)
- Explain fee structure and payment procedures

Information-Gathering Role
- Determine parties
- Early issue identification
- Demographics of disputants
    Culture
    Language
    Gender
    Age
- Types of disputants
    Voluntary versus captive —→ *voluntary vs. court.*
    Conflict styles ——→ *assertive / emotional / passive*
- Contact information
- Schedules

- Time constraints and deadlines
- Referral agencies
- Determine ability to pay

Assessment Role (Mediators role)

- Determine issue appropriateness (can it be mediated (by me))
- Assess history of and threat of violence
- Ascertain the decision makers and affected parties
- Determine the appropriateness of mediation over other resolution processes
- Explore advocacy needs children
- Review legal issues (restraining orders, children, illegal activities)
- Compare power resources and ability levels (cognitive, communicative) equal?
- Assess levels of distress and resistance entusiastic, want to be there?

Education Role

Explain the Process of Mediation. Even disputants who seek a mediator require some information about the process. Mediation often is misunderstood to be synonymous with arbitration or litigation. The intake coordinator explains the process of mediation to the prospective client. If asked a direct question such as, "Do you know what mediation is?" most clients would respond in the affirmative.

Batna: best vs worst outcomes
watna: worst

Success of mediation + cost + challenges never encour attorney discourage.

	MEDIATOR NOTEBOOK 4.1 **Mediator Supplies**
◯	Create a checklist of supplies that a mediator should bring to each mediation session. Place the list in your mediator's notebook. For example, the checklist might include:
	- Paper/notepads (for mediators as well as disputants) - Writing utensils (for all parties)
	- Calculator - Calendar (two year)
	- Schedule of room availability for future mediations - Tissues
	- Watch or clock - Receipt book - Mediators notebook

Instead of asking disputants if they understand mediation, the intake coordinator briefly explains the process to all new clients.

The education function should be concise and adapted to the disputant's needs. For example, a brief statement might explain: "Mediation is a process where a third party helps people discuss their unique situation and creates a place for the two of them to work through possible solutions to meet their needs. The mediator will not make decisions for the parties, but will help them through a process to reach their own decisions." In Case 4.1, Roland, having initiated this call, may be willing to accept the inherent neutrality of the mediator. Janet, however, may require more information and assurances about the balanced nature of the process. Generally, if the disputants need information beyond a simple explanation, they will request it.

ACTIVITY **4.1**

Role play with a partner the phone call between Roland and the intake coordinator. Place your chairs back to back so you can simulate a phone call while you talk.

Establish Boundaries.   Disputants occasionally try to "lure the mediator" to their side. Janet or Roland may feel the need to paint the intake coordinator a picture of how things "really are." The intake coordinator views these persuasive efforts as an opportunity to *establish boundaries* by validating their concerns without agreeing and by encouraging the parties to come to the table to discuss what is important to them. A statement about the role a mediator will and will not play can help clarify misconceptions. For example, the intake coordinator could explain: "Your mediator is not a judge or decision maker. Instead, you and the other party will offer and evaluate any solutions that the two of you propose." Some disputants can be very persistent in their efforts to persuade a third party to their side. A statement that explains neutrality and puts the onus of responsibility back into the disputant's hands is helpful. For example:

JANET: "Roland is being completely unreasonable. You have to at least agree with that!"

INTAKE COORDINATOR: "My job and the mediator's job is not to pick a side between the two of you. What the mediator can do is help the two of you explore your challenges in-depth and arrive at a solution that meets the needs of both of you."

The intake coordinator should correct disputants immediately if they make the assumption that the mediator is biased toward one party or the other.

ACTIVITY **4.2**

Role play with a partner the cold call between the intake coordinator and Janet. The person who role plays Janet should be tentative about mediation, concerned about bias, and insistent on telling her side of the story. The person role playing the intake coordinator should validate without agreeing, using the skills in Chapter 3. Place your chairs back to back so you can simulate a phone call while you talk.

Establish Credibility. During intake, the coordinator conveys the credibility of the mediation process and the mediator. Sharing statistics about the growth and success of mediation helps people feel more confident about choosing mediation. Establishing the training and credibility of the mediator fosters the clients' trust in his or her abilities.

Persuading disputants that mediation can be helpful is an integral intake co-ordinator role. In Fisher and Ury's *Getting to Yes* (1981), the concept of BATNA (the Best Alternatives To Negotiated Agreements) is provided as a key negotiation tool. Other scholars later created WATNA (the Worst Alternatives To Negotiated Agreements). The best (and worst) alternatives for clients sometimes mean proceeding to court or having the conflict continue. Presenting mediation in comparison to other alternatives may persuade disputants to try mediation. If Janet replies that she already has an attorney working on the case so she doesn't need a mediator, pointing out the unpredictability of the courts may be convincing.

An ethical mediator, however, never disparages another vocation to bolster the attractiveness of mediation or discourages disputants from contacting attorneys. For example, the intake coordinator may prompt further consideration by saying, "Tell me how this situation will play out if it goes to court." The answer may offer an opportunity to discuss the benefits of mediation. For cases involving money, the intake coordinator can explain that: "In court, even if you do win a judgment, you still have to collect. In general, mediated agreements are kept by the parties more often than those ordered by the courts." Be careful, however, of overstating the success or expectations for resolution in mediation. Another caution for intake coordinators is never to speculate about the worth of disputant's case in a court of law as in, "You seem to have a pretty good case and would probably win in court." Even if the intake coordinator has legal experience, speculation is inappropriate. Instead, the intake coordinator emphasizes that mediation allows for self-determination instead of having a judge make a decision.

Another avenue of persuasion to entice disputants to the mediation table lies in the emotional and relational aspects of the case. Bush and Folger (1994) explain that success in mediation is not measured solely in settlement rates. Success of mediation can be evaluated by the greater understanding between parties that it creates, the improved mental health of individuals, and the promise of better relationships. If Janet and Roland want their remaining relationship as their childrens' parents to be more amiable, mediation may be more helpful than litigation.

ACTIVITY **4.3**

In a telephone role play between Janet and the Intake Coordinator, the intake coordinator explains BATNAs or WATNAs inherent in her situation to Janet. Place your chairs back to back so you can simulate a phone call while you talk.

Explain the Clients' Responsibilities.   In addition to educating parties about mediation, the initial communication with the disputants is an ideal time to set forth the disputants' role in the mediation process. In mediation, disputants present their own story in a quiet and private setting. Defining what will be expected from the disputants helps create momentum for a successful mediation session. Failing to inform disputants about who should attend can result in a party bringing young children to the mediation. Another time, a disputant in a neighborhood dispute arrived with three of her other neighbors to speak as witnesses against the other disputant. Ferreting out problems and educating disputants about their responsibilities and roles is part of the intake coordinator's job.

Mediators typically don't hear "testimony" from third parties because they prefer to have the parties tell their own stories from their own perspectives. Usually, a disputant can provide all the information needed without bringing other individuals. If expert consultants are required, agreement on selection of the expert generally is a part of the negotiation process rather than chosen by one party.

The intake coordinator must inform disputants that if they make an appointment they are responsible for either appearing or canceling. When only one of the parties appears, a higher level of tension is heaped onto an already strained relationship. Parties also should be apprised about what information they should bring to the table. In divorce mediation, for example, parties should be able to produce a list of assets and liabilities, income statements, and other pertinent information. In the case of Roland and Janet, being prepared to discuss real numbers (not just projections) and real schedules (not just memory) may make the process flow more smoothly.

Discuss Billing and Charges.   Most codes of mediator conduct are clear that clients should be informed of the mediator's rates and how they will be billed for the mediation service. For example, the Texas Association of Mediators' *Standards of Practice for Mediators* (2001) states: "As early as practical, and before the mediation session begins, a mediator should explain all fees and other expenses to be charged for the mediation." A pricing structure should be easy to communicate and fair to the parties. Typically, fees contingent on settlement are considered unethical. Some mediators charge a per hour rate or per mediation session fee. Others offer a sliding scale based on the income levels of the parties. Questions about the method of payments should be addressed. For example: Are parties to bring payments to the mediation session or will they be billed? Will each party be responsible for part of the bill? If the mediation is hourly, is there a minimum and a maximum charge? Does the mediator charge for formalizing agreements? Some states have specific instructions for when and how rates and billing information are disclosed. Consult your state's codes of conduct for the rules that apply in your jurisdiction.

VISIT SEVERAL mediation companies on the Internet. Find three different methods of establishing fees for a mediation. How can fee structures affect the fairness of the mediation for the parties?

Make Referrals.   Through the education process, disputants may find that mediation is not right for them. The intake coordinator also has a responsibility to educate callers about other processes and resources available in their community. Effective intake coordinators are informed about community and service resources (legal aid, victim's advocacy groups, small claims court, homeless advocates, and so on) so they can help individuals problem solve. Assessing the appropriateness of mediation will be discussed later in this chapter.

WHAT RESOURCES should the intake coordinator be aware about in the community? What circumstances may arise that would require the intake coordinator to explore options other than mediation? Is it ethical to recommend for or against another course of action besides mediation?

Formalize the Agreement to Mediate.   Once both parties agree to mediate, the intake coordinator formalizes the agreement to mediate. One method is to mail or fax both parties follow-up correspondence including: a congratulations to the parties on their decision to mediate, a brief statement about the nature of the process, the specifics for the meeting time and place, a reminder of materials to bring, and contact information if there are any questions or concerns. In the case of Janet and Roland, Janet asked if she could bring her attorney. This is not common, but does happen. Many mediators do make room for attorneys in the mediation room, but clearly outline the attorney's role as advisor. The intake coordinator explained these rules to Janet. She consented to proceed, so the intake coordinator then informed Roland that he also could bring an attorney, but that the mediation process would not utilize the attorneys directly in the discussions. If attorneys are not present, a mediator will encourage disputants to consult counsel if they have any legal questions or concerns.

Many mediators request that clients sign an *Agreement to Mediate* or a *Waiver and Consent* form. The agreement to mediate form customarily includes confidentiality policies, discloses fees and payment, and contains a statement that parties are welcome to seek legal counsel. These forms also may indicate the client's responsibilities, such as agreeing to bargain in good faith, to meet as scheduled, and to pay a certain percentage of the total costs. Many mediators will not mediate until both parties sign a waiver and consent form. Good practice dictates that disputants should have a copy of the form for their records. Others who are present at the mediation also may be required to sign a confidentiality agreement.

Mediators should be aware of laws governing the issue of *mediator privilege* as it pertains to confidentiality. Most mediators include a statement in their waiver and consent form indicating that disputants agree not to subpoena mediators to testify in a court hearing. State laws treat mediator privilege differently, and mediators should investigate regulations in their jurisdiction.

Information-Gathering Role

While educating disputants, the intake coordinator simultaneously is gathering information about the nature of the dispute and the parties. Through the process of active listening, the intake coordinator builds a detailed picture of the conflict and determines the primary parties, level of emotionality, special needs of the disputants, obstacles to settlement, and suggestions for structuring the mediation session. The intake coordinator also elicits information on times each party is available for mediation and briefs the parties on how to prepare for the mediation.

Determine Demographic Information.   Basic questions about each disputant may reveal important demographic information. Are the disputants from the same root culture? What is the first language of each disputant? What genders are represented? What ages are the disputants? What is the occupation and status of each disputant? If the mediator is not familiar with the cultures represented, he or she may need to research or locate a co-mediator from that culture. If the disputants and the mediator do not all speak the same language, a translator trained to be faithful to the mediator's comments must be scheduled. Gender or age differences can affect the dynamics of the mediation. A male-female co-mediation team is prudent in some cases with female and male disputants. Juveniles require different skill applications than adults. The occupation of each disputant may give the mediator hints about power or status differences that could affect the session.

Having enough information can aid mediators in making significant decisions about the structure of the mediation. For example, an employment dispute involving respect issues between male and female coworkers might function best with male and female co-mediators, to reduce the appearance of a single mediator siding with her or his own gender. Some college mediation programs balance student-teacher disputes by assigning a student and a professor as co-mediators. In cases where cultures differ, matching the demographics of the mediator to the disputing parties may be helpful.

Explore the Clients' Expectations.   In talking with Roland, the intake coordinator determined that he wanted his eleven-year-old son, Rob to come to the mediation table, so Rob could decide where he was going to live. Determining the primary parties who should attend the mediation is not up to the intake coordinator, but asking appropriate questions can assist disputants in choosing where the decision-making power should lie. Roland was adamant that Rob have a voice in the process. The intake coordinator and Roland discussed *when* in the process Rob should participate. They determined that a later session might be better. Rob's presence was determined to be a topic for discussion between Janet and Roland during the mediation.

Juggle Schedules.   The intake coordinator asks detailed questions to gather information about the parties' schedules and general availability. Disputants often do not think of "end times" when offering times to mediate. One mediator was surprised to learn on beginning a mediation that a disputant needed to leave in 40 minutes to pick up her child from school. Many mediators prefer a two-hour session, but do not tell disputants that the session will last exactly two hours. Disputants may feel like failures if they need more time, or feel they are not getting their money's worth if they finish in 25 minutes. Informing Janet and Roland "the room is scheduled until 3:00 for our mediation starting at 12:30" gives a deadline, but a flexible one. The intake coordinator asks key questions to locate times when both parties are available and then searches for a match in the mediator's available schedule. Finally, the intake coordinator notifies the parties and the mediator of the chosen time.

ACTIVITY 4.4

In groups of three, role play negotiating the time when Janet and Roland will meet with the mediator. How can the intake coordinator manage competing schedules? After the separate calls to Janet and Roland have agreed on a time, brief both parties and help them to prepare for the mediation. Be sure to work through some obstacles, such as competing obligations, desire to bring witnesses, and not knowing what to bring to the mediation. Place your chairs back to back so you can simulate the separate phone calls while you talk.

Determine an Appropriate Structure.   Decisions about the formality of the mediation process are shaped by the information garnered in the intake process. For example, if disputants have little trust and a history of high tension, the mediation may require more formality and structure. On the other hand, dormitory roommate disputes may benefit from a more relaxed mediation process and less formal structure. In a mediation program designed to handle disputes for a state medical association, the process may call for great formality due to the professional and technical nature of the cases. However, for a welder's association, disputants may feel more comfortable in a less structured approach. Knowing about the disputants can help mediators tailor the structure to meet their needs.

*I*N WHAT *ways can a mediator affect the formality of the mediation? Consider behaviors and environmental factors in your answer.*

Determine Disputant Style and Degree of Freedom. Not all disputants are volunteers to the mediation process. An intake coordinator should assess if the disputants are volunteers or if a third party mandates their participation. Many associations, divorce courts, and organizations require all parties to go to mediation before moving to another form of dispute resolution. In victim-offender mediation, mediation may be somewhat coerced from the perpetrator's perspective but voluntary from the victim's perspective. Mediators should know if the disputants are resistant to them or to the mediation process. Intake coordinators must explain to mandated disputants that agreement to outcomes is not mandated—even if disputants are not attending the mediation "by choice," the process of coming to *agreement* always is voluntary.

Developing a sense for the conflict style and emotional state of the disputants may be helpful in determining initial moves by the mediator. Disputants who are highly agitated and verbally aggressive may need clear and formal boundaries about appropriate venting. If disputants are highly competitive or rigid, coaching may be required in making apologies or offers to settle.

Assessment Role

Explore the Appropriateness of Mediation. While educating disputants and gathering necessary information, intake coordinators evaluate if the case is appropriate for mediation. Through the process of gathering information, the intake coordinator looks for issues that can be mediated. In one situation, the intake coordinator determined that a young man was attempting to mediate with an ex-girlfriend simply in order to see her again. He claimed that she still owed him $28 on a past phone bill, but told the intake coordinator that he "wasn't worried about the money since she didn't have a job." While he may have benefited from meeting with his ex, mediation was not the appropriate venue for such a reunion. Mayer (2000) concludes that the "mediator's decision not to mediate or to suggest some other form of intervention is in itself an important contribution to a conflict resolution process" (pp. 202–203).

The *Standards of Ethics and Professional Responsibility for Certified Mediators* (Judicial Council of Virginia, 2001) articulates three criteria in assessing whether to take a case:

1. Mediation is appropriate for all of the parties.
2. Each party is able to participate effectively within the context of the mediation process.
3. Each party is willing to enter and participate in the process in good faith.

Determining whether mediation is appropriate is linked directly to the *principle of self-determination*. The Oregon Mediation Association's *Standards of Practice* (2001) is representative of how mediators define self-determination. "Each participant should be able to fully comprehend the process, issues, and options for settlement, to make decisions, and should not be acting under fear, coercion, or duress. If the mediator believes that a participant is unable or unwilling to participate effectively in the mediation process, the mediator must suspend or terminate the mediation." Separate recommendations and rules for judging the capacity of persons who qualify under the Americans With Disabilities Act have been created so mediators can evaluate the capacity of ADA-qualified disputants to exhibit self-determination (The Alliance for Education in Dispute Resolution, 2002).

Assess Relationship History and Threats of Violence. The intake coordinator is a detective who determines if the relationship between the parties is appropriate for mediation. For example, if there has been abuse, violence, or a threat of abuse or violence, specialized training is essential before a mediator attempts the case. Most novice mediators are not equipped to navigate such delicate situations. However, assessing the level of threat is something that an intake coordinator must do. In a case over a barking dog, one neighbor held a black belt in Karate. He was so furious about his neighbor's barking dog keeping him up all night that he kicked his neighbor's mailbox post, snapping the four-inch post in half. The violence frightened the owner of the mailbox. The intake coordinator evaluated the level of threat, discussed the situation with both parties, and made a judgment that the threat of violence to the neighbor was negligible. Nonetheless, the intake coordinator scheduled a volunteer, off-duty police officer to co-mediate that dispute.

Acts of abuse and violence themselves cannot be mediated. One cannot allow threats of violence as a bargaining chip. An offer to "not to hit the neighbor if he agrees to keep the dog inside" never is acceptable. While victim-offender mediation, for example, does engage in mediation in cases where violence may have occurred, the violence itself is not the negotiated item. Victim-offender mediation is about restitution to the victim and society (Umbreit, Coates, & Roberts, 2000). A primary concern is ensuring that the victim is not re-victimized during the mediation. Victim-offender mediation is a highly specialized form of mediation requiring extensive training far beyond a basic mediation course. Intake coordinators in victim-offender mediation receive specialized training to distinguish cases appropriate for mediation from those that are not appropriate. Likewise, intake coordinators in family mediation should understand and screen for family and spousal abuse dynamics (Girdner, 1990).

WHAT SHOULD an intake coordinator do if it is determined that Janet and Roland had an incident of physical abuse in their marriage? Is it appropriate to mediate this dispute?

Assess Advocacy Needs. When people are in a dispute, they frequently seek support from friends and family. Intake coordinators balance the needs of disputants to feel supported and the mediator's need to have only decision makers at the table. In one mediation, the mediator chose to have a family advocate attend with a disputant as she negotiated with her ex-husband. The ex-wife felt intimidated because her husband was more educated and more confident than she, and all parties agreed that, in the interest of balance, having the advocate present was desirable. Assessing the advocacy needs of disputants is a necessary requirement for the case manager/intake coordinator.

If extreme power differences divide the parties, balancing power becomes a major concern. Inviting an advocate is one possibility to empower a party. The intake coordinator or mediator, however, should brief the advocate on the nature of mediation and her or his role in the process. Disputants with disabilities too may require the assistance of an advocate.

Establish Legal Issues. The intake coordinator will ask questions that are customized to the context of each case (divorce, neighbors, child custody, roommates, environment). Questions to reveal the nature of the relationship between the parties or past legal actions are critical. For example, in a divorce situation, mediators need to know: "Are there any restraining orders in place?" "Have there been any incidents involving police?" These questions can uncover how volatile or strained the relationship is between the parties. In one case involving unhappy neighbors, police had been called numerous times for various complaints by each neighbor. One call prompted the police to recommend mediation. A neighbor, unhappy about the other neighbor infringing on his parking place (even though he himself did not have a car), took a laser pointer and flashed his neighbor in the eyes through the windshield as he pulled into the disputed parking spot. A restraining order was issued against the laser-pointing neighbor and the case was forwarded to mediation. Mediators need to know these circumstances to provide safe environments for themselves and the parties.

Intake coordinators may determine that a threat of abuse or actual abuse is present in the relationship. Only a highly trained specialist should contemplate mediating cases involving a history of abuse. However, all intake coordinators should be prepared to refer callers to appropriate help if an abusive situation or other impairments to self-determination are revealed.

For mediation to work, the parties must be able to make informed choices and represent their own interests in a safe environment. If the mediator cannot provide a safe environment, the mediation should not occur. Mediating a case where one party is impaired by alcohol or drugs is unworkable. Parties must be responsible for their own decision making and those who are chemically impaired have questionable accountability for decisions. Intake coordinators refer contacts who are not eligible for mediation to other service providers or to the courts.

Ascertain the Affected Parties and Decision Makers. Ascertaining the decision makers is another assessment step for the intake coordinator. For example, a group of students are living in a rented six-bedroom house. Rent is divided six ways. One roommate is unable to meet her obligations for paying one-sixth of the rent. The reason she can't make the rent is due to an extended illness, which also

---

MEDIATOR NOTEBOOK 4.2
Mediation Forms

Create a checklist of forms and supplies the intake coordinator should have. Next, create a sample of each item on the checklist. You may find samples of many forms on the Internet. Put the checklist in your Mediator Notebook. For example,

- Intake form (design a form to use during intake coordination to solicit all the information you need)
- Waiver of rights to subpoena the mediator and consent to mediate forms (design a sample waiver and consent form)
- Schedule/planner (Design a form to use when juggling schedules)

---

prevents her from coming to the mediation table with her five roommates. Can we mediate this case without the roommate who isn't paying her share? Of course not. The key individual who will be affected by the outcome is not present. In another case, a mobile home park tenant's association was in conflict with the owners over landscaping issues. The tenant's association wanted to send eight members to meet with the one owner during mediation. However, the mediator was concerned that the power imbalance (of having eight people on one side with only one on the other) would be too difficult to overcome.

In each of these cases, with the sick roommate and with the tenant's association, a similar solution was found. Each appointed a representative to attend the mediation. The sick roommate had her mother attend the mediation. The tenant's association elected one tenant to represent the entire association. It is critical, however, that the representative is delegated bargaining and decision-making power. Without the power to negotiate and make decisions, having a representative at the mediation table is meaningless. Intake coordinators ensure that the right people are at the table or have appropriate representation.

A strategy that may be attempted by disputants is to send someone who is not a decision maker to the mediation. Companies may send representatives who either do not have the power to negotiate creatively or who are not able to alter policies. Intake coordinators should determine the level of decision-making power representatives have prior to the mediation session.

WHAT PROBLEMS may occur if a party's representative does not have decision-making power in the mediation?

Create a Preliminary Issue List.   The final assessment task for the intake coordinator is creating a preliminary list of procedural, psychological, and substantive issues in the case. The preliminary issue list is used to build the mediation plan, which is discussed in Chapter 5.

Intake coordinators have the job of educating parties about mediation and the mediation process and gathering information from disputants to aid in structuring the mediation. They assess the issues, disputants, context, needs, power dynamics, and decision-making abilities of the parties to determine if mediation is appropriate. The role of the intake coordinator should not be undervalued in the success of the mediation process.

Setting the Stage

Once the intake coordinator has determined the appropriateness of mediation, the time, place, and environment of the mediation session are established.

Time and Timing

At what point in a conflict is mediation appropriate? *Recency* (how recent is the conflict?) and *ripeness* (how ready are disputants to work on problem solving?) are two means to analyze the timing of intervention. Intake Coordinators can assess recency by asking questions about when the dispute manifested. If a roommate contacts a mediation program and wants to mediate a dispute because his roommate moved out yesterday, the events are recent. Tension is high, trust probably is low, and feelings are freshly hurt. The recency of the event may make problem solving more difficult. Some conflicts can be managed between the parties without intervention once the initial shock surrounding the incident has moderated; other conflicts where disputants have immediate needs should be scheduled quickly.

Where the passage of time does not seem to be moving parties toward solution, the ripeness of the conflict may help gauging the readiness of the case for mediation. Intake coordinators assess ripeness of a conflict by determining if the parties have reached an impasse on their own or have other motivation to settle. Asking questions can establish if the situation is ripe for mediation. For example, the intake coordinator may query: "How long has this situation been going on?" "What steps, if any, have you taken to resolve this issue so far?" "What other alternatives have you tried to settle this dispute?" "Are there critical deadlines that are looming?" When asked to "describe the communication that has occurred between the two of you since he moved out," one roommate said: "Well, I never talked to him and told him he owed me this money." The conflict was not ripe. The intake coordinator encouraged the caller to contact his ex-roommate himself and return to the mediation center if they still needed to mediate. He never called back.

Place

Establishing the best place to mediate is critical to the process. The location must be neutral, safe, and convenient for the parties. Two neighbors were having a dispute over the property line dividing their two homes. One neighbor was elderly, didn't drive, and wasn't interested in coming into town for the mediation. Neither neighbor was interested in mediating in the other's house. The challenge for the mediator was to locate a space that was convenient and neutral to both parties. The mediator brought a folding table and set it up outside between the two properties, seating each disputant in his own yard. The neighbors not only negotiated an agreement, they also established a neighborly tone with each other (culminating in one bringing over fresh garden tomatoes to the other in exchange for a prized salsa recipe). The setting of a mediation is important to establish a sense of fairness in the process.

> *A*SSUME THAT *there is a dispute between a manager and her employee. What might occur to each of the parties if the mediation takes place in the manager's office or if it occurs in one of the party's work area? Where would be a good place to mediate, and why?*

The disputants in any mediation should feel equally comfortable, or equally uncomfortable, with the surroundings. They may each travel to a neutral setting away from locations where one party would have the "home court advantage." Additionally, the convenience of participants should be part of the planning process. In a mediation involving six parties in different towns across a large geographical area, the mediator selected a central location that was equally inconvenient to all of the parties. The next sessions were moved to accommodate different parties in an attempt to even out the travel distance between all of the participants over time.

While not ideal, mediators can work to overcome the potential harm of mediating in nonneutral places. One strategy is to recreate the environment as the "mediator's" space. If a nonneutral location must be utilized, the mediator makes it his or her space by establishing a formal means of inviting parties into the room, by moving furniture to meet the mediator's space and seating requirements, and by having the mediator take charge of directing disputants to their seats.

Environment

The *mediation environment* includes all of the other factors in the setting—size of the room, seating arrangements, temperature, noise levels, privacy, and distractions. Each decision about the environment can affect the disputants and the overall tone of the mediation. For example, mediating in a room with a large window can be distracting. In a mediation about household obligations, chores, and appropriate communication, a fifteen-year-old male and his mother met in a room with a large window. The teenager could see people walking outside. Unfortunately, there were no blinds to be pulled or curtains to shut. In retrospect, changing the seating so the boy had his back to the window would have helped him to be more engaged in the process.

A quality mediation environment will have free parking, enough seating for all parties, and guaranteed privacy. Other items that may affect the tone of the mediation are the availability of water or vending machines, noise levels in the surroundings, restroom availability, and the formality of the setting.

While there is no one "right" way to seat disputants and mediators, seating is a strategic element that the mediator can control. The mediator must consider the implication of who sits in *power chairs*. Chairs that are larger, more luxurious, or at the head of a table may be perceived as more powerful and create a visual advantage to the party that sits in the power chair. Some mediators choose not to have a table or to have parties sit side-by-side with the mediator working from behind a desk. Other mediators prefer a round table where all parties can see each other and there are no power positions available. Each choice creates a different dynamic for the mediation. Some seating arrangements are designed to keep disputants physically apart; some are designed to keep them in close proximity. Some are arranged to encourage disputant eye contact with each other; some are designed to encourage disputant eye contact with the mediator.

WHAT FACTORS should affect the mediator's choice of seating arrangements?

Practical concerns for the mediator include accessibility of a computer, printer, and copy machine. A place is needed for one party to go if the other is in a private meeting with the mediator. Don't make the mistake of one mediator who scheduled only one small room for a session: When he needed to meet privately with one party, the other party was required to go outside on a cold, winter day.

Access to a telephone can be valuable if disputants need to arrange for more time, secure additional information, or clear a schedule for a future meeting. In one mediation, having access to the Internet helped parties to learn about current interest rates and to make a decision about whether to put their house on the market and move into two different houses. Each choice in designing the mediation environment is worthy of attention.

ACTIVITY 4.5

Given a round table and four people (two mediators and two parties), how could the parties sit? Draw a round table and place the disputants and mediators in different seating arrangements. What would the effect be of the different arrangements on ease of conversation?

Draw a rectangular table and place two disputants and one mediator in different seats at the table. What would the effect be of the different arrangements on ease of conversation? What would the effect be of the different arrangements on who appears the most powerful?

Ethical Issues for Pre-Mediation Caseworkers

Leitch (1987) makes a compelling case that mediation is a dangerous place for those who are disenfranchised or underpowered in a society. Mediators may bring with them the biases of their culture. For example, in a patriarchal society, men are better equipped and socially trained to negotiate using power tactics. Those who have not learned rules for negotiating may find that without a mediator aware of cultural inequities, those same inequities manifest during mediation. For this reason, mediation may not always be an appropriate place for those in low power to seek a fair settlement. Furthermore, mediation requires the ability to know one's own needs, assess a satisfactory solution, and not be bulldozed into agreement by a higher-power party. Individuals who have been in abusive situations may suffer from low self-esteem and a decreased sense of self-worth, and thus may not be in a good psychological position to negotiate on their own behalf. In order to create the most equitable mediation environment, mediators and intake coordinators must be aware of inherent cultural biases. Biases can only be moderated through awareness and training.

Some cases should not be mediated because of their social importance. Ms. Rosa Parks refused her bus seat to white passengers in segregated Montgomery, Alabama in 1955. Her action and the legal decision that followed was a turning point in the modern civil-rights movement. The publicity of her case brought to the forefront the inherent inequities of segregation. Consider what might have happened if Ms. Parks had decided to mediate with the Montgomery transit authority. In a private context, the bus company or the city may have agreed to let Rosa sit where she wanted on one particular route, and the spark that ignited public exposure and scrutiny of segregation might not have occurred. Similarly, cities with landlord-tenant mediation programs must be vigilant that unsavory landlords do not repeatedly use mediation as a tactic to avoid public and legal obligations to improve substandard housing. Good mediators know that mediation is not appropriate for all cases. Ethical mediators are aware of the systematic, cultural factors that advantage some groups over others.

MEDIATOR NOTEBOOK 4.3 ~optional

The Referral Sourcebook

Create a list of resources available at your college and in your community. Where possible, include phone numbers and contact individuals. Place your community resource list in your mediator notebook.

Summary

Pre-mediation casework or intake activities involve specialized skills. The intake co-ordinator may be an intake specialist or a mediator. There are advantages and disad-vantages to separating the intake and mediator functions with two different people.

Intake coordinators fulfill three roles: educating the disputants, gathering information, and assessing the conflict. While educating the disputants, intake co-ordinators explain the process of mediation, establish neutral and impartiality boundaries, establish the credibility of the mediator and the mediation process, explain the clients' responsibilities, discuss billing and fees, make referrals to other services, and formalize the agreement to mediate. Information-gathering functions include active listening to gather demographic information, exploring clients' expectations, discovering if bringing witnesses is contemplated by any of the parties, scheduling the session, and establishing if the context or the parties call for a formal or informal style of mediation. Within their assessment role, intake coordinators explore whether mediation is appropriate for the disputants and if the disputants are in a position to exert their own self-determination. Intake coordinators also screen for past violence, advocacy needs, legal issues, establish that the key decision makers will be present or represented at the mediation, and check for power imbalances among the disputing parties.

The setting of the mediation includes timing, place, and the overall environ-ment. Timing is judged by whether cases are appropriately recent and sufficiently ripe to motivate the disputants to work in good faith toward a mutually desirable outcome. The location of the mediation must be neutral, safe, and convenient. Other aspects of the environment that affect the mediation include the seating ar-rangement, size of the space, distractions, privacy, and the availability of private meeting rooms.

Pre-mediation and the decision of which cases are appropriate involve unique questions of social equity and social power. While mediation is helpful in many contexts, those who are otherwise disenfranchised from a society may also be disenfranchised in mediation if the mediator is not vigilant.

*import. to know.

mediator manager: mediator that mediates employees.
, know partic. w/ bias (@work.) bias for organit.

5 Mental and Tactical Preparations for the Mediation Session

roles

Once the pre-mediation activities are complete and the mediator holds preliminary information about the case and the disputants, the mediator plans the first session. Preparation involves both psychological and tactical aspects. Psychologically, the mediator must refresh her or his awareness of what is and is not the mediator's role, disputant roles, and the ethical boundaries of professional mediation. Tactically, the mediator analyzes the stakeholders in the conflict, creates a plan to guide the mediation, compares the case to common causes of conflict, analyzes the conflict, and screens for cultural dissimilarities that might create barriers to communication.

Mediator Roles

Mediators have numerous responsibilities throughout the course of a mediation. These responsibilities can be divided into specific roles the mediator assumes during the course of a mediation. However, psychological awareness of the limits and boundaries to the mediator's role is critical to professional conduct. Mediators

CASE 5.1

The Roommates at Odds

Juanita and Julie are first-semester college students living in the dorm. Both were excited to be accepted at college, but sad to leave their families and friends back home. Both are from small towns about two hours' drive from campus, but in different parts of the state.

Juanita became distressed that Julie's many friends seem to drop by the room at all hours of the day and night. Sometimes Juanita doesn't mind studying down the hall or across campus at the library, but not all the time! Julie's boyfriends also visit the room and Juanita never knows whether it is "safe" to come in. Juanita is a little uncomfortable with all the boyfriends visiting late into the night—she's just not used to that type of "free" relationship and is a little embarrassed. Besides, when is she supposed to sleep and get her homework done?

Julie doesn't understand what the problem is with Juanita. She's always been nice to her and willing to share her clothes. Lately, Juanita has been borrowing things without asking and leaving snippy little notes taped to the mirror about Julie's boyfriends and complaining that she can never study. Juanita goes home every weekend to see her family—she should just study while she's home, in Julie's view.

Juanita approached the resident advisor for her floor and asked for a roommate change and told the advisor that her roommate was like a prostitute having so many men in the room at all hours. One of Julie's friends overheard the comment and told Julie. When Juanita got back to the room, Julie first yelled at Juanita and then started crying. Juanita left for the weekend without saying anything to Julie. The resident advisor asked both roommates to come to her office for a mediation.

---

must choose, develop, and maintain a strong sense of each of their roles. Role awareness is critical for three reasons. First, how the mediator interprets his or her role guides choices about which skills are developed, what behaviors are embraced or avoided, and what one expects of the disputants. The mediator role that is adopted will align the mediator professionally with like-minded mediators and potentially alienate the mediator from those who adopt an incompatible role.

In many ways, "What should my role be as a mediator?" is the essential question that guides a mediator's strategies and behaviors. As we discussed in Chapter 2, different philosophies bring different values to mediation. Transformative mediators believe their role primarily is to "transform" the participants—a perspective that is encapsulated in the book *Mediating Dangerously* (Cloke, 2001). Changing people is a more profound goal than assisting in problem solving. Some mediators believe that they merely should play the matchmaker role—scheduling the time and place where disputants meet and then passively sitting back unless a fight erupts. Problem-solving mediators believe their role is to help the parties reach a resolution to their problems by facilitating their communicative process.

The second reason for role awareness is that the mediator's role varies by the type of mediation conducted (Moore, 2003). Typically mediators in the European American model are impartial and neutral—having no connection to the disputants and no personal interest in the outcome. A growing trend in business called manager mediation embraces a mediator role that is neither neutral nor impartial, as the mediator is the employees' direct supervisor and has a bias in favor of the organization's interests (Cohen, 1999).

Third, mediators must ensure that their chosen role matches the rules and regulations of their state, province, or administrative district. For example, Hawaii's Supreme Court advisory for public and private mediators states: "The role of the mediator includes but is not limited to assisting the parties in improving the definition of issues, reducing obstacles to communication, maximizing the exploration of alternatives, and helping them arrive at agreements" (Standards, 2002).

The balanced approach used in this book acknowledges that mediators assume many roles that are selected strategically, depending on the mediator's level of skill, the desired results, and the type of mediation. We encourage beginning mediators who are acquiring their skills to focus on the role of an independent, problem-solving mediator. Once basic skills are mastered, the novice mediator can consider taking on roles that are more complicated. In the ethics section of this chapter, we discuss the ethical boundaries and dilemmas of more complicated mediator roles.

Numerous researchers discuss mediator roles (Domenici & Littlejohn, 2001; Isenhart & Spangle, 2000; Kheel, 1999; Ponte & Cavenagh, 1999). Typical mediator roles for beginners include:

- *Facilitator* who makes communication between the parties possible
- *Impartial third-party* who has no stake in the outcome
- *Neutral third-party* who does not favor either disputant
- *Power balancer* who levels the playing field when one party has more power than the other (see Chapter 7)
- *Face manager* who helps the parties settle without undue embarrassment (see Chapter 8)
- *Role model* who demonstrates constructive communication skills
- *Process controller* who orchestrates the ebb and flow of the discussion
- *Resource developer* who encourages the parties to consult outside expert when necessary
- *Legitimizer* who maintains each party's perspective and rights
- *Catalyst* who spurs the parties to perceive the problem differently
- *Innovator* who builds a structure for creative thinking
- *Trainer* who educates the parties about the process
- *Coach* who helps the parties talk directly to each other when appropriate
- *Agent of reality* who helps parties recognize unrealistic goals or unobtainable settlement options

The Mediation Center of Kentucky's Standards of Professional Conduct (2000) elegantly summarized the role of a mediator: "The role of the mediator is to reduce obstacles to effective communication, assist in the identification of issues and exploration of alternatives, and otherwise facilitate voluntary agreements resolving the dispute. The ultimate decision-making authority, however, rests solely with the parties."

WHAT TYPICAL mediator roles apply to Case 5.1?

Ethical Considerations for Mediators

Awareness of the mediator's ethical responsibilities is central to any discussion of the mediator's role. Unfortunately, professional and state codes of conduct provide no systematic message about mediator ethical standards. The 2001 Uniform Mediation Act recommended by the National Conference of Commissioners on Uniform State Laws (2001) may provide some consistency if it is adopted. Some states have state code that covers mediator responsibilities and qualifications or licensure of mediators. Some states have codes of ethics created by a state professional association. However, other states provide little or no guidance to mediators or consumers. Mediators should consult the ethical guidelines or standards of practice in their state, province, or administrative area.

While the ethical codes within each state, judicial district, or professional associations will differ on some specific points, common threads are woven among the many documents. When examining the ethical considerations within a mediator's role, questions about neutrality, competence, dual-role relationships, and truthfulness are prominent:

1. Are there limits to mediator neutrality?
2. Do mediators always need to be impartial?
3. Can mediators be ethical practitioners if they lack particular skill competencies?
4. Should mediators be required to adhere to nondiscriminatory practice in acceptance of clients?
5. Should mediators be expected to do *pro bono* work?
6. Is it ethical if mediators have a bias toward settlement of the problem?
7. Does the mediator have responsibilities to external parties?
8. Do mediator-provider organizations have their own, separate ethical responsibilities?
9. When should a mediator withdraw from a session?
10. Should different contexts of mediation require different standards of practice?
11. Are there limits to the concept of disputant informed consent?
12. Should there be limits to a mediator's promise of confidentiality?
13. Is dual-role mediation ethical? No Never

> ### MEDIATOR NOTEBOOK 5.1
> #### Codes of Conduct
>
> *[handwritten: Idaho mediation.org or Association]*
>
> What are the rules and regulations for mediation in your state?
> Discover if your state has a professional mediation association with a
> code of conduct through an Internet search. Print out the relevant
> codes and requirements and put them in your mediator notebook. If
> your state has no regulations or codes, go to the national Association for
> Conflict Resolution Web site (http://acresolution.org/) and print out
> their code of conduct recommendations.
>
> *[handwritten: Standards of practice]*

14. Are mediators ethically responsible for the fairness of the outcome of a mediation?
15. Are referral fees or fees based on settlement appropriate?
16. What ethical standards apply to caucuses?
17. To what standard of truthfulness should a mediator be obligated? (McCorkle, 2001)

Ethics and Mediator Neutrality and Impartiality

Textbooks and most codes of conduct repeat the mantra that "ethical mediators should be neutral and impartial," but do not always discuss the conundrums inherent in that simple statement. Power balancing, where the mediator helps the low power or less verbally skilled disputant as he or she expresses interests or makes offers, could be seen as a breach of neutrality. Should the mediator be impartial to outcomes that obviously are unfair to one of the parties or that may harm others who are not at the negotiating table? If the parties decide to take care of their mutual litter problem by collecting it and dumping the garbage in a nearby gully, does the mediator have a responsibility to question the fairness of the decision to the unknown property owner of the gully?

Mediators also arrive at a session with their own past experiences, biases, and opinions. While mediators strive to minimize their own visceral reactions to the stories disputants tell, mediators are humans who cannot avoid being affected by information that strikes an emotional chord from their own life histories. Some authors suggest the term *equidistance* between the parties may be a more accurate description of the mediator's relationship to each party than is neutrality (Beck, 1999; Cohen, Dattner, & Luxenberg, 1999). If a mediator is equidistant, he or she maintains the same level of partiality and connection to both parties. Mediators should consult the code of conduct in their jurisdictions for further guidance on neutrality's limits.

CASE 5.2

A Mediator's Story of the Golden Retriever

I mediated a case about a barking dog. The disputant who complained about the barking professed to hate all dogs. The other party, a husband and wife, had a ten-year-old golden retriever who meant the world to them. I have two retrievers of my own, and I felt some kinship with the owners of the dog. The issue was that the dog was barking while the owners worked, and the plaintiff in this small claims court case was a writer who demanded absolute quiet in the neighborhood during the day while he worked at home. He had filed suits against four other dog owners in the same neighborhood. This case was the first to come to mediation through the court.

Through the emotional disclosures in the storytelling phase, I learned that the dog owners had made several attempts previously to appease the neighbor. They brought the dog inside during the day. Their efforts were not enough for the writer who could still hear the dog barking at the mail carrier and kids who passed by. The dog owners then agreed to put the dog in the bathroom of the house, where there were no windows or walls to the outside. Over the course of two months, the dog gained considerable weight and this worried the owners.

These efforts were not enough for the writer. During the mediation the writer expressed a demand that the dog wear a shock collar that would shock the dog each time he barked. The owners were opposed to this in principle, but decided that keeping peace with the neighbors and avoiding court was more important, citing their religious belief that people were more important than pets.

I brought the dog owners into caucus and shared my concerns that they seemed very distraught over their agreement to use a shock collar. They said they were, but wanted the conflict to end. The woman cried throughout the caucus. I informed them of their options: that they didn't have to make a decision today and that we could postpone or they could go to court. They said, "No. Getting this over with and not dealing with this jerk anymore was more important." I asked questions about the workability of the decision for them and their dog. I laid out their BATNAs and WATNAs.

As a mediator, my unspoken bias was that they should take this guy to court, as I believed they would prevail. I felt badly for the dog. I felt badly for the couple. I really disliked the plaintiff and believed him to be a bully. But ultimately, I wrote up the agreement. Of all the mediations I've done—including divorce and child custody—this was the one that caused me the most angst and had me question my own ethical responsibilities.

Ethics and Mediator Competence

Competence is divided in some ethical codes into *mediator knowledge* and *mediator skillfulness*. While some states have no technical requirements for mediator knowledge or training, the obligation to be knowledgeable about mediation theory and practice is integral to professional behavior. Cupach and Canary (1997) and Domenici and Littlejohn (2001) maintain that keeping within the limits of one's own competence is a challenge for mediators. While mediating any type of case may be tempting, it is doubtful whether a mediator unaware of the dynamics of child development and the effects of various models of split parenting on children should be conducting child custody mediation. Some argue that child custody mediators must carry both enhanced information requirements in family law and child development and enhanced competency requirements in high-conflict mediation (Irving & Benjamin, 1995). Roberts (1997) argues that all mediators have the responsibility to become educated about, and respond to, cultural differences that might affect the outcome of a mediation. For example, individuals from cultures where authority figures should be obeyed and respected might be disadvantaged in mediations where the other disputant is an attorney, teacher, or police officer.

In some jurisdictions the competence issue is regulated by mediator certification. In Australia, family mediators are expected to demonstrate competence in nineteen knowledge areas on family theory and law and forty-nine communicative skills (Bagshaw, 1999). Mediators should consult their state or territory for applicable rules.

Ethics and Dual-Role Relationships

Dual-role relationships exist when someone who represents one or both parties in one professional role, such as an attorney or counselor, also becomes their mediator. The codes of conduct that address dual-role relationships universally state that dual-role relationships are not appropriate. Some codes state that taking on a disputant as a client in a counseling relationship or as an attorney, after first meeting him or her in a mediation session, is not appropriate.

Ethics and Mediator Truthfulness

As you consider your role as a mediator, how truthful must you be with disputants? Most codes of conduct are clear that the mediator must disclose any potential conflicts of interest, prior knowledge of one of the parties, connection to some stake in the outcome, and fees that will be charged. Other questions remain murky, however. How truthful must the mediator be in talking with the disputants about other issues or in representing offers made in caucus? Is it appropriate to try to motivate the parties by saying they are very close to coming together during a monetary negotiation when the parties actually are quite far apart? Attorney-mediators are trained to accept a level of deception in their role as advocates for their clients (Cooley, 2001). Should attorney-mediators or judge-mediators who run settlement conferences be held to the same standards as lay mediators? If deception is a part of the "game" in some types of mediation, should that fact be disclosed to the disputants? Mediators must confront these questions and mentally prepare to maintain their practice within boundaries accepted by the profession and their peers.

A common feature of codes of mediator ethics is *informed choice*. The mediator has some obligation to ensure that parties have enough data so their choices are well based, rather than permitting the disputants to make decisions based on partial or erroneous information.

Conclusions about Mediator Ethics

While the landscape of ethics for mediators remains unmapped, beginning mediators can be guided by eight basic principles:

1. *Do no harm.* It is better not to mediate than to mediate and make the situation worse.
2. *Uphold the parties' right to self-determination by assisting parties to make informed choices.* Roberts (1997) summarizes this viewpoint by saying: "The mediator's first responsibility is to protect the right of the parties to be the architects of their own agreement" (p. 104). The mediator is responsible to respect and maintain the disputants' rights to determine their own solutions and decisions, as well as to be sure they have the information and capacity to make an informed choice.
3. *Work within your own level of competence.* Withdraw from cases for which you do not have specialized training or topics about which you cannot be neutral because of your own life history or values.
4. *Disclose any limits to your neutrality or impartiality.* Any past associations with the parties, their businesses, or potential outcomes must be disclosed.
5. *Disclose your limits to confidentiality and then maintain that confidentiality.* Many states' laws require mediators to report child abuse or threats of physical danger to self or others. Confidentiality applies to casework and caucus session, as well as to the primary negotiations. Mediators should not divulge the names or details of cases in ways that harm the disputants' anonymity.
6. *Avoid professional dual-role relationships.* Do not act as the counselor, attorney, or in other professional capacities for a client during or for a reasonable amount of time after a mediation. Do not solicit mediation clients for other professional relationships. The exception to the dual-role relationship principle is a system of manager mediation specifically designed to manage conflict at the lowest level where direct supervisors mediate their own employees. In Case 5.1, Julie and Juanita's resident advisor might mediate their case if the college has provided specialized training to permit mediation even though the advisor knows both roommates.
7. *Withdraw from the case when you cannot maintain your professional role or when withdrawal is best for the disputants.* While mediation works wonders for many cases, it is not always the right choice. Likewise, continuing a mediation that is outside one's comfort zone is unwise. The Kansas Dispute Reso-

potential trust/care [handwritten marginal note]

CASE **5.3**

Reverend McDonald's Mediation

Bob MacDonald has been counseling one of his parishioners, Maggie Smythe, who has been unhappy with her marriage and family. Bob has taken a four-hour mediation workshop and is eager to put his new skills to work. He persuades Maggie that family mediation is a good idea and to bring her husband and thirteen-year-old daughter together to discuss some issues that might help the family. Maggie agrees and brings the family to mediation. Bob acts as their mediator. He is happy to finally meet Dan and the daughter, Marquerida, who do not attend services with Maggie. During the session, Maggie and Dan discuss how their marriage has been unhappy and how stressful it is for the whole family. Marquerida is withdrawn and hardly speaks. The parents decide to send Marquerida to live with a cousin in Nevada over the summer so they can work on their marriage. They haven't talked to the cousin for a while, but he is family. Maggie, Dan, and Bob all are happy with the outcome of the session.

lution Advisory Council (2002) concluded, "Mediation is an appropriate method to use when parties wish to preserve their ongoing relationships or terminate an existing relationship in the least adversarial and most cooperative way. Solutions arrived at in mediation tend to last over time because the people affected by the decisions are the ones making them. Because the parties are responsible for making their own decisions, mediation may not be appropriate if a party is unable to negotiate due to substance abuse, psychological impairment, physical or emotional abuse by the other party, or ignorance." In the latter cases, the mediator should withdraw from the case.

8. *Know the law and any mediator codes of conduct binding on those who practice in your state or territory.*

Review the code of conduct for your state or territory. If your state or territory has no code of conduct, examine the Association for Conflict Resolution Standards of Practice. Then, analyze Case 5.3 for any potential ethical dilemmas.

Disputant Roles

Cupach and Canary state, "Although mediators garner the majority of research attention, much of the credit for the success (or failure) of any mediation rests with the disputants" (1997, p. 229). Preparing the disputants to hold up their part of the mediation is an essential task for the mediator. Sometimes, preparation begins during casework and pre-mediation interviews; sometimes individuals learn about their role on a Web site; sometimes the mediator must coach disputants on their role during a mediation session.

Disputants have their own role during mediation. They have responsibilities to themselves to know and convey their interests and issues. They have responsibilities as problem solvers to seek creative solutions. They sometimes have responsibilities to constituencies they represent in the mediation or to others who will be affected by the outcome.

Disputants need to be able to:

- Explain their interests and tell their story
- Follow the instructions of the mediator
- Listen to the other party and the mediator
- Seek and consider creative solutions to problems
- Be willing to access the facts and information necessary to make informed choices
- Communicate well enough to express themselves to the mediator and the other party

Haynes (1994) commented that a mediator who enters a dispute faces clients who are invested in their own side and are motivated to convince the mediator that their side is right. Disputants need to be guided to see their role differently and to alter their perspective from advocate to negotiator and from opponent to participant in mutual problem solving.

In the case of Juanita and Julie, the mediator would explain her or his own role and the disputants' roles during the mediator monologue. If Julie repeatedly interrupted Juanita while she was telling her perception of their roommate situation, the mediator would remind Julie her role is to listen while Juanita was speaking and that she would have an opportunity to give her perceptions later. A part of mediator preparation is reviewing the roles that disputants should play in order to be fully prepared to communicate those roles to disputants.

Analyzing Stakeholders

A *stakeholder* is any person who has a "stake" or holds a substantial and direct interest in the outcome of the mediation. Generally, beginning mediators work with cases where only two disputants come to the table. Mediation cases, however, may include any number of potential stakeholders who could be disputants. For example, in a juvenile victim-offender mediation case where a swimming pool was damaged and taken out of service during a hot August week, an entire family might be the victims. If the pool was owned by the city, an entire community may be victimized. There also may have been more than one offender who committed the crime. While it is possible to *fractionate*, or break the case down into one person representing a family or the community and one offender, the mediator must realize that other stakeholders in the family or the community exist who are not at the table. In mediations involving spouses or business partners, the mediator always must analyze who has a stake in the mediation and whether the person who comes to the table has the authority to negotiate on behalf of a larger group of stakeholders. If the swimming pool case involving damage to a city pool were mediated within the community mediation model utilized in some areas, representatives of each group having a stake in their community may come to the mediation: the offender's teacher, parents, the pool manager, someone representing others who use the pool, and perhaps someone from the faith community. In another case, two juveniles broke thirty car windows in one night throughout their neighborhood. Because having thirty car owners lined up on one side of the table and two adolescent boys on the other was not workable, the program coordinator scheduled each boy separately with each car owner who was willing to mediate—resulting in sixty potential mediation sessions, each with its own different personal dynamics and restitution plan. In another example, all relevant parties to a large-scale environmental issue are brought together at once to negotiate a creative solution to what should become of rusting, abandoned factory sites that are labeled Brownfields by the Environmental Protection Agency (Branham, 1999). Parties might include the city, county, state, federal agencies, nearby businesses, neighbors, tribes, and so forth.

Who Should Come to the Mediation Table?

Those who come to the mediation table should either be the direct stakeholder in the case or have authority to make binding decisions on behalf of the stakeholder. A common frustration in small claims court mediation is finding out part way through the session that the person who came to court that day representing a business does not have authority to negotiate an outcome. Discovering whether the party who comes to the mediation table has authority to make a decision is critical. Disputants who are ordered to small claims court mediation by a judge commonly obey the command to appear at the designated time or send a representative. All too often, however, the representative will know nothing about the case or the real disputant's wishes and does not feel as though he or she can negotiate.

Determining who should *not* come to the mediation table is equally important to determining who should come to the table. While friends, attorneys, or other support networks sometimes are allowed in the mediation room, they may or may not sit at the table where negotiations occur and typically are not allowed to speak as a party to the negotiation. The individual disputants, of course, always will be permitted time to speak privately with an attorney or a support person to help them make an informed choice.

Just as it may be ill advised to have people who are only loosely connected to the conflict sitting at the table, it is problematic to exclude someone who has a direct stake in the outcome. When three roommates are having a conflict over their common finances, it is wrong to have only two of the roommates negotiate a decision that is binding on the third. Analyzing the conflict and the potential issues will help the mediator determine who the stakeholders are and who should be involved in the mediation.

The Mediation Plan

Many mediations are conducted with the benefit of the insights gained through analysis of the pre-mediation casework data. The mediator compares the information gained during pre-mediation to one or more structured analytical tools and then deduces probable interests, issues, commonalities, and stumbling blocks. Moore (2003) lists ten critical questions to use when creating the mediation plan.

1. Who should be involved in the mediation effort?
2. What is the best location for mediation?
3. What physical arrangements need to be made?
4. What procedures will be used?
5. What issues, interests, and settlement options are important to the parties?
6. What are the psychological conditions of the parties?
7. How will rules or behavioral guidelines be established?
8. What is the general plan for the first joint negotiations in the mediator's presence? How will specific agenda items be identified and ordered?
9. How will parties be educated about the process, and how will they arrive at agreement to proceed with negotiations?
10. What possible deadlocks could occur, and how will they be overcome? (pp. 146–147)

Based on the analysis of the case information, the mediator strategically creates a preliminary plan of how, when, and where the mediation will unfold. Like most good plans in fluid situations, the plan is only a starting point and source of initial structure. As new information emerges during the session, it could appear that the mediation plan is unraveling. We prefer to think that the mediation plan is fluid and changeable.

Advantages and Disadvantages of Prior Knowledge and Mediation Plans

Having the opportunity to talk to the disputants in advance and research the case offers several advantages. The mediator can create a theory about the case, prepare for predictable outbursts if emotions are high, stockpile questions to elicit information, and make other strategic preparations. The disadvantages occur when the mediator begins to believe the theory he or she created. The result of the case analysis is just a theory—a tentative explanation of what the mediator speculates is occurring. When the mediator sticks to the plan, despite new information provided by the disputants, the session is sure to go awry.

Cold-mediation sessions, where the mediator has no prior knowledge of the case or the disputants, have the advantage of permitting the mediator to "fish" for very general stories at the beginning of the session and to model positive communication behaviors as each party's story unfolds. The disadvantage is that the mediator must be able to analyze the case quickly and have a deep mental storehouse of techniques and tactics to apply to many types of cases. The mediator notebook is particularly useful as a reference for cold mediation sessions.

Common Causes of Conflict

Knowledge of the causes of conflict and basic conflict analysis tools assist in the preparation of the mediation plan. Each conflict cause requires a separate strategy.

Wilmot and Hocker (2001) imply that all conflicts boil down to one of two causes—either a power struggle or a self-esteem issue is driving the conflict. While there is an elegance to reducing all conflicts to one of two causes, mediators usually find broader typologies useful when analyzing cases.

Mayer's (2000) _wheel of conflict_ locates conflict in unmet needs that are expressed through one or more of five clusters. Locating which cluster dominates a conflict helps the mediator determine a plan of how to proceed.

name + describe all 5 Essay

- _Communication:_ Humans are not always skilled at communication and often misperceive each other's intentions or behaviors.
- _Emotions:_ Fear, hurt feelings, anger, and other emotions drive and sustain some conflicts.
- _Values:_ Values are deeply rooted concepts tied to core beliefs and often are defended vigorously when threatened.
- _Structural Conflicts:_ External rules and frameworks can precipitate or sustain conflicts, such as resource distribution, decision-making processes, time constraints, physical settings, law, political pressure, and geography.
- _History:_ Conflicts always occur in a context with a past. (pp. 8–13)

By locating which cluster or clusters are driving a conflict, mediators can plan where to begin their work. If the conflict between Julie and Juanita seems to center around hurt feelings, the mediator would choose different strategic options than if the conflict were about core values. Chapter 7 will present how the wheel of conflict can be utilized during the storytelling and issue identification phase.

A pattern of conflict that mediators often see is labeled by Lulofs and Cahn (2000) as the _competitive conflict escalation cycle._ A problem emerges and the parties try, unsuccessfully, to work it out. A conflict results. The conflict escalates, and one or both parties feel emotionally threatened. Face-saving strategies are suppressed or fail, resulting in emotional grievances on top of the original issue. Participants assume a win-lose orientation that leads to one person winning, leaving an unresolved conflict that sets the stage for the next conflict episode. What began as a conflict over a tangible interest became a relationship problem dominated by emotional hurt.

Folger, Poole, and Stutman (2001) describe another pattern of conflicts commonly seen by mediators. They claim that a perception of differing _goals_ can lead one party to resist the other, precipitating a power struggle. The roommates Juanita and Julie may have different goals about their relationship or about how to use their mutual space. If Juanita's goal in the relationship is to have Julie as her best friend and Julie just wants to share a room for financial reasons, they may be trying to pull each other in different directions. Likewise, an overt or subtle use of power to restrict the other parties' choices may also lead to resistance and enhanced conflict. If Juanita is using the room as a social or recreational area, her presence precludes Juanita's ability to use the room as a place to study or rest.

Deducing the disputants' goals is one of many important elements to analyze before creating a mediation plan. Style differences also can be a contributing cause of conflict. Folger, Poole, and Stutman (2001) define *style* as a "consistent, specific orientation toward the conflict, an orientation that unifies specific tactics into a coherent whole" (p. 219). Thomas and Kilmann (1977) identified five primary approaches to conflict that have become commonplace in discussions of conflict style:

- *Avoidance:* pretending the conflict does not exist
- *Competitiveness:* opposing the other's goals in a desire to win on all issues
- *Compromise:* splitting the difference on issues to achieve a settlement
- *Collaboration:* working until a solution is reached that all parties will agree to
- *Accommodation:* agreeing to whatever the other party wishes

Style differences function as a cause of conflict when the style inhibits productive communication about the problem. Two competitors may become stuck in a destructive win-lose pattern of interaction. Any conflict with an avoider may need a third party to persuade and cajole the avoider into showing up and participating in the mediation. Over-reliance on compromise can lead to resolution that satisfies no one and does not really address the core issues. Accommodators faced with competitors may need the power balancing assistance of a mediator to have a fair chance to have their needs met during negotiations.

If you have ever worked with someone whose style is dramatically different from your own, you know how style differences can drive people crazy and create the illusion of problems or insults where none really exist. While we do not concur entirely with the popular literature that suggests the genders have completely different communication styles, we do agree with Cooks and Hale's (1992) observation that some men and women exhibit differences that exacerbate conflict and that mediators should be aware of gender dynamics.

WHAT "STYLE" differences in communication patterns might create barriers to individuals managing their own conflicts? Hint: Think about the ways that others communicate that are different from how you communicate or that you find irritating.

Conflict Causes and Mediator Moves

As the mediator discovers which general causes of conflict are sustaining and driving the conflict, the mediator knows which first moves to try during the early phases of the session, which skills might be most useful, which barriers to settlement will probably emerge, and which types of outcomes are likely. For example, if the conflict arises because one party has information that the other party does not have (a data conflict), having the disputants share information early in the process is a natural first step. If the parties share deeply rooted, mutually exclusive value systems, resolution by transforming one or both parties' value structure is unlikely, so the mediator knows to frame the resolution stage in terms of getting agreement on how the parties can work together even though they have strong value differences. In all cases, the mediator must remember that the cause of a conflict and its barriers to settlement will be a combination of actual events and the disputants' *perceptions* of those events. Uncovering and managing different perceptions is an important mediator skill. Van Slyke (1999) comments:

> Constructive conflict management depends significantly on our emotional awareness and social interaction skills, and less on our cognitive capabilities. A high IQ may, in fact, interfere with positive interaction because conflict is not always rational, and an analytical approach may overlook significant emotional needs. While we can break every conflict down into its structural components, isolate the variables, identify the problem, and develop systematic solutions, we are still dealing with humans. And no matter how "right" our answer may be, if we have not satisfied the other party's temperamental, peculiar, exacerbating personal issues, we have not resolved the conflict. (p. 32)

Specific mediator moves will be discussed more in later chapters.

Cultural Awareness

Cultural awareness must be an element of any mediation plan. Mediators should screen to determine if the disputants are from dissimilar cultures. In this context, culture can be defined as how race, ethnicity, background, socioeconomic status, family of origin, environment, and gender affect how one perceives the world. If the disputants' cultures have different norms about authority figures, public loss of face, how to express conflict, or appropriate nonverbal behaviors, the mediator will need to prepare to manage the differences—through power balancing techniques or finding a co-mediator who better understands the cultures. While there is a risk of stereotyping all persons from a general geographic area as being essentially the same, an awareness of cultural variability is essential for mediators. If two immigrant families are referred to mediation by the police and one is Russian and the other is Chinese, the mediator should consider the probable cultural differences that might affect the mediation. Russian root culture permits more vocal and emotional expression of conflict than root Chinese culture. Both, however, share values in working and sacrifice for the good of the greater group. In Case 5.1, if Juanita comes from a traditional Hispanic or Mexican American family, her values toward premarital relations *may* be quite dissimilar to Julie's values.

While the mediator should not assume that exhibiting a particular ethnicity or geographic homeland automatically means a disputant will share the dominant culture and values of that group, the mediator should ask questions to screen for cultural dissimilarities. The mediator should be aware of the communication patterns and attitudes that might accompany specific cultural backgrounds. A mediator should learn about the specific cultural groups that dominate his or her community. There also are general techniques a mediator can apply during a session to discover cultural traditions and values. The mediator might ask each disputant: "When you were growing up, what did you learn about how neighbors should interact with each other?" "What would an ideal roommate situation be like for you?" "How were problems settled back home before you moved here?"

WHAT CULTURAL groups dominate your geographic area? How can you learn more about each cultural group and the values and communication patterns that they might bring to a mediation session?

Conflict Analysis

Conflict Assessment Tools

Numerous tools have been developed to assist in the analysis of interpersonal conflict. In this section, we discuss how tools developed to assist individuals in analyzing their own interpersonal conflicts can be adapted for use by mediators when analyzing a case and creating the mediation plan.

Metaphor Analysis.   *Metaphor analysis* (McCorkle & Mills, 1992; Wilmot & Hocker, 2001) examines the language used by the disputants as diagnostic of their perceptions of the conflict. If conflicts are described as "war," a competitive, win-lose approach probably has dominated their past experiences, and the mediator would plan to intervene to alter the metaphor and open a door to perceive the conflict differently. If in Case 5.1 Julie refers to their living situation as "two inmates in a prison cell" and Juanita labels them "a family having a squabble," the perceptual differences illustrated in their metaphors provide an important clue to the mediator about the conflict.

System Rules.   *System rules* may provide barriers to productive problem solving. Asking what the implicit rules are for solving disagreements in an established group reveals the system rules. Some mediators will ask disputants to describe a typical communication between the two parties. Descriptions of these *microevents* provide clues to style and substance of a conflict (Wilmot & Hocker, 2001). When implicit or structural rules have inhibited resolution of the conflict, the mediator must create a plan to negotiate structural elements.

Maps. Conflict maps are tools for detailed systematic analysis of conflicts. Wilmot and Hocker (2001) provide a map suitable to interpersonal conflicts that asks a series of questions to build a comprehensive picture of the past conflict by listing the disputants' attitudes, *triggering events* (the conversation or behaviors that precipitate eruption of the conflict), goals, power structures, styles, past tactics utilized by each party, and past solutions disputants have tried. The Australian Conflict Resolution Network (2002) promotes another mapping tool that disputants can utilize to analyze their own cases that also is useful for mediators. A description of the issue is written at the center of a page. Each disputant's perspective is given half of the page. Each disputant then lists what he or she needs at the end of the negotiation and what they fear will or will not happen. A series of other questions helps the disputants think through their own and the other party's needs and fears: What is my real need here? What is theirs? What is it like to be in their shoes? What do I want to change? Am I (or are they) using power inappropriately? What am I feeling? What do I want to change?

Elements of the Case Theory

Whatever tools are used for conflict analysis, the mediator should create a theory about nine key factors in the case and a tentative plan for how to manage each factor during the mediation session:

1. Is emotion high in this conflict? Are there psychological barriers to settlement?
2. What are the probable interests of each party?
3. Do all parties have the same information?
4. How have the parties attempted to communicate in the past? Did it work for them?
5. Are the parties embedded in a structural system that will affect the choices they can make?
6. What is the nature of the relationship between the parties? Do they have a good or bad history? Will they have a sustaining relationship in the future?
7. What do the parties have in common?
8. What specific issues will need to be negotiated?
9. Are the disputants from similar or dissimilar cultures?

ANALYZE CASE *5.1 to discover Julie and Juanita's probable perspectives on each of the nine elements of the mediation plan.*

Summary

Preparation for a mediation involves both psychological and tactical aspects. Psychologically, the mediator must review his or her role boundaries, impartiality, neutrality, and state- or province-specific regulations. Beginners should assume the role of an independent, problem-solving mediator. Psychologically, the mediator must review the standards of practice in her or his state or province and personal considerations of neutrality and impartiality, competence, dual-role relationships, and truthfulness. Eight ethical guidelines for beginning mediators were suggested. Finally, the mediator psychologically reviews the disputants' roles, so he or she is prepared to explain their roles as disputants and maintain disputants within acceptable boundaries during the mediation.

Tactically, the mediator must analyze the stakeholders in the mediation to ensure that the correct parties come to the table, as well as ensuring that superfluous parties are not present. Those who come to the mediation table as representatives of other parties must have the authority to negotiate outcomes. Tactically, the mediator then creates a tentative mediation plan, keeping in mind the advantages and disadvantages of prior knowledge of the case. Some mediations are conducted cold, with no prior knowledge of the case or the disputants. Tactically, the mediator compares the most common causes of conflict to the case to determine probable barriers to settlement. Common causes presented in the wheel of conflict include: communication, emotions, values, structure, and history. Other common causes of conflict are competitive conflict escalation cycles, perceived goal differences, and style differences. Each potential cause of conflict requires a different opening move by the mediator.

Cultural awareness must be integrated into the mediator's psychological and tactical preparations. Mediators should be aware of the communication patterns and cultural assumptions of the groups they work with.

Several conflict assessment tools can assist the mediator with analysis of the case. Metaphor analysis, system rules, and maps can provide insights into how the disputants perceive the conflict.

CHAPTER

6

The Mediator's Opening Statement

*T*he words that begin a mediation are critical. The opening statement establishes the tone and protocol for the session. A good opening statement builds trust and puts the mediator in control of the session. A poor opening statement erodes disputant confidence and permits the eruption of power struggles between the mediator and the parties. Domenici and Littlejohn (2001) established three purposes for the mediator's opening statement: introduce the disputants to the mediator and to each other, explain the mediation process, and establish trust (p. 40). The symbolic value of the opening statement should not be undervalued. The symbolism of the opening statement creates the first visible commonality for the parties: both are listening to and conceding process control to the mediator; both are developing a common trust in the mediator. Additionally, the content of the opening statement establishes important procedures and rules, setting the tone and expectations for the mediation. This chapter presents the functions and practical realities of the first phase of mediation—the mediator's opening statement.

Functions of the Opening Statement

The mediator's opening statement must accomplish several functions:

- Introduce the parties and the mediator to each other as a team working on the parties' issues
- Model a positive tone
- Build trust and rapport between the mediator and each party
- Establish the mediator's control of the process
- Educate parties about mediation as a process
- Reduce anxiety about what will occur during the mediation
- Discuss the role of mediator
- Discuss the role of the disputants
- Transition to the phase where the disputants tell their stories

Moore (2003) recommends that the mediator's opening remarks "should set a positive tone and meet the basic needs of the parties for comfort and safety. To establish a safe environment, the mediator should consider both emotional and physical safety" (p. 212). Physical safety concerns, according to Moore, are accomplished nonverbally "through the physical arrangement of the parties in the room and verbally with his or her opening statement" (p. 212). In Chapter 4, we discussed the importance of seating arrangements in the creation of a mediation environment. Establishing an emotionally safe environment also is accomplished through the mediator's words and behaviors. The mediation context must be a place where parties feel secure enough to share information about themselves and their issues. The mediator establishes this environment by appearing fair, consistent, and inclusive of both parties.

CHOOSE ONE of the mediation cases presented in the previous chapters. Identify the safety issues that should be considered by the mediators. How can the mediator's opening statement address those safety concerns?

The opening statement also fulfills the critical need of educating disputants to make informed choices. To have *informed choice*, disputants must able to anticipate what will occur during the process, what the mediator will and will not do, and how decisions might affect their rights. Informed choice is so critical that some states have specifically identified the topics to be covered in the mediator's opening statement. The Arkansas Alternative Dispute Resolution Commission (2002) *Requirements for the Conduct of Mediation and Mediators* asserts: "In order for parties to exercise self-determination they must understand the mediation process" (p. 3). Arkansas requires mediators to discuss:

- The role the mediator plays to assist the parties in their own voluntary decision making
- The difference between a mediator's role and the role of a legal authority

- The procedures that will be followed
- The mediator's pledge of confidentiality
- That the mediator does not represent either party
- The mediator's responsibility to foster a reasonable negotiating atmosphere
- The mediator's ability to stop the process for a variety of reasons
- How parties not represented by an attorney may consult legal counsel at any time
- The binding nature of mediated agreements once signed

Lulofs and Cahn (2000) note that if disputants doubt the process or the credibility of the mediator, the information and tone of the opening statement may help to build trust (p. 351). The opening statement fulfills many functions for the mediator.

Opening Statement Styles

Monologue Style

Mediators have choices about how to deliver the opening statement. As the term *monologue* suggests, the mediator can be the one who does most, or even all, of the talking. In mediations that are highly structured, and where consistency is paramount in each and every mediation, an opening monologue may be scripted. For example, in state agencies dealing with discrimination issues, a pure monologue where only the mediator speaks may be necessary. When the mediator chooses to deliver a strictly one-sided monologue, she or he sets a more-formal and less-flexible tone. The mediator is communicating that he or she is in strict control of the mediation process.

In the pure monologue style, the mediator prepares a short speech that is delivered in a conversational tone to the disputants. The monologue sometimes is written and memorized or may be spoken from a list of subjects that the mediator needs to address. In this style, the mediator does not permit the disputants to speak, except at carefully chosen points. The disputants become accustomed to listening to, and heeding, the mediator's control of the process. The mediator might only permit the disputants to speak during the monologue to ask how each one wishes to be addressed, if they agree to the ground rules, and—at the conclusion of the monologue—if they have any questions about the process or timing.

Interactive Style

In an interactive approach, the mediator includes the disputants in a conversation. After providing information about his or her role, confidentiality, or some other element of the opening statement, the mediator asks questions such as: "Is the goal of the mediation clear?" or "Do you have any questions about my role?" An interactive opening statement encourages the parties to take part in the creation of the process. Mediators may explain mediation in segments and invite the disputants to "buy in" to the process by soliciting their approval. In sales, this process of gaining agreement early and often is called getting the *yes response.* The interactive style is less rigid and allows the mediator to convey the information and functions inherent in the opening statement through a dialogue with the disputants. For example, after explaining why ground rules are necessary, the mediator might ask the disputants what ground rules they would find useful. Creating a dialogue with the disputants has the additional benefit of checking understanding and keeping disputants focused on the main points of the opening statement. In a mediation where an informal tone is desired, more interaction between mediators and disputants may help establish an informal tone.

IDENTIFY AN example where a strict monologue approach would be most appropriate. Identify when a more interactive approach would be appropriate. How would a mediator know which style would be best?

Opening Statement Dynamics

Every opening statement will address several key issues. While opening statements are modified in specialized contexts, such as juvenile victim-offender mediation, a general opening statement will follow this outline:

Welcome
Introductions
  Self
  Center or agency (if working as an agent for a larger group)
Credibility statement
Establish stakeholders
Overview of mediation
  Voluntary
  Parties create solution
  Caucus
  Role of outside experts
Explanations of mediator role
  Not attorney or judge
  Impartial and neutral
  Confidentiality (mediator and parties)
  Note-taking procedures
Ground rules
  Respect
  Honesty
  Speak one at a time
  Breaks and facilities

> Time constraints
>   Agreement to ground rules
> Commitment to begin
> Transition to storytelling

Length

While the list of basic components may seem complicated, most elements are described quite briefly. A mediator's opening statement should be long enough to cover all points, yet short enough not to bog the disputants down in unnecessary details. Opening statements typically run one to three minutes in length, and rarely more than five minutes. Opening statements will be longer if many questions are asked or if the function of the opening statement must also fulfill goals of educating the disputants about some aspect of mediation.

Order

The order of the topics in the opening statement can be modified. For example, in a mediation where there is high tension between disputants, a mediator may decide to address ground rules early in the opening statement. If mediator credibility must be established, more time may be spent to build confidence in the mediator. The sample opening statement in Figure 6.1 is a compact presentation of the basic elements.

Key Components of the Opening Statement

Welcoming

Mediators begin by welcoming the parties to the mediation. A simple statement such as, "I'd like to welcome the two of you to our center" can set a positive tone. A common addition to welcoming the parties is to praise them for coming to the mediation table. These "welcoming" comments add a positive note to the mediation at a time when the parties probably are feeling uncertain. The mediator might say, "I'd like to commend you for coming here today in an effort to work on your concerns together." The first words should be delivered conversationally, with the mediator's attention split evenly between the two disputants. Speaking only to one disputant might imply favoritism or lack of neutrality. The mediator has considerable influence at this point in the mediation to affect the overall tone of the session. An approachable mediator with a friendly tone can set the stage for positive interactions throughout the mediation.

Introductions

The next task in the opening statement is to ensure that all parties are introduced to each other and to the mediator. Several factors need to be considered as an

FIGURE 6.1   Sample Opening Statement

Hello. My name is Carol Hutchison, and I would like to welcome you to the campus mediation center. I trust that you didn't have any difficulty finding the office. Good. I'd like to commend you both for coming to mediation in an effort to work out a solution to your issues together. I've been mediating cases for this center for two years now, and am a big believer in the mediation process. I am confident that this process will be helpful to you both.

Introduces self, informally introduces center, builds rapport, congratulates their choice, and briefly outlines mediation goal

Again, my name is Carol. You must be Aaron Randall. And you are Selena Wright. May I call you both by your first names? Great, thanks.

Determines formality of names

As a mediator, I am going to walk us through a process that will ask each of you to help me understand what brought us here today. The plan will then be to explore what each of you needs and to see if we can come up with a resolution that meets each of your concerns. I'm not here to make decisions for you, nor offer you legal counsel. My job is to help the two of you come up with a solution that works for you both. In that role, I intend to be neutral and impartial, meaning that I will not favor either one of you or champion any particular solution. If you have any concerns about how the process is going or what I am doing, please let me know so we can discuss it.

Briefly explains process

Establishes role

Explains neutrality and impartiality

You have each been sent a copy of the waiver and consent form. Did you get a chance to look it over? Are there any questions? I would like to draw your attention to the confidentiality clause, under point eight. I intend to keep anything that you say in here confidential and am asking that you are willing to do the same. The only reason I would break confidentiality is if I were to be informed of harm or threat to harm another individual. I also want to inform you that in the event we don't resolve your dispute here and this case proceeds to court, I cannot be subpoenaed by either side. As such, I will likely take notes through the course of this mediation, just to keep my thoughts straight, but will destroy those notes following this session.

Explains confidentiality issues

Explains note-taking procedures

At some point I may find it necessary to meet with you individually. If so, what is said in those meetings also is confidential, unless you choose to share it with the other person.

Explains caucus

I've reserved this room until 4:30 today. Are there any time constraints? Good. If you need a break, let me know. Bathrooms are just across the hall.

Discovers time constraints, explains facilities and breaks

Just a couple of items before we get started. I expect that you will speak honestly and bargain in good faith. I've found it easier to understand if only one person talks at a time. Please write down concerns you have if the other person is talking. I promise we will address any concerns you have. Also, if we could promise to be respectful to each other, even if we don't agree, this would be very helpful. Do either of you have any thing to add? Okay. Are you both willing to following these guidelines? Great.

Overview of ground rules

Are there any questions before we get started? Okay, if you are both willing to start, let's begin with Aaron since he called the center first, if that is all right with you, Selena? Aaron, what prompted your call to the mediation center?

Gains agreement to rules, asks questions before beginning, gains commitment, transition to next phase introduction strategy is devised. When high tension abounds or the context requires more formality, the mediator might use a title, for example by calling herself Ms. Hutchison, and address each party by their formal names, Mrs. Wright and Mr. Randall (or Ms. or Miss, depending on the wishes of the parties). If you choose to use a title for yourself, then referring to your disputants as Ms. or Mr. also is advised.

If an informal tone is desired, the mediator may introduce his or her first and last name, and then let the parties know that she or he would like to be called by the first name. Informality opens the door to having the parties call each other by their first names as well. For example, "Hello, my name is Sean O'Reilly. Please call me Sean. And you must be Ms. Davidson. May I call you Ann?" Another approach could be, "My name is Sean O'Reilly. Please call me Sean. Which of you is Katherine Bradshaw? Is it okay if I call you Kathy or would you prefer Katherine? And you must be Camilla Wilson. May I call you Camilla?" If you would prefer, you can avoid the guesswork by simply stating, "Hello, I'm Sean O'Reilly. Please call me Sean. And you are?" and wait for them to introduce themselves.

Formality of address also has cultural implications. For parties who are older, issues of respect and being addressed by title may be important. Elderly disputants may perceive being addressed by their first name without permission as rude. Not using formal titles may be seen as disrespectful in a cross-cultural mediation. If you are unsure about decorum in this area, we recommend erring on the side of formality.

Once the mediator has determined the names the disputants, recording the names is a good idea. The mediator can place the names on his or her mediator's note-taking form, which will be discussed later in this chapter.

Building Credibility

Mediators may opt to integrate a credibility statement into their monologue. Referring to the program or center through which you mediate may be one way to establish credibility. For example, a campus mediator might say, "Thank you for choosing the Campus Mediation Center. We've been helping university students like yourselves resolve disputes for over a decade."

Another means to build credibility is to refer to one's credentials. The mediator may make a statement about certifications or titles held, by saying, "Hello, my name is Wanda Smith. I'm a certified mediator in the Commonwealth of Massachusetts and member of the Massachusetts Council on Family Mediation." Beginning mediators might say, "Hello, my name is Wanda Smith. I'm a mediator trained by the University Dispute Resolution Program and an intern for the university in the Small Claims Court Mediation Program."

Establishing Stakeholders

If pre-mediation has not established who the relevant parties are, the mediator will check to be sure the right parties are at the table and that they have the authority to negotiate a settlement. The decision makers and those affected by the decisions made in mediation are called *stakeholders*. In small claims court, where the person who appears at court may or may not be authorized by the business being sued to negotiate creative solutions, a mediator commonly will ask, "Ms. Bradshaw, are you authorized to negotiate the issues of the case today and do you have the ability to make decisions? Great. Ms. Wilson, are you authorized to negotiate the issues of the case today and do you have the ability to make decisions?" Using precisely the same phrasing with each party demonstrates the mediator's equal treatment of both disputants.

Explaining the Nature and Scope of Mediation

Part of upholding the disputants' rights of self-determination is ensuring that they understand their rights in the process. Even if the disputants are required to appear at mediation by a judge or other authority, they are not required to reach an agreement. The mediator explains that the negotiation process is voluntary. If the mediation was self-selected by the parties, the mediator might say, "I commend both of you for choosing to come to mediation today to try to work out your differences. As you probably know, the negotiations today are entirely voluntary and you can leave at any time." If the mediation was mandated, the mediator could state, "Today's mediation involves a process where you can choose to work out the issues between you, and you may or may not reach an agreement. The negotiation part of the process is entirely voluntary and does not deter you (or the courts) from pursuing other actions if you don't reach agreement in this session."

In addition to describing the basic premise of mediation, many mediators also give the disputants a brief overview of the process. As mentioned in previous chapters, different mediation contexts use slightly different mediation models. A mediator utilizing the balanced mediation model might relate, "What will happen is that each of you will have a chance to tell me what brought you here today and the issues that are important to you. Once we've identified issues that need to be worked out, we'll set an agenda of the items that the two of you need to negotiate. I will then help you through the negotiation process and help you document any agreements you may make." A simple explanation of how the mediation will unfold assists the disputants to know what to expect and to reduce concerns about time spent initially on one party's story—the other party knows that his or her chance to speak will follow.

Explaining the Mediator's Role

Explaining what the mediator will and will not do helps the disputants understand the difference between the role of mediator and the roles of judges or others who make decisions for the parties. Mediators must be very clear in communicating their role to the disputants. If mediators are not attorneys, they must be vigilant to avoid presenting themselves as such by giving legal advice. Even when mediators are attorneys, separating the role of attorney and the role of mediator is advised. Nonattorneys who dispense legal advice may be guilty of the unauthorized practice of law (Peace, 2002). Make sure your clients know your role. "My role here today is to assist you in discussing the issues that brought you here and in helping you formulate any decisions the two of you might reach. I am not a judge or attorney and I will not make any decisions for you. Any decisions that you make are your own. Additionally, I do not offer you any legal advice, but know that you may seek advice from outside parties if you wish."

Explaining the Caucus

If the model used permits or requires a caucus, disputants need to understand what a caucus is and what might happen during a caucus. The term *caucus* may be substituted with *private meeting* if preferred. "There may come a point in this process where I'll want to meet privately with each of you." The mediator also should explain the rules of confidentiality during caucus. For instance the mediator may relate, "The same rules of confidentiality apply to the caucus and I won't tell the other party what you say without your permission."

Explaining Impartiality and Neutrality

Disputants should be made aware of the mediator's commitment to fairness in the process. The mediator explains: "During the mediation, I am impartial—meaning I don't have any stake in the outcome of the issues you decide here today—and neutral—meaning I have no bias toward either of you personally." The explanation of impartiality and neutrality should be accompanied with a disclosure of any factors that might limit neutrality or impartiality. If the mediator has seen one of the disputants before in a professional capacity or has some stake in the issue of the case, he or she must disclose those factors. "Now that I see Ms. Bradshaw, I recollect that I have mediated a case before when she also was representing the QuickRent Management Company. I don't feel that this affects my neutrality. Ms. Wilson, do you feel comfortable proceeding with me as your mediator?" If there is a connection between the mediator and the issue, the mediator might disclose, "I see that this case is regarding a rental in the Summer Winds subdivision. I have a home in that subdivision. In the nature of this case, I don't perceive any conflict that would cause me to recuse myself. Are both of you comfortable with me proceeding as your mediator?"

In some cases, the mediator may not be neutral or impartial. If the mediator is a first-level supervisor mediating for his or her own employees or a college dormitory resident advisor mediating for two roommates, the mediator will have both personal knowledge of the disputants and a stake in an amiable solution to the conflict. Under these conditions, the neutrality and impartiality statement must be altered. "As you know, the university wants difficulties between roommates to be resolved, when possible, by the people who are closest to the issues. In this mediation, I'll be fair and equal in my treatment of both of you as you work toward a possible solution that works for you and makes our dormitory a better place to live."

Giving a Confidentiality Pledge

As we discussed in Chapter 5, mediators must consider what they are willing or able to keep confidential. What is and is not confidential is detailed in the mediator's *confidentiality pledge*. Many state laws require any person with knowledge about harm or threat of harm to another person to alert proper authorities. Mediators must know what limits to confidentiality are required by state, province, or local laws. Additionally, mediators must consider where they personally stand in areas that may not be delineated in the law. For example, if a mediator finds out that one party is engaging in underage drinking, should she or he break confidentiality to report this violation? Parties must be informed about the mediator's confidentiality policy and the limitations to the pledge of confidentiality. For example the mediator may promise, "Anything you say to me today I will hold confidential. The exceptions to my confidentiality are [insert the exceptions in state, local, or province law]. In addition, as a Resident Advisor for this dormitory, I am also under obligation to report underage drinking and illegal drug use."

If the mediator required the disputants to sign a confidentiality pledge (such as the waiver and consent form discussed in Chapter 4), the mediator should review that pledge. "Both of you have signed a confidentiality pledge before we met today, saying that you will hold any information you learn today strictly confidential." A mediator may choose to add a statement that allows flexibility to this pledge by making disclosure to outside parties a negotiable issue to be discussed during the mediation.

Not all states offer *mediator privilege*, a protection for mediators against being called to testify about what they heard in mediation in the event the disputants go to court. Mediators who are not protected by their local laws may wish to seek some protection by having disputants sign a waiver and consent form stating that they will not subpoena the mediator or mediation records. How effective a waiver might be, however, depends on the laws in each jurisdiction.

Disclosing Note Taking

Disputants will be curious about why the mediator is writing while they are speaking and interested in what will become of the notes. A campus mediator could comment, "I'll be taking personal notes during the session just to keep things straight in my own mind. I'll destroy the notes at the end of our mediation. The only information I will report to the Dormitory Grievance Board is that the two of you did meet and if you came to agreement."

Destroying notes offers further protection for mediators in the unlikely event that they and their records are subpoenaed for court. While it is unlawful to destroy records once the courts have requested them, many mediators make a habit of destroying all personal records of the mediation event immediately following the mediation. Some mediators even request the personal notes of the parties be destroyed with their own. On some college campuses and in many government agencies, all documents may be considered part of the public records available for public disclosure. If agency documents are classified as a public record, it may be illegal to destroy them. Therefore, a court subpoena may not be the only threat to the confidentiality of the mediation session. Keeping only the copy of the intake information and the agreement is a common practice for many mediators. Mediators are encouraged to research the laws in their own jurisdictions to ensure that their record keeping and destroying practices are legal.

Establishing Ground Rules

Ground rules create expectations for courteous behavior and inform the disputants what is expected and what is not appropriate behavior. Most mediators have a list of ground rules in mind before they begin the mediation. Isenhart and Spangle (2000) identify four typical ground rules:

- Only one person speaks at a time
- No interruptions while someone else is speaking
- No personal attacks will be allowed
- Information shared during the mediation session will be treated as confidential (p. 79)

We recommend modifying the phrasing of these general ground rules. Saying that there will be "no interruptions while someone else is speaking" is not entirely true, as the mediator may interrupt the parties frequently to guide and control the flow of the session. A more accurate ground rule is that the disputants should allow each other to speak uninterrupted. Likewise, saying that information shared during the mediation session will be treated as confidential may not be accurate. Mediators must differentiate between their own confidentiality (and its limits under state or territorial law) and confidentiality expected of disputants or others in the room. Unless the disputants and others at the session sign a confidentiality agreement, there is no reason to expect them to keep secret about what has occurred. To be more accurate, mediators can say that they will keep information shared in the session confidential, except as required by law.

We further recommend that mediators refrain from sounding punitive in their establishment of the ground rules. Stating desired behavior instead of unacceptable behavior seems less parental. For instance, instead of saying, "Do not interrupt when the other is speaking," say: "When one of you is speaking, it is important that she is allowed to finish. If you have something you want to add when someone is talking, please write it down and I promise we will get to your concerns."

Maintaining civility is an important goal for the mediation. A ground rule about respecting each other may be presented as, "In my experience, these sessions work best when we are respectful and courteous to one another, even when we don't agree." Using the term "we" here includes the mediator in the rules and sounds less dogmatic.

Another area for discussion in the ground rules section of the opening statement is a brief description of the surroundings and if disputants may take care of their own personal needs during the session. Mediators may mention bathrooms, water fountains, and telephones, for example, or inform disputants of how breaks will be managed. A mediator may say, "If you need a break, please let me know. Bathrooms are down the hall to the left, and soda machines are across the foyer."

Having each party agree to the ground rules is critical and can be accomplished by asking a direct question such as, "Can we agree to these ground rules before we begin?" If a party becomes unruly, one strategy is to take some of the blame for the need to adhere to the rules. For example, the mediator could say, "I'm finding it very difficult to follow this conversation when more than one person is talking. Could we go back to one person speaking at a time? Jessie, please continue with your explanation." Asking for compliance to rules should be handled carefully, as the "scolded" party may perceive bias from the mediator. Major infractions may be handled most effectively one-on-one during a caucus.

An optional strategy for establishing ground rules allows the disputants to set the rules. The mediator would tell the disputants that the sessions work better when the parties agree on how they will treat each other in advance, then ask each party what rules of behavior would be important to them. The mediator then helps the parties negotiate the rules they will adopt. Once the parties agree on their own rules, the mediator can add any other rules critical to the model being applied and praise the disputants for working together to reach their first agreement. Keltner (1987) notes that in some instances rules are written and signed by all parties.

Discovering Time Constraints

Mediators must ensure that there will be sufficient time to explore issues and negotiate effectively. In one instance, a disputant was feeling that the negotiations were not going in her favor and informed the mediator that she had to leave to pick up her daughter. This tactic caused the negotiations to stall on the spot, and the mediation ended.

During pre-mediation, the disputants may have been informed of a typical range of time for the mediation, but reminding them of their time commitment is helpful during the opening statement. Be cautious, however, not to set up an expectation in your disputants for *exactly* how much time the mediation will take. We advise not giving disputants cause to worry that they are taking too long or, if they are fast, not doing it right. Commenting, "We have scheduled the room until

4:00, so we can take the time we need to work on your concerns," will give disputants an idea of the expectations on their time. Do ask directly about their time constraints. "Are both of you alright with that time frame?" You also may wish to address avoiding distractions: "If you'll turn off your cell phones and beepers, I think we're ready to begin." Occasionally, disputants cannot turn off their phones for emergency purposes, but typically it is best to reduce distractions by having communication devices turned off.

Explaining the Role of Outside Experts

At the onset of mediation, disputants may believe that they have all the information and advice that they will need during negotiations. However, during the mediation, they may find that access to more resources is necessary to make informed decisions. Mediators can include a statement that addresses their right to seek counsel such as: "Each of you should know that any agreements you reach today may be binding and that agreements may restrict your rights in later actions. You are both encouraged to seek legal counsel before finalizing any agreements if you have any doubts or need the advice of counsel." If the issue is complex enough to require impartial experts to establish facts in the case, the disputants should be briefed on how experts would be used. For instance, the mediator may relate: "Should there be a dispute about facts in the case that both of you decide needs to be resolved, we may bring in an impartial outside expert to assist the two of you. If that time comes, I'll assist you in jointly choosing an expert that you both feel will give fair and impartial facts and how you will pay the expert." The desire of the mediator is for disputants to be well informed and comfortable in the decision-making process.

Securing the Commitment to Begin

By this point, the disputants have received a considerable amount of information that may or may not be new to them. Asking for their commitment to transition to the next phase of the mediation provides the mediator with a verbal commitment to move forward. The commitment to begin statement should be simple, such as: "Now that we've covered the basics, are there any questions? (pause) Are we ready to begin?"

Transitioning to Storytelling

In transitioning to the storytelling and issue-identification phase, the mediator must decide who should talk first and present some rationale to the disputants for the choice. If one disputant is visibly agitated, sometimes it is best to start with him or her, as people who are agitated rarely can listen to the other party before

---

MEDIATOR NOTEBOOK 6.1

Creating Your Own Opening Statement

Examine the opening statement elements and the sample opening statement in Figure 6.1. Create a version of the monologue that covers the required elements, but is adapted to your own personal vocabulary and way of speaking. After you have written your personalized opening statement, examine the functions of an opening statement presented in this chapter to be sure each function is included in your personal opening statement.

Write an outline *add follow outline*

their own fears and emotions have been moderated. Other strategies for deciding who will speak first include selecting:

- The person who first contacted the mediator
- The plaintiff in a court case
- The individual with less power

The mediator may or may not reveal his or her true motivation in selecting who speaks first. In a mediation with a professor and a student, the mediator may wish to power balance by having the person with less institutional power—the student—speak first. The explanation given to the disputants, however, might be: "You were both referred to the Mediation Center by the Academic Grievance Board, so I'll have the person on my right [or left] go first. John, could you tell us what brought you here today?" Beer and Stief (1997) suggest two other basic opening prompts: "Please explain to us what has been happening" and "Can you give us some background?—tell us your view of the situation?" (p. 106). More details about storytelling and issue identification will be presented in Chapter 7.

Building Credibility and Rapport

Throughout the opening statement, the mediator strives to build rapport with each disputant and a perception of competence and credibility. Donohue, Diez, and Weider-Hatfield (1984) argue that "the mediator must encourage each of the disputants to attribute trust to him or her so that both parties will comply with the mediator's requests" (p. 230). The mediator may need to interrupt the parties, encourage changes in how the parties perceive the facts in the situation, coach the parties in how to hear each other's concerns, or ask the disputants to make difficult choices to transform the pattern of an intractable conflict. All of these actions require trust between the parties and the mediator. Disputants must trust that the mediator will be fair to both and will keep the process under control and on track. Keltner (1987) notes "there are many ways the mediator can build such a trust factor into the relationships. These include such things as friendliness, acceptance of the clients' ideas and feelings, use of non-aggressive questions, showing concern for the problems of clients face, and accuracy of feedback" (p. 26).

Dominici and Littlejohn (2001) also view the opening moments of the mediation as key to the building of trust: "If a trust relationship is created, the disputants can participate openly while seeing the mediator as competent. All components of the introduction work together to set the tone and to establish trust. If a trusting environment is evident from the start, it will facilitate the entire process. People often have misconceptions about mediation, and this is the time to get everyone on the same track" (pp. 65–66). The mediator's demeanor during the opening statement cues the disputants that the mediator is trustworthy and competent.

ACTIVITY **6.1**

Practice your opening statement aloud until you are comfortable with the words and phrasing. Find two partners in the class with whom to practice your opening statement. Deliver the opening statement to your partners, striving for a personable tone that will build trust and confidence in you as a mediator and for an equal division of your attention between both parties.

The Relationship between Opening Statements and Mediator Control

By definition, mediators control the process of the session. The balanced mediation model recommends a fairly active role for the mediator to guide the disputants through the phases in the model and to intervene to keep the session on-task and moving in productive directions. Donohue, Diez, and Weider-Hatfield (1984) define relational control as the "right to direct, delimit, and define the action of the relationship" (p. 229). They continue, "in mediation, control of the interaction is a key objective for the mediator to increase his or her flexibility in pursuing some particular pattern of questioning or topic development. The opposing parties may also be trying to compete with the mediator for control depending upon their objectives. Nevertheless, negotiating control is one of the relational parameters that the mediator must be able to manage" (p. 229).

The mediator establishes control during the opening statement through the creation of ground rules and by building confidence in the minds of the disputants. Isenhart and Spangle (2000) argue the function of ground rules is to provide

◯	**MEDIATOR NOTEBOOK 6.2** **Creating Your Own Note-Taking Form**
	Create your own note-taking form based on the sample in Figure 6.2. Place the form in your mediator notebook and use it during practice mediations.

a safe and predictable space for the disputants to negotiate their differences. A composed and confident presentation of the opening statement implicitly says to the disputants, "I will keep your conflict under control and create a safe space for you to work things out."

Note Taking for Mediators

During the mediation session, the disputants will disclose many facts, fears, solutions, or other information the mediator needs to remember. While some mediators can retain all the information mentally, most mediators need to take notes. A mediator's notes are a combination of facts and the mediator's own analysis. Donohue, Diez, and Weider-Hatfield (1984) explain that the mediator "uses his or her skills to listen for potential links, to sort and analyze elements of the discourse, synthesizing or structuring the information to delete the 'hidden' principles clouding the assessment of potential solutions. This is a critical interpretation skill, requiring the ability to analyze and synthesize on the spot" (p. 235).

As the mediator progresses in skill and confidence, each will develop his or her own unique method of taking notes. Beginning mediators can profit from a simple structure. Figure 6.2 illustrates a sample note-taking form for beginning mediators. This general format can help keep notes organized, but the actual "form" is typically plain, lined paper.

As the disputants are introduced, the mediator will fill in each party's name at the top of the page, typically with the name of the person on one's left in the left column and the person on one's right in the right column. As the storytelling and issue-identification phase proceeds, the mediator will note a word or short phrase in the "interest" section whenever a key need is disclosed by one of the disputants.

Issues will be recorded in the center of the page. Issues are common to both parties and hence are recorded in a space that represents both of the disputants. Any other observations the mediator wishes to remember (such as settlement offers made early in the process that the mediator tabled at that time but may wish to bring back into the discussion later) can be noted at the bottom of the page.

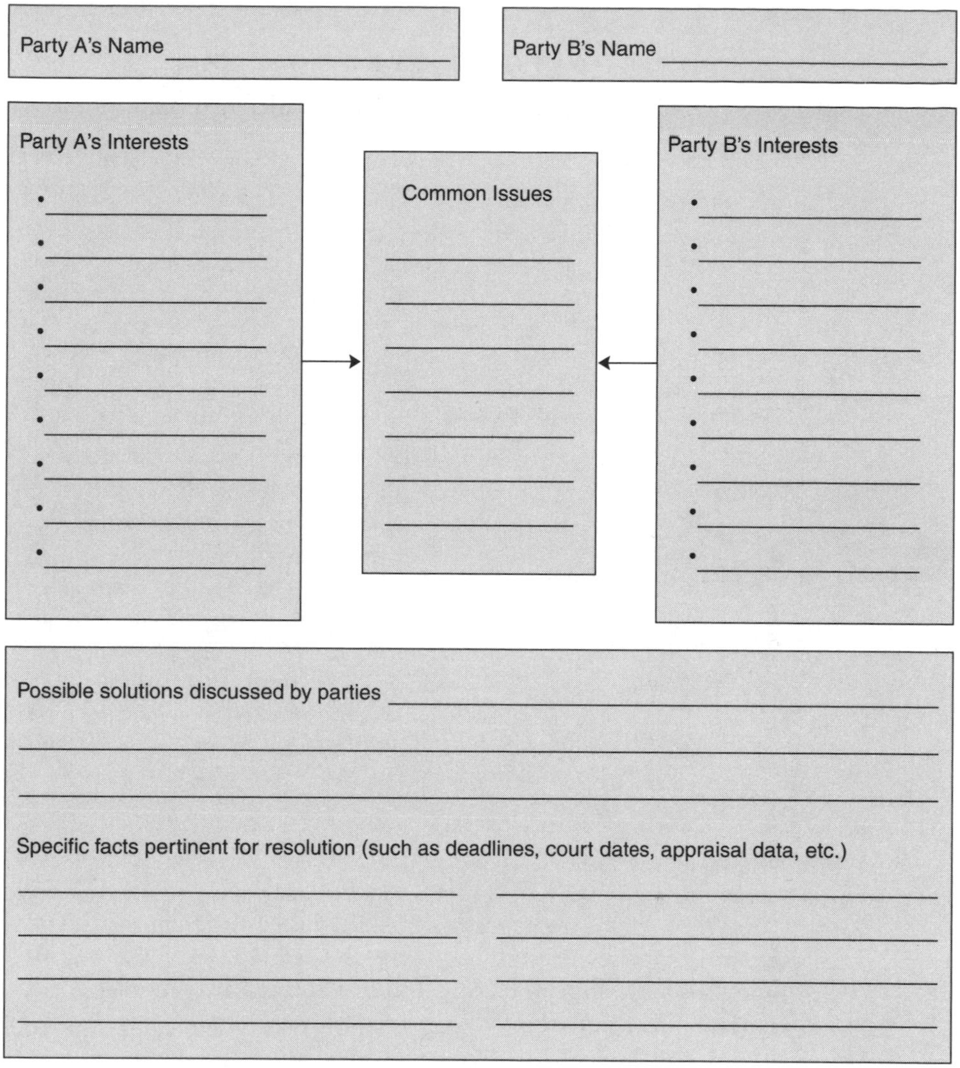

| Party A's Name _____ | Party B's Name _____ |

Party A's Interests	Common Issues	Party B's Interests
• _____	_____	• _____
• _____	_____	• _____
• _____	_____	• _____
• _____	_____	• _____
• _____	→ _____ ←	• _____
• _____	_____	• _____
• _____	_____	• _____
• _____	_____	• _____
• _____		• _____

Possible solutions discussed by parties _____

_____

_____

Specific facts pertinent for resolution (such as deadlines, court dates, appraisal data, etc.)

_____   _____

_____   _____

_____   _____

_____   _____

FIGURE 6.2   Sample Note-Taking Form

Mediators will want to make a special note of commonalities among the parties. These very important revelations are simple, but profound. *Commonalities* are practices, values, traits, goals, or other discernible facts shared by both parties. Commonalities can be indicated in the mediator's notes by connecting two interests or facts with lines across the page or by writing them separately somewhere else on the page (either in the center with issues or at the lower section of the page). Mediators treasure commonalities and will insert them strategically into the mediation, as we will discuss in later chapters.

Summary

The mediator's opening statement begins the mediation by informing the disputants about the mediator's role and the process that will be followed for the mediation session. Opening statements may be a monologue or interactive. The opening statement serves to introduce parties, set the tone, and establish the mediator as the process facilitator for the session. Informing disputants about their rights and responsibilities is accomplished in the opening statement. Disputants should know what is expected of their behavior and how much time a mediation may take. Disputants also should be made aware of the role attorneys or outside experts may play in the mediation. One important area that deserves careful attention is the issue of confidentiality. Mediators must share with the parties their confidentiality promises and their limitations. Disputants should also be informed about their obligations in terms of confidentiality.

The opening statement is the part of the mediation where the mediator establishes his or her credibility and control of the process. Making sure that disputants are on board with ground rules and are educated about the process enables mediators to create a safe and productive mediation environment.

The notes that mediators take during a session function as a reminder of facts and a storehouse of the mediator's insights about the case. Typically, the mediator's notes are destroyed after the session.

7 Storytelling and Issue Identification

*A*t the heart of the mediation process is the time and energy spent discovering the individual stories of the participants. While listening to how each party has experienced the conflict, the mediator validates where needed, explores when more clarification is required, and identifies key issues or interests that must be highlighted throughout the rest of the process. New mediators have a tendency to rush through this critical step to bring parties to quick resolution. What usually results from a rush to problem solving, however, is that the process begins to unravel when disputants discuss solutions. Parties who do not have an adequate chance to explain their views and concerns may end up cycling back to their story. Thus, effort in this important stage is time well spent, making the rest of the mediation flow much more smoothly.

CASE **7.1**

The Privacy Fence

The Holleys and the Wallaces have been next-door neighbors for over twenty years. Each had two children and over the years several incidents occurred that caused tensions between the families. When the children were small, the Holley boy and the Wallaces' son were playing with matches behind the Holleys' shed. In fact, they burned it down. Each boy blamed the other, and their respective families believed their own child's version of events. Since that time, the children were not allowed to play together. The kids have grown and moved away, but tensions still exist between the two neighbors. Mrs. Wallace grows prize roses and the rose garden is on the line between the two properties, currently marked by a three-foot-high chain-link fence.

Mr. and Mrs. Holley are planning to build a new fence between the properties and are irritated that the Wallace's refused to pay for half of the new fence. Mrs. Wallace doesn't want the fence, as the shade will destroy her garden that currently receives lots of sun. The Holleys have wanted a fence for twenty years, so they can have additional privacy for their yard and, now, a new hot tub.

In most mediations, the majority of the mediation time is spent in the story-telling and issue-identification phase. In contexts such as victim-offender mediation, the interest and issue identification can occur in extended pre-mediation sessions (where the mediator meets individually with parties before bringing them together). However, in the balanced model of mediation, the mediator strives to complete this crucial phase in the presence of both parties.

According to the Pepperdine University Institute for Dispute Resolution (1995), the parties' opening statements offer valuable psychological benefits for the disputants as well as critical information for the mediator. Specifically, the storytelling offers:

- A chance to get a "flavor" of the case, as well as offering insight into the parties' conflict management styles, personalities, and what is most significant to the parties
- A forum where parties are required to hear opposing ideas and respond to the issues in the presence of a neutral party
- A place to compare and contrast opposing views and identify areas in common
- A context where parties disclose the bases for their claims, allegations, and conclusions, and can assess the efficacy of those assumptions
- An environment where parties can feel that they have their "day in court" (p. 8:2)

This chapter presents two theories useful for understanding storytelling: symbolic interaction and attribution theory. Additionally, it presents the basic functions of storytelling, the importance of separating interests from positions, strategies for encouraging parties to tell their stories, and tips to avoid common pitfalls in this phase of mediation.

Theories of Storytelling

Theories of human communication can inform our understanding of what happens during storytelling. When looking through the lens of a particular theory, certain elements of the event are revealed. Theories help mediators see the process from a different perspective. Understanding several theories offers options for making sense of human behavior. Two theories that inform the storytelling phase are *symbolic interaction* and *attribution theories*.

Symbolic Interaction

Symbolic interaction is a broad-based theory of how humans create meaning. Although more complex than will be explained here, symbolic interaction provides mediators with a core understanding of the importance of the storytelling event. According to Ballis Lal (1995), three tenets of symbolic interaction are of particular interest to mediators:

1. Individuals act according to how they understand the world based on their own subjective interpretations of their circumstances
2. People understand and interpret their world through language (symbols)
3. Through social interaction we construct (and re-construct) meaning

Individuals come to mediation with a particular view of the conflict. In essence, two different stories of the conflict exist for the disputants. Subjective interpretations of experience are a primary focus of mediators. Disputants see the world independently and uniquely, and understand their world through language. Mediators attempt to understand how each disputant has constructed his or her reality and how each has created meaning with the symbols used.

Disputants enter the mediation with separate stories that have been constructed independently. In the storytelling phase, the mediator draws out the individuals' stories and weaves the two into one story that they create together. The goal through the lens of symbolic interaction is to create a *shared meaning* (or story) from which both parties can function. The new story, now including the meaning of each participant, provides a common reality on which to build the rest of the mediation event.

*W*HY WOULD *creating a shared story be important to the mediation phases of generating possible options and negotiation? What is a probable outcome of a mediation where parties continue to operate from their own perspectives without being able to see the other's view?*

Attribution Theory

Humans naturally try to understand what motivates behavior. When we are not certain of why someone acted a certain way, we have a tendency to guess. Heider's (1958) attribution theory provides insights into how disputants may create meaning from each other's behavior. Heider offers several ways in which people attribute motive. Two common types of attributions people make are personality and situational. A *personality attribution* manifests when a party assumes that an element of a person's personality, something *inside* of that person, is responsible for a behavior. A *situational attribution* assumes that a person's behavior is a result of some *outside* circumstance or situation (see Figure 7.1).

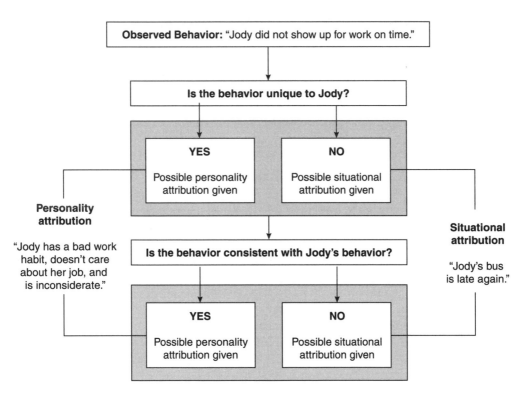

FIGURE 7.1   Situational and Personality Attributions

Personality and situational attributions frequently are at odds with one another. They also may be a key to how each party perceives the other. For example, a professor notices that a student is sleeping in her class. A natural human tendency is for the professor to assign a motive to that student. A possible attribution by the professor would be that the student is lazy or disinterested, both attributes of the student's personality. From the student's perspective, however, a situational attribution may be more accurate. Due to a friend's car breaking down on the freeway (a situation), he had to go help out his buddy at 1:00 A.M., drive an hour and a half to rescue him, and tow his car back to town.

In addition to evaluating behaviors according to a person's personality or situation, humans also consider two other variables, *consistency* and *uniqueness*. Consistency speaks to the stability of the behavior over time. The student in the previous example has taken two other courses with the professor and has not fallen asleep before in class. The sleeping behavior would be inconsistent, and cause of the behavior probably would be attributed to the situation. Uniqueness refers to the idiosyncratic nature of the behavior in question. If the same professor has noted that all of her students are nodding off during a lecture, the sleeping student's behavior is not unique and probably would not be attributed to personality (the cause is affecting all students, therefore the heat in the room must be the reason for the sleepiness).

The *fundamental attribution error* is that people generally consider personality attributions to others' behavior when they make mistakes (they are lazy, rude, insensitive, uncaring, and irresponsible). However, a *self-serving bias* occurs when an individual has to account for his or her own mistakes. Generally, we do not blame our own personality, but instead provide a situational attribution or something outside of us as the motivation.

*P*ROVIDE AN *example where two competing attributions were operating in a conflict in which you were involved. What happened? Do you think the effect occurred because the individuals were not aware of the differing attributions? How would (or did) the conflict end?*

Knowing the human tendency to favor one's self in attributing motive to situation and in blaming other people's personalities when their motives are called into question helps mediators recognize and deal with attributions. For example, Janelle sees Mac using new office supplies. When she goes to the supply closet to get some markers, pens, and tape, there is little there. She sees Mac has new supplies all over his desk. Janelle may see Mac as selfish and inconsiderate (personality attributions). However, Mac, unbeknownst to Janelle, has taken over a sick colleague's account and is working overtime doing his work and his colleague's. He has taken most of his supplies home so he can work on the project, and he has restocked his desk with new supplies from the supply closet. He sees his use of supplies as part of his situation, not his personality. The mediator, on hearing

Janelle's personality attribution, "Mac is being so piggish with the supplies!" could then ask Mac to explain from his perspective, thus revealing the situational circumstances. The mediator could say to Mac, "Janelle has noticed a change in the use of supplies. Could you tell us how you see this situation?"

> *What could occur when a mediator shapes the story of participants in the viewpoint or the language of one disputant?*

Mediators should have an understanding of how disputants frame their experiences from their own subjective points of view. With the insights gained from theory in mind, the mediator can better understand the functions of storytelling.

Functions of Storytelling

The storytelling and issue-identification phase offers important benefits for the individual disputants. It also provides information to guide the mediator in how to focus the mediation.

The Individual

The needs of the disputants in mediation can vary, but generally fall into three categories: to be safe, to be heard, and to be acknowledged.

The Need to Be Safe.   Through the mediator's opening statement, disputants should be aware that the process of mediation is to create a fair, equitable, and safe forum for the exchange of ideas. Mediators work to maintain the safe psychological environment of the mediation by being encouraging, displaying empathy, maintaining a neutral and impartial demeanor both verbally and nonverbally, and keeping control of the mediation process. Disputants need to feel confident that the mediator can handle any changes in dynamics that may result if they make themselves vulnerable to attack or share information that may be difficult for the other party to hear.

The Need to Be Heard.   Parties may also need to be heard and to have a place and time to vent their frustrations with the current situation. The disputants' opening statements during storytelling may be their first chance to tell their stories in full. It may, in fact, be the first time that they have considered their own experiences fully.

The Need to Be Acknowledged.   Parties have a need to be acknowledged and to feel validated about their concerns. Parties may need to have their story recognized as having value and being important. They may worry that their ideas will be seen as inconsequential or trivial and need the mediator to acknowledge the worth of their ideas and feelings by giving them space and time for their hearing.

Mediators, however, must adapt to the cues from disputants about what is important to them. In one mediation, a new mediator, equipped with a toolbox of listening skills, entered the session eager to validate. The disputants were not friends, did not have an ongoing relationship, and were only in disagreement about how much money should be returned for a defective piece of construction equipment that was rented to dig a trench. The mediator, with the best of intentions, continued to validate the parties' emotions and attempted to create a shared relationship where none existed. When the disputants grew tired of the mediator focusing on feelings while they wanted to focus on the content issue of money, they both became mad at the mediator. One exasperated party said, "Look. I don't care about how she felt, and it's none of her business how I felt. I just want my money back!" Storytelling offers the individual disputants the chance to highlight what is important to them. It should not be a showcase for the mediator's skills or focus on what is important to the mediator.

The Mediator

The storytelling phase allows mediators to identify issues to be negotiated, to determine underlying interests, and to establish common ground, if possible. The mediator accomplishes these tasks while at the same time keeping the mediation process focused and productive.

Separating Interests from Positions.   As discussed in Chapter 1, mediation is an interest-based conflict management process, specifically focusing on substantive, procedural, and psychological interests. Unfortunately for mediators, disputants do not automatically come to the mediation table with their *interests,* or needs, identified. Most people in conflict approach negotiations from a *positional base,* considering what they want or expect to occur to resolve the conflict. Working with positions and interests during negotiations is discussed in Chapter 9. However, at this point, knowing that parties see the conflict differently is important. There are three parts to their typical complaint: their version of events, their complaint about the other, and their definition of the problem.

Haynes (1994) points out that "the hallmark is that each person defines the problem in such a way that the problem can be solved only by a change in the behavior or position of the *other*" (p. 8). For example, a disputant may come to the mediation table believing that the only way to be satisfied is if the other party apologizes. This position usually comes in the form of a demand: "She should apologize to me." Parties are adept in making demands for particular solutions. Examples of other positional statements are:

"We won't sign a contract that does not include a dental and vision plan."
"I won't take a dime less than $800.00 for the damage she did to that carpet."

"He can see the kids every other weekend and two weeks in the summer."
"She needs to move that wreck of a car from in front of my house."

Behind every positional statement is an interest waiting for the mediator to uncover. Interests are what drive positions—the needs that underlie the demands.
Skilled mediators listen for positional statements so they can explore the interests
that brought the parties to those conclusions. Instead of repeating positional statements, mediators reframe positions through validating or paraphrasing.

The listening skills presented in Chapter 3 come into play for the mediator
during the storytelling phase. When a position is stated, the mediator considers
which tools would best draw out the interest and shift the focus away from the
stated position. Mediators may ask questions to clarify or expand information for
understanding substantive interests. Mediators may need to validate the speaker
by identifying a psychological interest (such as respect, safety, inclusion, self-
determination). In all cases, mediators strive to reframe positions into interests,
without restating specific positions. For instance:

Wrong

DISPUTANT: "I won't pay her a dime for those calls. They're not all mine."

MEDIATOR: "So you don't want to pay her for the calls." [A content paraphrase restating the position.]

In the above example, the mediator repeated the position of the disputant by stating the solution that the disputant brought to the table—he didn't want to pay for
any calls. By restating the position, the mediator adds power to that position,
making it more difficult for the disputant to consider other options. Instead, the
mediator could reframe the statement into an *interest* and work to clarify more of
the story:

Correct

DISPUTANT: "I won't pay her a dime for those calls. They're not all mine."

MEDIATOR: "You're looking to be treated fairly and have a concern with the
request for payment. Tell me, when did you first find out about the phone
bill?"

Interests become a key element in the evaluation of possible solutions later in the
negotiation stage. "Fair treatment" is an interest that can be explored by the mediator. The criteria by which options are evaluated primarily are the interests of the
parties. If one party, fearful of being robbed again, bought a big dog for protection,
the underlying interest may be feeling safe in his home. If, through negotiations,
the same party agrees to give up the dog because the neighbor is afraid of it, the
home security interest may re-emerge. Consequently, establishing criteria may be

useful in this mediation: any solution would need to meet the safety issues of both parties. More about establishing criteria and evaluating options will be discussed in Chapter 10.

Identifying Issues.   In addition to addressing the emotions that the parties may bring to the table, the mediator also must determine the issues to be negotiated. *Issues* are the topics of the mediation, those items that will be negotiated. Mediators constantly are identifying issues that are important to the parties and further separating them into categories of what can and cannot be negotiated. The mediator tracks these issues and uses them later to frame the negotiation agenda (discussed in Chapter 8). In the storytelling and issue-identification phase, the mediator locates issues and explores them so all parties understand the basic facts, interests, and considerations connected to the issue.

Issues that can be negotiated include those where the parties at the table have power to affect change. A buyer and seller of a small business who want to change the reporting requirements to the state about the details of their agreement really have no control over that requirement. However, the two at the table could negotiate their own responsibilities about which party reports to the state.

Moore (2003) identifies three types of issues that can be negotiated: substantive issues, negotiation procedures, and behavioral changes for improving the psychological conditions of the parties (p. 75). According to Moore, most mediators begin with the *substantive issues,* focusing on the cause and desired outcomes of the dispute. In the case of a divorcing couple, the substantive issues may include the division of property. However, focusing too early on this substantive issue may create problems in the negotiation if the parties are not in a psychological space conducive to negotiating. Mediators must evaluate the needs of the disputants to attend to other nonsubstantive issues. Consequently, the mediator fully explores the nature of a substantive issue during storytelling and issue identification rather than immediately moving to negotiation once an issue is discovered.

Procedural issues evolve around how things are done: how agendas will be created, when and where events occur, how information is shared, how a process is governed by ground rules, or how records are kept. According to Moore, when procedural issues are identified during storytelling and placed early on the negotiation agenda, a history of successful negotiation is created and trust in the mediation and the parties is built. Examples of procedural issues include discussing who else, besides the parties, will be privy to the mediation agreement; determining the amount of time available for the mediation session; and developing rules for the mediation concerning how parties will communicate with each other. By exploring the nature of any procedural issues during storytelling and issue identification, the mediator is prepared to decide where to place procedural issues on the negotiation agenda.

Psychological (emotional) issues emerge from paying particular attention to the relationship of the parties and creating a safe environment where the mediation can unfold. Hurt feelings often impede the parties' abilities to talk together. In neighborhood disputes, mediators may highlight the ongoing neighbor relationship that the parties share and determine the importance of this relationship for each neighbor. The focus on linkages provides a superordinate, or umbrella, issue under which the other issues can be framed.

A second function of focusing on the emotional issues is helping the disputants create a space where they can communicate effectively. Mediators may take time early in the mediation to train disputants and to establish behavioral codes. The mediator may teach disputants to exhibit ownership language through "I statements," such as: "This is how I see it," or "From my perspective, this occurred." Mediators can encourage validation and active listening behaviors from both parties. In this way, the mediator aids the parties in creating a communication environment where their emotional issues can be heard.

According to Cloke (2001), "the poses" the parties take, or the face they show to the other party, affect the entire mediation process. Cloke writes, "As long as parties hold on to their poses, whether of injured virtue, anger, or self-righteousness, honest communication will be blocked and conflicts left unresolved. The mediator's role is to assist parties in dropping their poses, communicating honestly and empathetically, and taking responsibility—not only for their intentions, but their words, actions, and effects they have on others, regardless of intention" (p. 35). The mediator must create a productive communication environment where the disputants can hear, and be heard by, all participants. Whether or not emotional issues appear on the agenda for negotiation, the mediator must work through these issues in storytelling and issue identification for the mediation to proceed.

Attending to the substantive and procedural issues, as well as creating a psychological space conducive to the productive expression of emotion, is crucial. Identifying interests and operating from an interest-based approach is another means of establishing a healthy psychological grounding from which to operate.

Establishing Common Ground.   Common ground encompasses any area where the disputants are in agreement or have similar interests, such as a desire to have a good relationship with each other, to have a successful business, or to be treated fairly. Common ground areas are considered by many mediators to be the "golden nuggets" of mediation. By framing issues and interests as common problems, the mediator is moving the problem psychologically to the "other side of the table," as illustrated in Figure 7.2. In the first box, Party A believes that Party B is the "problem" and that the way for the problem to be fixed is to fix Party B. Party B, however, sees Party A as the source of the problem, and both parties are looking to change the other instead of focusing on the problem itself. The second box illustrates what the mediator is attempting to do with the disputants—metaphorically put both parties on the same side of the table facing the problem to be fixed. If the mediator can identify a common concern, interest, or problem to be addressed, this shift becomes much easier to accomplish. According to Haynes (1994), "Neither A nor B will change unilaterally, and neither will change to conform with the other's definition of the problem, since both have their own definition. Therefore,

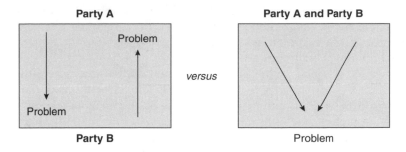

FIGURE 7.2   **Establishing Common Ground**

the mediator's task is to help the participants discard their individual problem definitions and adopt a mutual and common definition of the problem. Only then can problem solving begin." (p. 9)

*I*N CASE *7.1, identify the substantive, procedural, and psychological issues that may need to be addressed. Which of these would you address first? Explain.*

*U*SING CASE *7.1, identify how each party sees the other as the "problem." What would be each party's solution to the fence situation? How would you move the problem to the other side of the table (Figure 7.2)? How would you frame the problem to include both parties?*

Mediator Strategies in Storytelling

Mediators must consider the consequence of any strategy employed to begin and continue the storytelling phase. For example, the simple act of choosing one party to speak first allows that party to frame the discussion. The other party is placed in the position of responding to the first speaker. However, one party may feel uncomfortable speaking first and would benefit from hearing the other side before responding. As with any strategy, mediators make choices about the use, effectiveness, and possible consequences of adopting one strategy over another.

This section presents several strategies for eliciting stories and uncovering information from the disputants. No single strategy will be useful all of the time. Saposnek (1998) uses an aikido metaphor for his approach to mediation, calling it the strategic approach. Saposnek claims that if something isn't working, don't do more of the same. Instead, think strategically by "maintaining an organized and goal-directed but flexible thought process that allows the mediator, in the face of obstacles, to shift gears, change tactics, and continue moving toward a preplanned goal" (p. 58). Thinking strategically means that mediators do not use a technique for its own sake; mediators must have an idea where the strategy will go and how it will move the parties forward.

One Storyteller at a Time

The one storyteller at a time strategy gives the floor to one disputant to express a personal view of the current problem and situation. After the mediator's opening statement, the mediator may say to one party, "Martin, you were the one who contacted the mediation center, would you please tell me what led to your call and what has been the situation as you see it?" The mediator then prompts and validates as needed, taking notes on issues and identifying interests as the speaker relays the story. Some follow-up questions can be included, but the mediator should not let one party monopolize a great deal of time. The other party is waiting for a turn to speak and refute. The mediator would then use the same prompt ("Tell me what the situation is as you see it") and give the floor to the other party.

The benefit of the one storyteller at a time approach is that parties each tell their stories with relatively few interruptions. Each has a chance to vent and receive the attention of the mediator, which, in turn, may create more trust in the process.

The disadvantages, however, also should be considered. In the one storyteller at a time approach, one person may attempt to monopolize the session. If one party is more articulate or prepared than the other, he or she will have more to say and can create an imbalance of power. The other party may become frustrated by not being allowed to interject until the end of the speaker's story or, if suffering from communication anxiety, may not be able to express him/herself. Additionally, in this approach, one party establishes the first framing of the story that the other party may feel a need to refute, rather than having a chance to develop her or his own story. Managing interruptions is a key skill when using this strategy.

Co-Constructing Stories

An alternative to the strict one at a time strategy is to have the parties present their perceptions of their stories at the same time. This strategy works better if there is a history of cooperation between the parties and tension is reasonably low. In this approach, one party begins sharing and then the mediator switches back and forth, making sure that both parties can add their perceptions to the story as it unfolds. This strategy of switching back and forth between the parties may have the added benefit of clearing up simple misunderstandings as the story is told. Another advantage is that since the story is created together, both parties are able to participate directly and are not relegated to a passive listener role. The goal of creating a shared meaning of the events is often easier when co-constructing stories.

However, co-construction is not an easy approach to manage, particularly when disputants disagree about key issues during the story construction. New mediators may have difficulty tracking the issues and interests of both parties at the same time. Another risk is that parties will become caught in details and begin arguing.

Once the storytelling process begins, the mediator must employ strategies to uncover hidden agendas, reveal important elements of the story, and gain a full picture of the situation to be mediated. The following strategies help the mediator get the whole story on the table.

General Inquiry Approach

The *general inquiry approach* is designed to build a sense of the "big picture." Questions such as, "What is the situation that brought you here today?" or "I understand that you are having concerns over the upkeep of the employee lunchroom. Explain a little bit about the situation," serve to paint the picture in broad strokes. In the initial storytelling, it is effective to create a general picture from both parties and then establish the specifics. In any approach the mediator must avoid having party A sitting silent for a considerably long time while party B lays out the details of the story. In general inquiry, the mediator attempts to get the issues onto the table. In the specific inquiry (discussed later), the mediator probes for the details and deeper interests.

Whole Picture Questions

Disputants may bog down the mediation in the details important to them. As the mediator works to get a sense of the bigger picture, *whole picture questions* may be helpful. Every story has a past, a present, and a future. In the initial storytelling, the mediator attempts to become current on the situation and understand what led up to the point when the mediation was scheduled. Disputants can be directed to focus on the past with direct questions such as, "What was the past situation with your boss like, prior to this incident?" or "Has there ever been a time when this wasn't a problem?"

Questions that focus the disputants on their current situation also shed light onto how they are experiencing the event now. Asking, "How is this currently affecting your business relationship?" or "What are the consequences to you now?" may present the mediator with the party's interests. Having parties consider the current ideal is another strategy. The mediator may ask, "What is your idea of a good neighbor?"

Future questions typically are saved for the option-generating part of the mediation (see Chapter 10). However, a well-placed future question may provide insight into how this affects the disputants' futures. For example, asking, "Can you see a time when this won't be a problem anymore?" may provide everyone with information about one party's plan to move to another state and shift the mediation to a short-term, problem-solving session.

Being Columbo

In the 1970s and 1980s, *Columbo* was a television criminal detective with a penchant for getting people to answer his questions, and in doing so, inadvertently giving up key evidence. Columbo adopted a naïve perspective to solving any case. He asked questions that seemed elementary, but were relevant. "Do these windows lock?" "How long did you know Ms. Gray?" "So you drive to work every day and come home for lunch?" His naïve perspective allowed Columbo to uncover information that others would deem irrelevant, but ultimately proved critical to the case at hand.

As mediators, we are offered this same latitude to ask seemingly irrelevant or elementary questions in order for us to gain a good understanding of the disputant's situation. We can ask for a party to draw a diagram of the placement of the office cubicles or to explain what they mean by "being uncomfortable around that equipment." Mediators are in a position not to take anything for granted—the details may uncover facts that neither party considered or may foster a more creative view during negotiations.

Specific Inquiry

As the storytelling progresses, the mediator elicits more details from the disputants. Specific inquiry questions ask for details and concrete information, such as "How much?" "When?" and "Where?" For example, the mediator may ask a question about a past assertion: "You said that the automobile does run, but you say there are still areas where it is having problems. Could you tell me about those?" or "How did you arrive at that amount?" or "Would you discuss your normal billing procedures?" Other information may be gleaned from specific inquiry as the mediator attempts to discern how the disputant experienced the situation, such as, "When you weren't paid for your carpentry project, how did that affect you personally?" "How has this situation affected your work?" "What do you need to do your job well?"

Establishing Agreed-on "Facts"

If parties are having a difficult time seeing each other's perspectives, one strategy is to establish clear places where they do agree and use these "facts" as springboards for discussion. For example, the mediator may state, "So there was a $300 deposit paid on July 14. What was the understanding about this deposit?" This statement allows both parties to see an established fact and then discuss their perceptions of that fact. Stating a fact and then asking for interpretations allows the disputants to see how the other party may view the same situation differently. Another example is: "From what I can tell, the original payment amount was to be $55 a month for the medical bills. There were ten payments made last year and no

---

MEDIATOR NOTEBOOK 7.1

Developing Questions to Elicit Stories

Having a list of prepared questions that might apply to any type of mediation is a useful tool in the mediator's skill set. Create a list of questions you can ask to elicit stories from disputants. Categorize the list into different types of questions. Begin with general questions that open the storytelling and issues identification phase (such as, "Can you tell me what brought you here today?"). Include questions to probe for more specificity in detail ("How did your arrive at that figure?"). Add questions to move parties to consider interests over positions ("How did that behavior affect you?"). Create statements that engage parties in taking the perspective of the other ("If you were the other person, explain how you would see this situation"). Finish with "what else" questions to check your assumptions about the case ("What other issues should the two of you discuss today?"). During the storytelling and issue identification phase, the mediation will progress better if general questions are used before specific or probing questions.

---

payments made since October. What changed in October?" Parties are focused on the month of October instead of solely attending to the money dispute.

Weighing the Importance of Disagreements

People disagree; otherwise mediators would not be needed. Determining the importance and relevance of such disagreements is instrumental to deciding when a "difference makes a difference." In one consumer mediation, a woman took a precious heirloom doll to a restorer to have the doll's eyelashes reconstructed. The woman claimed that not only did the eyelashes fall out again, but that the restorer switched the entire eyes, which were brown when she brought them in, and now were blue. The restorer adamantly denied switching the original eyes. The mediation quickly began to dissolve into a name-calling situation where both claimed the other lied. The mediator deftly stepped into the fray and reframed the discussion stating, "We are not here to determine what color the original eyes were. Obviously there is disagreement and no way to resolve this issue. Can we move past this area of disagreement and determine where we go from here?" The mediator must ascertain if areas of disagreement are tangential or critical to problem resolution. In this case, the disputants agreed to disagree.

Another strategy for working through impasse is unpacking the disagreement over specifics by asking questions about how a "fact" was established. "How did you learn about the extent of the damage?" or "You estimate the damage at $4,000. How did you arrive at that figure?" When the onus of responsibility is placed on the disputant to explain, the disputant may become less fixated on specifics, allowing the mediator to move the process forward.

Perspective Taking

Perspective taking activities require the disputants to see the world from the other's view. Saposnek (1998) identified *interactional* questions as a means to achieve such perspective taking. The question, "What do you see the other parent as doing?" requires the disputant to see the world through the eyes of the other. Another more direct strategy involves one party reacting from the perspective of the other party. For example, the mediator may ask: "Let's say for a moment that you are the boss. Sales are down and you are required to make changes in the sales force. How do you go about making these decisions?" Some mediators will require disputants so speak as if they were the other person: "Let's say you are Jenny. Jenny, what would be a fair settlement from your perspective?"

Caution is required when employing perspective-taking strategies. If the parties aren't willing to go along with the strategy, it can backfire. In one instance, a disputant responded to this strategy with anger saying, "Look, I don't have the foggiest idea why he thinks the way he does. A normal person wouldn't have gotten us in this situation in the first place." A general sense of cooperation and trust by the disputants is a prerequisite for employing perspective-taking strategies.

Conflict Causes and Mediator Moves

As the storytelling and issue-identification phase progresses, the mediator may discover that the conflict is based in one of the primary causes of interpersonal conflict (Mayer, 2000). Through identification of the cause of the conflict, the mediator can determine a strategy to move the mediation process forward. According to Mayer (2000), the primary causes of conflict are:

- *Communication:* poor communication, mistaken assumptions, lack of communication, differing perceptions
- *Emotions:* hurt feelings, anger, and other feelings that preempt the ability to negotiate in good faith
- *Procedure:* disagreements on how to make decisions or rules that prevent creative solutions to problems
- *Value:* core beliefs, customs, or strong preferences about what is right and virtuous
- *History:* how the conflicting parties have interacted in the past

TABLE 7.1 Mediator Moves and Causes of Conflict

Conflict Cause	Indicators	Mediator Move
Communication Conflicts	Parties have difficulty listening to each other, misunderstand each other, exhibit communication apprehension, or are using information differently.	Validate and paraphrase Suggest parties reverse paraphrase each other Coach parties in how to make comments more productively Establish how each is interpreting information differently
Emotion Conflicts	Parties blame or attack the other, express high feelings, exhibit anger or sadness.	Validate and emotionally paraphrase Adopt a future focus Highlight positive remarks made about the other party Work for acknowledgment or apologies Coach parties in "I" language
Procedure Conflicts	Parties agree on goals but not on methods; parties are fighting about how decisions should be made.	Make differences in criteria transparent to both parties Validate common goals Set criteria for good decisions Assist the parties in selecting a procedure that is mutually beneficial
Value Conflicts	Parties denigrate each other's background or assume that the other should think and feel exactly the same. Parties may be from different age, ethnic, religious, or national groups.	Make value differences transparent Validate both perspectives Emphasize commonalities Focus on a larger, common goal
Historic Conflicts	Parties have a long relationship or exhibit a cycle of conflict that repeats.	Make the cycle of conflict transparent by asking parties to describe how it usually unfolds Assist parties in locating a place to transform the cycle through new responses Reveal and transform unproductive or conflicting conflict metaphors used by the disputants

name each + name 2 moves

Conflicts stemming from different causal clusters require different skill applications from the mediator. Table 7.1 suggests moves to respond to each type of conflict. Even with a tool chest full of strategies, problems can arise at any point in the mediation. The following section addresses some of these sticky situations.

Overcoming Common Pitfalls in Storytelling

Mediators experience many bumps on the path toward peaceful settlements. New mediators find it helpful to collect a set of tools to employ when faced with these common pitfalls in mediation. The following section describes common problems faced during storytelling and in other stages of mediation.

Pitfall 1: Unchecked Power Differences

Parties do not necessarily enter the mediation process with the same power resources. One party may be a stronger communicator and have greater negotiation skills. One party may have higher status, for example, where one party is the employer and the other the employee. A cultural bias may exist for disputants. A member of the dominant culture in any area may feel more comfortable than one who is part of a minority culture. Additionally, cultural power may be unevenly matched when one party is like the mediator in gender, race, age, or social background. Left unchecked, these power differences detract from building fair agreements.

Mediators must be acutely aware of the place and construction of power in any relationship and make critical decisions based on power differences. One strategy in balancing power is to let the lower-power party speak first. According to Merry (1990), the first person to frame the story has more power. Another strat-

---

MEDIATOR NOTEBOOK 7.2
Avoiding Common Pitfalls

Create an organized list of tools (strategies and actual phrases) that you could use to mitigate the common pitfalls. Create a chart with the pitfalls in the left column and strategy to respond to pitfall in the right column. After each strategy, illustrate the concept with an actual phrase that you might use. For example, under the pitfall "allowing blaming and attacking," you might identify the strategy, "educate parties to use I statements," then provide phrases you could employ, "I would like you to try to explain how this affected you personally. I want you to try using, 'I' statements such as, 'I felt____,' to explain your story." Be sure to use language that would fit your personal style and that you would be comfortable delivering. Creating tools and phrases in advance helps you build your repertoire of skills. Feel free to share your list and adopt tools from other students that would work for you.

egy, however, is to do the opposite. In some instances letting one party lay out her or his argument allows the other party to contemplate a response, thus creating less pressure. A third strategy is to co-construct the story, so that neither side is advantaged by the "first to go" phenomenon. As you can see, no one strategy is a panacea for overcoming power differences. Mediators must ascertain the root of the power imbalance and consider the consequences, risks, and advantages to any course of action (Gewurz, 2001).

Being neutral does not necessarily require treating people the same or spending the same amount of time with both parties. In order to balance the power and create a fair environment, the mediator may spend more time helping one party identify areas of concerns, articulate ideas, express emotions, and identify interests. If one party is particularly adept at communicating, the extra time spent with the other party may seem lopsided. However, such attention is a reasonable and necessary course of action. The mediator can overcome perceptions of bias by making sure that the other party's interests and concerns are kept in the forefront while working with the less-communicative party.

Pitfall 2: Allowing Blaming and Attacking

Earlier in the chapter the ways in which individuals attribute motive to the other's behavior were discussed. Because of this natural tendency to blame others, the mediator must develop strategies for overcoming defensiveness in disputants. Often, the disputants see the other as the sole cause of the problem, taking no responsibility for their own feelings or perceptions. Cloke (2001) notes: "A desire for revenge is present in every conflict, though it is more significant in divorce, sexual harassment, wrongful termination, discrimination, victim and offender, and neighbor disputes" (p. 74). Dealing with such raw emotions and the destructive behaviors that accompany them is a necessary skill for all mediators.

Some educational coaching may be helpful in cases where parties are not accepting responsibility for their own emotions or are using considerable "attack" language (typically in the form of "you statements" or other defensive strategies). The mediator might teach parties to use "I" language and help them identify their own emotions. Another less direct method is to help the party give voice to a feeling. For instance, when a disputant says, "Erin is so lazy. She comes into work late every day and sits around instead of finding work to do," the mediator can respond with a question about how the situation affects the speaker. "How does it affect you when Erin comes to work late?"

Another strategy is to reframe attacks and blaming as interests or validate the other party. A loaded statement such as, "He's a sexual harasser and should be fired," can be reframed as, "You want to be respected and to have a fair outcome to this mediation. Let's discuss how you were affected by those comments."

In a related pitfall, called the *second party paraphrase*, the mediator miscasts a paraphrase to include a blaming statement. Paraphrases that begin "You feel that he…" repeat one party's perspective of the other party. Paraphrases should focus on the feelings of the person speaking, not their opinions of the other person.

Pitfall 3: Acting on Overstatements or Generalizations

Disputants habitually use absolute terms like "never" or "always" to paint the other party's behaviors with the broadest brush possible. If absolute statements are not addressed, resentment and lack of trust in the mediator's ability to facilitate the process fairly can result.

The primary strategy for dealing with overstatements and gross generalizations is asking for examples. The mediator then can prompt disputants to focus on the consequences of the behavior. For example:

> PARTY A: "Geoff never picks up the kids on time and they're always left waiting for him. He's so inconsiderate."
>
> MEDIATOR: "Could you tell me a time when the kids were left waiting and what happened as a result?"

In this situation, the mediator focuses the parties on the problem behavior and the consequence without addressing Geoff's overall past record. Geoff is more likely to hear the consequences of his actions if it is no longer framed in a global attack on his personality.

Pitfall 4: Taking Sides

As disputants tell their story, they may become more and more convinced that their actions and feelings are justified and want the mediator to agree. A disputant might say, "Do you see my point?" or "You can tell that this is a problem, can't you?" The disputant is attempting to get the mediator on his or her side. The danger for the mediator is appearing or being partial to one party. The mediator cannot take sides, even when asked.

When a disputant attempts to elicit an agreement or opinion from the mediator, he or she can validate the interest and redirect the query back to the party. For example, the mediator could say, "I can see that this has been a frustrating time for you. How have you handled the situation up until now?" Another strategy is to reassert your neutrality by saying, "My opinion is not really relevant. How did you feel about your choice?" Should a disputant become insistent, the mediator can repeat the mediator's roles and responsibilities, clarifying the purpose of the mediation.

Pitfall 5: Permitting Interrupting and Bickering

Sometimes parties have a difficult time listening without responding or correcting the other's perceptions. These interruptions can poison an environment so ideas cannot be expressed freely and open dialogue about issues cannot occur. If bickering or arguing becomes a fixed feature of the mediation, the danger of becoming bogged down in details is high.

One strategy is to blame yourself as the mediator for the disputant's inability to follow certain procedures. You can explain that you have trouble following the conversation when two people are talking at once and reassure the interrupters that you will get to their concerns. Have them write down their concerns so they can be sure to express them later. If continual bickering is a problem, the mediator can add more structure by establishing ground rules to counter the effects of the bickering. Mediators can validate concerns by writing down the topic and reminding the disputant that everything can't be discussed at the same time and we'll get to that topic in due time. If interrupting and bickering becomes a block to moving the mediation process forward, the mediator may caucus (meet privately) with the individuals to help them move beyond their disruptive behaviors.

Pitfall 6: Mismanaging Emotional Outbursts

In a particularly difficult divorce and child custody mediation, the husband had enough of listening to his wife disparaging his parenting skills. Spurred by fear of losing his kids and feelings of being painted unfairly, he jumped up suddenly from the table, forcefully pushed his notebook across the table to the floor, and yelled, "I'm done with this crap! I'm leaving!" The individual began walking toward the door. The mediator, thinking quickly, said, "You know, you're right. I think we could use a break. Let's take a breather and meet back here in ten minutes." Much to the surprise of the other party and the mediator, the man returned in ten minutes ready to negotiate calmly.

Maintaining control in the face of emotional outbursts can be taxing and tricky. According to Kosmoski and Pollock (2000), "Anger is about power. The angry individual who is acting inappropriately does not feel that his or her opinions or feelings are being recognized, adequately considered, given any weight, or accepted" (p. 4). Kosmoski and Pollock agree that anger has a tendency to beget more anger and that angry individuals often invite others to engage in escalating behaviors.

When considering options to respond to emotional outbursts, the safety of all parties is paramount. A mediator who assesses that anger may turn to violence should immediately end the mediation session, giving an outlet for future sessions or other interventions, if appropriate. Other safety measures include keeping a barrier between you and the agitated individual and maneuvering yourself and the other party toward a doorway.

If safety is not a pressing concern, key strategies for managing emotional outbursts include:

- Keep calm in the face of emotional displays
- Be aware of your own language choices
- Use inclusive language
- Postpone discussions when emotions are high
- Know your own emotional reactions
- Practice calming techniques

- Create psychological distance
- Collect tools and phrases
- Use strategic breaks
- Educate parties in effective communication

One strategy for dealing with emotional people includes keeping calm in the face of emotional displays. Keeping safety issues clearly in view, the mediator can de-escalate emotions by not getting pulled into the fray. Often the disputant will feel embarrassed after the incident, but will be more likely to return to the table if it seems a safe place. A calm mediator encourages calmness in others.

Mediators should be hyperaware of their language choices in the face of emotional outbursts. One client, who was feeling attacked, stood up with such force he tipped over his chair. The mediator looked at him and said, "You seem really upset." This understatement elicited a violent retort of, "Don't try your mediator BS on me!" The mediator, turned the table back on herself and said, "I'm sorry. I'm really confused. I am trying to understand what just happened, and I see you are really upset right now." The new phrasing of the same emotion was easier for the disputant to hear, allowing for some metacommunication about what had just occurred.

Using inclusive language such as "we" and "us" can help reassure the emotionally charged individual. For example, the mediator may say, "This topic is pretty tense for us right now. Let's move to another issue and come back to this one in a bit." This example illustrates another strategy of postponing discussions when emotions are high. In some cases, coming back to the issue at some future meeting is appropriate.

Mediators should be attuned to their own reactions to emotional displays, know their triggers and how they react when attacked. Mediators can practice calming techniques like breathing exercises and collect phrases to handle difficult situations and to postpone or end mediations. Mediators should be able to create psychological distance from the other party by recognizing that their anger usually is about the problem and not about the mediator. Another key strategy is to use strategic breaks. A break from the heat of mediation can add perspective to the situation. Finally, if disputants cannot engage each other civilly, then the mediator can attempt to educate the parties in effective communication skills as part of the mediation or in caucus.

Pitfall 7: Letting One Party Monopolize Time or Control the Process

Occasionally mediators face a party who attempts to "out talk" the other party or tries to control the flow of the process. Both of these actions usually are the result of one disputant trying to establish authority or power. Mediators must assert themselves into the process with authority when disputants try to take control.

The primary mediator strategy for parties who monopolize time is to summarize and redirect conversation. Sometimes parties repeat the same issues and ideas and tell more stories. This could be a hint for the mediator that the party needs to be validated. If validating does not work to stem the flow, the mediator can attempt to get the second party to acknowledge the concerns (keeping in mind that there is no requirement for agreement, just acknowledgement of one party by the other). However, if after validating, a party continues to belabor the topic, mediators can summarize to break the pattern of complaint. A numbered list is one means of accomplishing this task. The mediator can jump into the conversation and say, "So you are concerned about four items: (1) the plumbing bill, (2) the damage to the drywall in the basement, (3) the process of having your complaint heard, and (4) the treatment you received by the office manager. Is there anything else?" When the party goes into another story, if the story is evidence of one of those four points, the mediator can say, "Okay, so you're wanting to make sure your bill is accurate. The other items to cover are the damage to the basement, the complaint process and the interaction with the office manager. So does this list cover your primary concerns?" Generally, this summarization process is an effective means to move parties to the next phase.

Haynes (1994) warns, "the mediator is constantly faced with choices as to what to summarize and what to ignore. Whatever the mediator focuses on becomes important in the eyes of the participants" (p. 14). With this caution, the mediator must be aware of the power of summarizing. Mediators can effectively shape the mediation by ignoring some information and focusing on other information. The mediator must be diligent in keeping the disputants involved in the verification of the summary statements, allowing opportunity for disputants to challenge or change the summary characterizations.

Pitfall 8: Being Overwhelmed with Evidence

Occasionally disputants will come to the mediation table with an excessive amount of material that they will try to present as evidence to support their case. This behavior may be motivated by the desire to intimidate the other party, may be designed to convince the mediator to see things "their way," or may be because the disputant is acting on a mistaken assumption of what is expected in mediation.

When overwhelmed with evidence, the mediator must ensure that their role as a neutral third party, not a judge or evaluator, is clearly established. The mediator can be forthright that her or her interpretation of evidence and data is not germane due to the nature of mediation. Another important strategy is to require that information shared during mediation be made available to all parties. Sometimes a single document can shed light on the circumstances for both parties. Once disputants are certain that the mediator is not going to assess their evidence, usually the fervor of presenting it dissipates quickly.

Summary

The storytelling and issue-identification phase of mediation usually comprises a large block of time during the mediation. Recognizing how disputants will frame similar events differently through their attributions of others' behaviors is key in developing strategies for creating a story shared by both parties. Symbolic interaction theory and attribution theory both help explain some disputant behaviors. Effective storytelling meets the safety, recognition, and acknowledgment needs of the disputants, while allowing mediators the opportunity to identify issues, interests, and establish common ground. Mediators work to separate *interests* from *positions* during the storytelling and issue-identification phase.

Mediators can choose to have disputants take turns telling their stories or choose to have them co-construct stories together. Basic strategies for storytelling include beginning with general inquiries, asking whole picture questions, using specific inquiry questions, being Columbo, establishing agreed on facts, weighing disagreements, and developing perspective-taking tools to aid the parties in seeing each other's side.

This chapter concludes by identifying eight common pitfalls and offering communication strategies for working past those problems. Storytelling, issue identification, and detecting common ground provide the necessary groundwork for later agenda setting and negotiations between the parties.

issues : behavioral
observable
concrete.

all need to be part of agreement.

Notes during S.T. phase. (identify issues)

8 Setting the Agenda for Negotiation

*T*he agenda phase is the shortest in duration, but is as important as any other phase. During the agenda phase, the mediator presents the issues that will dominate the negotiation. How the mediator frames the agenda can restrict the disputants' thinking about potential outcomes or expand opportunities to approach their difficulties in new ways. The phrasing of an agenda should continue the mediator's role as an impartial and neutral third party. If worded improperly, an agenda can bias the negotiation toward one side or subtly move the disputants toward solutions the mediator prefers.

This chapter examines when to shift to the agenda phase and presents the techniques mediators use when framing the agenda. The agenda itself is composed of two parts: a commonality statement and a list of issues to be negotiated. Before discussing the components of the agenda, we will present strategies for mediator note taking to assist in remembering issues raised by disputants during storytelling and issue identification.

CASE 8.1

The Estate Settlement

find commonalities
validated Sophia

After the issue identification and storytelling phase, your notes indicate that there are several potential issues to be settled in the estate of Sophia and Rashid's mother. Sophia is mad at her brother, Rashid, for not being around very much while their mother was ill and thinks that Rashid should get less of the estate because Sophia carried all the burden of their mother's care. Rashid was going through an unpleasant divorce at the time and was battling for full custody of his twin sons. Rashid feels badly that he wasn't around more. Rashid and Sophia haven't been talking much, which is why the case finally came to mediation. Rashid and Sophia both seem to have emotional connections to particular items. For example, Sophia has fond memories of working with her grandfather in the woodworking shop and wants some items as a remembrance of her grandfather; Rashid hopes to travel with his sons in the motor home. Rashid lost his own house and furniture in his divorce and needs furniture. Some positional statements were made during the opening phases of the mediation. Each party made demands about which items of the property they wanted to receive.

Sophia Wants	Rashid Wants
Table valued at $4,000	Table valued at $4,000
All the $100,000 cash	Half the $100,000 cash
All the jewelry ($10,000)	The gold watch ($800)
All of the photographs	The diamond ring ($4,000)
¾ of the value of the estate	½ of the value of the estate
The antique mirror ($1,000)	Refrigerator/freezer ($1,000)
The car ($15,000)	The car ($15,000)
The table saw and shop equipment ($8,000)	The motor home ($70,000)
The entertainment system ($4,000)	Most furniture ($15,000)

Mediator Note Taking and the Agenda   *final exam*

Potential TF

The mediator listens to each disputant during storytelling while simultaneously searching for negotiable issues. *Negotiable issues* are within the disputants' control and can be framed in behavioral, concrete, and observable outcomes. "Respect" is not a negotiable issue. One party cannot be forced to feel respect. However, a mediator may reframe the issue into one of "appropriate behavior" and ensure that discussions about respect ultimately result in *behaviors* perceived to exhibit respect. For example, in Case 8.1, Sophia and Rashid describe their past relationship as acrimonious and unsatisfactory. If Sophia repeatedly states that Rashid doesn't value and respect her care of their mother, "showing respect" might appear in the mediator's notes. When the mediator deduces that reviving a previously warmer relationship is an important issue for the two parties, the mediator might record "improve relationship" on the note-taking page and note specific behavioral issues to discuss. Behavioral issues could be "How are the parties going to communicate with each other about the estate?" or "What specific contact or e-mail etiquette will be used when talking with each other?" When the mediator realizes that "what is a fair distribution" of the estate is an issue for one or both parties, the words "criteria of a fair settlement" might be recorded in the issue section.

The mediator's notes are the starting point from which an agenda is built. Fortunately, mediators always will check with the disputants to ensure that all of the important issues are contained in the agenda. If something is missed or forgotten, the disputants will raise the issue.

When to Shift to the Agenda Step

Spending insufficient time in the storytelling phase of a mediation can be a problem. Disputants who are moved to the agenda or negotiation phases too soon often cycle back to earlier issues and disrupt the problem-solving process midway through. Several indicators help to cue the mediator when it is time to move to the next phase. Wildau (1987) identified five signs that indicate the time to move to the agenda has arrived:

1. Parties begin to repeat themselves
2. The mediator has enough material to work with, and the main issues appear to be on the table
3. Parties state they feel they have been heard
4. Parties allow the mediator to define the issue as a joint problem or remove the egocentricity from a party's issue definition
5. Parties indicate, either verbally or nonverbally, that they are ready to proceed with joint problem solving (p. 8)

[handwritten margin note: issues med. brings up @ joint level they are ok...]

Parties may indicate their readiness nonverbally by conversing congenially or turning toward each other in their chairs. Generally, when the parties have had sufficient time to tell their stories and when the mediator assesses that all of the basic issues have been uncovered, it is time to move to the next phase and establish the agenda.

WHAT ARE the probable consequences if the mediator moves to the agenda step too quickly? Discuss how a premature agenda could affect the parties, the process, and perceptions of the mediator.

Components of the Agenda

When the mediator determines that all of the issues have been raised and she or he has a general understanding of each party's needs, the mediator will move to the agenda step. The mediator will give a transitional statement such as, "I think I have a general understanding of the issues that brought you here today. Let me see if we can summarize what you've expressed in the shape of an agenda." The mediator may take a moment to organize his or her notes or work from a list prepared during the storytelling and issue-identification phase. The mediator sets the agenda in two steps. First, the mediator presents a commonality statement. Second, the mediator lists an agenda of items to be negotiated. The commonality statement may be either a two-way commonality statement or a general commonality statement.

The Commonality Statement

A commonality statement is the mediator's summary of characteristics, attitudes, or context that are shared by the parties. Neighbors share a common boundary line; disputants may share a desire to resolve the difficulty; employees may both want to excel in their work. The mediator may state either a two-way or a general commonality statement.

The Two-Way Commonality Statement.   One way to begin the agenda phase is to use a variation of the commonality statement called the two-way commonality statement. The *two-way commonality statement* links the goals of each party together and is built from the interests expressed by the parties during storytelling. It is a method of expressing the general goals of the negotiation in mutual terms. Two advantages of a two-way commonality statement are to interweave the needs of the parties together conceptually and to encourage cooperative problem solving and negotiation. It creates a common anchor for both parties and orchestrates an agreement that they have a common overriding goal.

MEDIATOR NOTEBOOK 8.1

Transitioning to the Agenda

Consider what you will say as a mediator to move the disputants from the storytelling and issue-identification phase to the agenda phase.

Write at least two transitional sentences to indicate that you are moving to the next step and place them in your mediator notebook.

For example, the mediator may hear that both Jake and Carl want to remain roommates, but that they have incompatible goals. The mediator might phrase the two-way commonality by saying, "It seems like the basic issue is how can Jake have social time with his friends and Carl have quiet time to study. Does that get at the heart of the matter?" An appropriate two-way commonality statement encompasses the goals and interests of the parties without implying a particular solution. If the mediator said, "The main issues seems to be how can the two of you split your time in the room so you can both pursue your individual interests," the mediator has suggested a solution. While the roommates may choose to divide the hours spent in the room, they may also discover more creative options such as socializing together or studying together either in the room or at different locations. Creative solutions are preempted if the mediator suggests a specific outcome. Mediators using the balanced model are prohibited from suggesting solutions.

The formula for a two-way commonality is:

How can Party A meet the goal of _____ while at the same time Party B meets the goal of _____?

Hopefully, both parties will nod or say, "Yes," to the two-way commonality statement. If not, the mediator may return to storytelling by asking, "What have I missed?" By laying the goals side-by-side with equal priority, the mediator validates both parties and encourages creative, mutual-gains thinking about potential outcomes.

General Commonality Statement. If a two-way commonality statement is not possible, a general commonality statement can be substituted. For example, "I see that both of you want to finish this issue today so you can get it behind you" or "I see that both of you want to do your jobs well and need each other in order to get your jobs done." General commonality statements highlight mutual goals and increase the probability of cooperation during the negotiation phase. The primary goal of the general commonality statement is metaphorically to move the parties to the same side of the table and place the problem to be solved on the other side (see Figure 7.2).

The Agenda List

The second task during the agenda phase is creating a list of items to be negotiated. The agenda is, as the name suggests, a list of the items to be negotiated. The list might be an exhaustive itemization of every small matter to be negotiated or might be presented as categories of items for negotiation. For example, in Case 8.1, if every disputed item appeared on the agenda, it would be a lengthy but exhaustive list of items to be negotiated. Typically, the mediator will cluster the items together, as illustrated later in this chapter.

Examine Case 8.1 and offer a two-way commonality statement for Sophia and Rashid. For additional practice, create a two-way or general commonality statement for the following cases.

1. During storytelling and issue identification, Bob repeats several times that he just wants to know where the property line is so he can build a fence and have some privacy in his backyard. Celia is very concerned that a fence would block her majestic view of the lake and hillside. What two-way commonality statement(s) can the mediator make?

2. During storytelling and issue identification, Naomi bluntly states that she wants $500 from Ty because Ty won't give her a receipt for the work. Naomi can't get reimbursed for the $500 from her supplier if she doesn't have a valid receipt. Ty won't give her a receipt because he could not get back into the house to finish the inspection and can't give a receipt for work he never finished. What two-way commonality statement can the mediator make?

3. Ramon and Henry both complain bitterly about the other's unkind remarks and slovenly work habits. Both like their jobs and feel they are good at what they do. What general commonality statement can the mediator make to open the agenda phase?

Ordering the Agenda

Who Decides the Order of the Agenda?

Once the items on the agenda are set forth, a strategy must be adopted to order the items and present them to the disputants. The mediator's first choice in the negotiation and problem-solving phase is whether to decide for the disputants the order in which issues will be addressed or to allow the disputants to choose. The advantages of mediator choice are threefold. First, the mediator maintains control of the process. Second, the mediator strategically can choose an issue to be first because it will be critical to the rest of the negotiation—because it is pivotal, or the logical place to start, or useful to get an early agreement, or because it is easy. Ultimately, the difficulty of any agenda item is a judgment call by the mediator. If the disputants are acrimonious, some mediators will start with small, easy items to build a history of negotiation success. For example, in Case 8.1, Sophia and Rashid have large differences on the amount of cash they request in the settlement, but may have fewer differences about items like the entertainment center or the refrigerator. Starting with less-contested items may build a pattern of cooperation. Finally, mediator control prevents either disputant from manipulating the order of the agenda to his or her advantage.

If the mediator determines that the disputants should choose the agenda order, the mediator assists the disputants in negotiating the order of the items on an agenda. Disputants might negotiate the order of all of the items to be negotiated or *freewheel*, where each would voluntarily select the next item for negotiation. There are two advantages to the mediator leading the disputants in choosing the agenda order. First, the disputants are involved in the decision, so they have ownership of the process. Second, working together on the agenda order is the disputants' first cooperative achievement. The mediator can praise their success and leverage the experience into a more cooperative negotiation phase. In both the mediator choice and the disputant choice strategies, it is the mediator's job to ensure that all agenda items receive attention.

Strategies for Ordering the Agenda

The mediator considers several questions in deciding how to order the agenda:

- Have criteria been established that will assist the disputants in their decisions?
- How divisive has the past relationship been?
- Have the disputants exhibited greater understanding for each other's needs through the storytelling phase?
- Is one party more adamant on particular issues than the other party?
- Is one item a linchpin that will affect all of the other items on the agenda?
- Is there an issue that is a Pandora's box that might explode if opened too soon?

After the mediator considers the strategic elements that affect the choice of which issue is first, the mediator selects a method of ordering the agenda.

How could a nonnegotiable issue such as "respect" identified during negotiation be incorporated into the agenda? Is it advisable to change the agenda order at all during negotiations? If so, under what circumstances?

Methods of Agenda Ordering

Some mediators begin the negotiation phase with specifying criteria that any decision must meet for both parties to be satisfied (discussed more in Chapter 9). The decision criteria should match the party's interests expressed during the storytelling phase. The mediator ensures that the criteria are goal-centered rather than restatements of individual positions. For example, criteria might include: the decision must be fair to both parties, or a decision must settle the issue so it doesn't continue.

The rationale for the order of the agenda may be:

- Criteria as the first issue (combined with some other method for the list of issues)
- In the order they were identified during the storytelling phase

- In the order in which they will be implemented, if adopted
- Alternating choice of the next issue to each disputant
- Most important to least important
- Least important to most important
- Linchpin items first
- From the most abstract to the most concrete
- Packaging similar items together

The various methods of ordering the agenda can be illustrated using Case 8.1. If the mediator asks what would characterize a fair decision, then *criteria* are addressed as the first issue. The mediator might list the agenda in the order of his or her notes *(order of identification)* or in two sections called estate settlement and future communication *(order of implementation)*. The *alternating selection method* would be used if the disputants decide who has the first choice and then Rashid and Sophia alternate in picking the next item to be resolved during negotiation. A mediator might ask each disputant what issue is most important and note the items that are common. Next, the mediator would move through the list from *most to least important*. If settlement of the criteria of a fair outcome is so important to Sophia and Rashid that it overshadows the negotiation on all of the specific issues, the mediator may suggest it be negotiated first and use the *linchpin* method. If all of the actual furnishings and items are negotiated before the more intangible issues of fairness and future relationship are addressed, then the *most concrete to most abstract method* is used. If all of the furniture is disposed as one negotiation item rather than breaking it down into each separate piece, then the specific items to be negotiated are *packaged*.

Regardless of which method of ordering the agenda is selected, the mediator must verify that all issues are on the list. Before transitioning to the negotiation phase, the mediator will summarize the agenda list and inquire: "Are there other issues that need to be added to the agenda?"

ACTIVITY 8.2

In Case 8.1, two siblings are in a heated conflict over their recently deceased mother's estate. The mediator's notes contain a long list of individual items to be negotiated. What agenda *strategy* (mediator or disputant choice) would you select? If the mediator chooses, which *method* of ordering the agenda would you utilize? Provide a rationale for your choices.

Issues for Continuing Relationships

In cases where the parties have a continuing relationship, we recommend an agenda item about future communication. As discussed in Chapter 7, disputants with a continuing relationship who come to mediation have experienced some breach of trust or lapse in effective communication. In cases where both parties have lamented the toll this situation has had on their relationship, the mediator can pursue a discussion about how to rebuild trust or improve communication between them. The mediator leads the parties in a discussion of what they would prefer their communication to be like in the future, how they wish to have future communication, or what they will do if another difficulty arises in the future.

Sometimes the mediator will ask disputants about guidelines for future communication. After listing the other issues to be negotiated, the mediator might say, "The two of you seem dissatisfied with your past interactions, should we discuss ideas for how to interact in the future?" At other times, the mediator will not list the item on the regular agenda, but may prompt future communication as an issue after the parties have experienced some success on other issues.

WHAT ARE the probable consequences if a mediator repeats negative phrasing as part of an agenda item? For example, what might happen if the mediator said: "Part of the solution is finding a way to balance Rashid's lack of help against Sophia's care for your mother"?

Packing and Unpacking

As the negotiation proceeds, the mediator may connect agenda items together if settlement of one issue is relevant or sequential to settlement of another issue or if having more than one item on the table at the same time is advantageous. Competitive negotiators may need to trade concessions on different agenda items to feel as if they are not giving in to their "opponent." For example, in Case 8.1, Sophia might be willing to settle for half the value of the estate, but only if that concession is traded for the right to select the first five items of property. Cooperative negotiators may need to link issues to spur creative thinking and mutual-gains options. For example, Sophia and Rashid might link all the items together that have sentimental value and negotiate their disposition as one decision, then deal with the rest of the estate.

Larger issues may need to be *unpacked* or unlinked when the items can stand alone and are not contingent on one another. After listening to Sophia and Rashid's demands for particular items during storytelling, the mediator may lump them together during the agenda under the headings of cash, vehicles, and furnishings. During the negotiation, the three large agenda items would be unpacked. For example, the large package of furnishings might be considered item by item.

In general, when framing the agenda, the mediator groups issues together into packages of similar items. For example, instead of listing every item of furniture, every electronic device, each photograph and painting, the mediator might group an estate agenda under the headings of "furnishings." As the negotiation proceeds, however, the mediator may need to adjust the agenda to pack or unpack items.

The Language of the Agenda

Framing the Agenda Mutually

It is tempting for mediators to keep separate lists of which issues are important to each disputant and then present the two lists to the disputants as part of the agenda. In Case 8.1, the mediator's notes contain the disputants' interests. The agenda, however, must be phrased as mutual issues rather than as a list of Sophia's issues and a separate list of Rashid's issues. By *mutually framing* the issues, both parties are advantaged equally and a competitive win-lose frame is avoided. By mutually framing the issues, the mediator highlights that both parties are interconnected in the outcome of all issues in the mediation.

Framing the Agenda Neutrally

The commonality statement and the items on an agenda list should be phrased neutrally and impartially. Failing to do so can create feelings of mediator bias or erode necessary trust in the mediation process. Pope and Bush (2000) comment: "Practice in extracting and neutrally labeling issues is one of the challenging and important aspects of a training program, particularly because the exercise is unique to the role of mediator and hence foreign to most newcomers to mediation" (p. 32).

Three common mediator errors occur when framing the agenda:

Error #1: The agenda is framed using one disputant's suggestions. When two siblings are mediating over the estate of a relative, the negotiation could be slanted toward one party or the other if the mediator used one person's words when framing the agenda. If the mediator labels one item on the agenda as, "What to do about the table that Sophia wants," the issue is advantaged toward Sophia. Instead, the mediator could deliver a more generalized statement, such as, "How will the two of you dispose of the remaining furniture items?"

Error #2: A mediator seeds the negotiation by putting his or her ideas into the agenda. If the mediator assumes that Sophia will eventually receive the table, the mediator might erroneously say, "One of the issues is what to balance against Sophia's receipt of the table."

Error #3: Mediators may exclude some avenues of creativity if they presume issues must be resolved in particular ways. If the mediator assumes that the parties can only find an equitable solution by dividing each piece of furniture between them, then the mediator has excluded some potential outcomes. Instead of framing the agenda item as, "Who will get which piece of furniture?" the mediator might frame the agenda item by saying, "What will the two of you do with the remaining furniture?" For instance, the parties

---

M E D I A T O R   N O T E B O O K   8.2

Methods of Ordering the Agenda

Create a one-page summary with a list of methods for ordering the agenda. Place the list in your mediator notebook.

---

may decide to each pick pieces of furniture in alternating turns, or one party could buy items of furniture from the other, or furniture could be traded for other items in the settlement, or they could sell all the items and divide the proceeds, or they could decide to donate all of the furniture to charity.

Summary

The agenda phase is short, but important. The shift to the agenda occurs after the parties feel they have been heard and the mediator determines all the issues have been uncovered. From the notes taken during the storytelling and issue-identification phase, the mediator forms either a two-way or general commonality statement that links the goals of the parties together and a compressed list of the items to be negotiated.

The mediator chooses whether to state the agenda for the parties or involve them in the decision of which items to negotiate first. The three advantages to mediator selection are: (1) The mediator maintains control; (2) The mediator strategically can select which item is addressed first; (3) It prevents disputants from manipulating the order to their own advantage. Two advantages of the disputant choice method are: (1) The disputants have more ownership of the process; and (2) Negotiating the agenda order creates their first cooperative success.

Several strategies exist for ordering the agenda. Key questions assist the mediator in considering which strategy is best. When the agenda is created, similar items initially are grouped together. The mediator may package or unpack items as necessary. Three common errors in phrasing the agenda are slanting an agenda item in one party's favor, suggesting outcomes, and deterring creative thinking.

CHAPTER

9 Problem Solving and Negotiation

[handwritten annotations: "fixed amount of resources, impossible for both sides to be happy / loose win / phil." "win/win - both needs satisfied." "2 views"]

[handwritten margin notes: "interests through story telling, what do they want?" "1. needs/goals 2. mutual gains / not win/loose" "see notes"]

Be patient. Some negotiators dance fast. Some negotiators dance more slowly.
—E. R. Galton, 1996, p. 374

Once the emotional and other barriers to settlement have moderated and the issue agenda is formulated, the mediator assists the disputants with problem solving and negotiation. If hurt feelings or emotional issues primarily caused the conflict, problem solving and negotiation over the remaining substantive issues may come easily for the disputants. Most conflicts, however, contain enduring thorny problems that are difficult for the disputants to manage. This chapter discusses the mediator's role in creating structures for problem solving, bringing specialized techniques to the table, and—when feasible—fostering a cooperative approach to bargaining.

The Two Worlds of Negotiation

An array of terms in the conflict management and mediation literature describe two opposite worldviews disputants bring to their negotiations. Labels for these worldviews include: competitive and coordinative, competitive and cooperative, adversarial and problem solving, hard and soft, principled and competitive, and distributive and integrative (Murray, 1996). In this book, the terms competitive and cooperative represent the two primary approaches to negotiation. Most conflicts, at one time or another, are *mixed-motive* conflicts that contain both competitive and cooperative elements.

Competitive versus Cooperative Negotiation

Bargaining involves a give and take of concessions to reach an agreement. By definition, bargaining includes compromise, or loss, in order to reach an agreement satisfactory to both parties. Traditional competitive bargaining is *distributive,* meaning the available resources are divided or distributed among the parties at the table. Competitive bargaining assumes there are a limited number of resources and that it is impossible for both parties to achieve all of their goals. A couple that receives $20,000 from a deceased relative may hold different opinions about what to do with the money. One may want to put the money toward a new car and the

---

CASE **9.1**

Not if He Wins

Jim Mallard and John Dillard were roommates in a house off campus for two years. They both moved out of the house to room with different people and have been embroiled in an acrimonious dispute ever since. Through the storytelling phase, the mediator determined that their mutual goal was to settle their differences so the two former roommates could clear their debts from the house without being taken to court or hurting either party's credit record. Both Jim and John agreed with the mediator's analysis that there were three primary issues to be negotiated: (1) How the landlord will be approached regarding the damages to the house; (2) What to do about an outstanding balance on the phone bill; and (3) The disposition of several items that the two of them purchased together while they were roommates.

The mediator opened the negotiation and problem-solving phase by selecting the phone bill as the first item to be addressed and asked: "Do either of you have an idea on how we can approach the phone bill in a way that is objective and fair?" John immediately replied, "I'm not paying any of it. I had my own cell phone and never used the phone." Jim retorted, "But you used the computer to go on-line all the time and it used the phone line!" The mediator asked John, "Did you use the phone line?" John did. The mediator then reframed: "It sounds like you both had some interest in having a phone line into the house. Given that fact, how can the two of you approach the outstanding bill in a way that is objective and fair?" John stuck to his position that he wouldn't pay any of the bill because it didn't cost Jim anything when he used the phone line with his computer, since it was already there. Jim asserted that John should pay half of the entire bill.

other may wish to save half of the money and remodel the bathroom with the other half. In traditional bargaining, one of two results typically will occur—the most powerful person will control the decision or both will compromise and split the available resources. For example, the most powerful person might want to buy a car and would spend all the money on that purchase. Compromise involves each party giving up something that was desired and might result in each party receiving $10,000.

Competitive negotiations typically are *positional*—disputants open with hard, inflexible, outcome-centered demands. Tactics in competitive negotiation include:

- Making concessions only when some principled rationale justifies the change
- Focusing solely on personal outcomes
- Blaming the other
- Arguing and debating
- Threatening and promising
- Real or feigned aggressive behavior
- Offering tit-for-tat (this-for-that trades)
- Fabricating information
- Withholding information

In Case 9.1, both disputants argue their side of the issue competitively and forge hard, positional stances.

Cooperative negotiation takes a different approach. The cooperative approach was popularized by Fisher and Ury of the Harvard Negotiation Project in their best-selling book, *Getting to Yes* (1981). The mediator who prefers a cooperative approach begins with the *interests* of both parties that were discovered during the storytelling phase rather than with the positions parties want. In cooperative bargaining, individuals focus on their goals and needs and the goals and needs of the other party. *Both* negotiators search for ways to maximize the outcome for *both* parties, called *mutual gains.* For example, a couple who receives a $20,000 insurance payment and takes a cooperative approach will discuss all of their goals and needs that might be met with the windfall. When approached creatively, they may choose to put $15,000 aside for a down payment on a condo, spend $1,000 on a vacation, and allocate $2,000 to each individual to spend as he or she desires.

Domenici and Littlejohn (2001) illustrate a typical opening to the negotiation section to encourage cooperative bargaining: "I see that John needs _____ and Manuel needs _____. If we are able to achieve a solution that meets those interests, would you be satisfied?" (p. 91). In Case 9.1, the mediator might apply this formula by saying, "I see Jim needs to have a clean credit record going into the future, and John needs a settlement of your mutual property so he knows what to buy for his new apartment. If you are able to negotiate a solution that meets both your needs in these areas, will you both be satisfied?"

By beginning with the interests, the mediator frames the negotiation as a search for creative solutions that might satisfy the underlying needs of *both* parties—to integrate their interests into an outcome that is mutually beneficial. Tactics of cooperative bargaining include:

- Focusing on the problem as a mutual issue
- Trying to meet both parties' needs
- Disclosing interests and needs
- Having more than one item on the table at a time so agreements can be packaged
- Generating several options for settlement
- Remaining provisional about solutions
- Bargaining in good faith

Fisher and Brown (1988) assert that the substantive issues must be separated from the relationship issues. For example, the issues surrounding money or household possessions should be separated from the issue of whether former roommates will remain friends. Further, they assert that the cooperative negotiator is unconditionally positive, eschews negative tactics, and listens to understand from the other's perspective.

Lax and Sebenius (1986) explain the three primary actions that create the mutual gains sought by cooperative bargainers: (1) Reaching agreements that are better for both parties than each individual's alternatives if there is no settlement, (2) Discovering an outcome that is preferable to each party, and (3) Discovering potential value by finding commonality and reducing differences so that each party gets the most they can from the agreement. The cooperative approach is less likely to work when one or both parties are focused on personal revenge or seek to establish precedents.

*A*RE *YOU comfortable with both competitive and cooperative negotiation styles? When would each style be most appropriate?*

How Involved Is the Mediator in the Negotiation?

The mediator chooses how actively to interact with the disputants during the negotiation. As we stated above, if the conflict primarily was spurred by emotional issues that have been moderated during the mediator's work in the storytelling and issue-identification phase, the mediator may be able to sit back and observe as the disputants conduct their negotiation. The parties might amiably work through their own problem solving and reach agreement. In many mediations, however, bad feelings continue, intractable issues persist, and the disputants have low communication or negotiation skills. In these cases, a more active mediator is required.

The degree of *directiveness* involves how much control the mediator exerts over the process. A high-directive mediator might lead the disputants through several problem-solving exercises to help them assess their options and to generate possible solutions. A high-directive mediator might continue to reframe and paraphrase offers throughout the negotiation phase. A low-directive mediator will lean back and let the disputants talk their way through the negotiation—acting only when the disputants become too emotional or become deadlocked. Most mediators will begin the negotiation and problem-solving phase somewhat directive and loosen that control as the disputants are able to work together successfully.

Mediator directiveness is different from mediator intrusiveness. An intrusive mediator inserts her or his own opinions and ideas into the substance of the settlement. When disputants are deadlocked, the intrusive mediator will suggest settlement options rather than lead the parties through a process to help them break their deadlock. If Jim and John in Case 9.1 can't find a compromise, the intrusive mediator might suggest they just split the basic phone bill, but have each party pay for his own long-distance calls. In the balanced mediation model, mediators are not intrusive and are prohibited from inserting their own ideas for solutions.

WHAT HAPPENS to a mediation when the mediator is overly intrusive? Do you think intrusiveness affects the probability that the disputants will carry though with their agreements? Do you think an intrusive mediator can work from the transformative perspective discussed in Chapter 1?

Mediator Techniques for Disputant Problem Solving

Starting the Negotiation

As stated in Chapter 8, sometimes the order of the agenda is the first item to be negotiated. Once the order is determined, the mediator opens the session for negotiation. At times, a general opening will suffice, such as: "What ideas do you have on how the two of you can achieve your mutual goal of settling this issue?" In negotiation, as in all phases of mediation, the mediator intervenes to deflect threats, reframe, and probe statements that merely repeat positions.

Garcia (2000) labels a general request for solutions directed at both parties a *collective solicit*. A collective solicit may be effective in eliciting offers from both parties. In other cases, one or both parties will avoid the mediator's solicit or not wish to be the first to make a concession. In these cases, parties often will repeat prior demands. If one party repeats a position, "I have to have $5,000," the mediator might redirect by saying, "You're looking for a fair settlement." The mediator might probe for the party's underlying needs by asking, "How did you arrive at that figure?" or "What will a monetary settlement do for you?"

When the disputants remain fixed on intractable emotional issues and demure from mediator solicits, the mediator may need to return to the skills and functions of the storytelling phase to work on the emotional or relationship issues or create face-saving opportunities. The section about face-saving, later in this chapter, delves into the potential of empathy and face-saving to transform conflicts.

Techniques for Cooperative Negotiation

When disputants are not progressing on their own, the mediator intervenes to assist the parties in discovering options. The competent mediator is adept at multiple strategies to enhance disputants' abilities to create ideas for settlement. Because each mediation and every disputant is unique, the technique that functions well in one mediation may be ineffective in the next. Eight common techniques are used to foster cooperative negotiation:

- Establishing criteria
- Brainstorming
- Linking and Unlinking
- Logrolling
- Role-reversal
- Focusing on the future relationship
- Cost-cutting
- Coaching

match

Establishing Criteria. Establishing criteria is useful in both competitive and cooperative bargaining, but may be essential to foster cooperation. Criteria connect directly to the interests that were uncovered during the storytelling and issue-identification phase. In Case 9.1, the mediator might state: "I have found that disputants make better decisions if they think about criteria for fairness before they begin the actual negotiation about money. You both have indicated that you desire a fair settlement. I need to understand what you both mean by fair. Please explain it to me." By discussing criteria first that are fair to both parties, the disputants have less opportunity to display competitive tactics. If the disputants adopt competitive tactics, the mediator attempts to move from positional stands to mutual interests by asking questions to determine the facts, moving the discussion to criteria that both would accept in judging the fairness of an outcome and reminding the former roommates of their common WATNA (Worst Alternative to a Negotiated Agreement). The mediator might ask: *match*

- "What prior agreements did you have about the phone?"
- "How was the bill paid in the past?"
- "Is the phone bill in both your names?"
- "You both indicated you may want to be able to get a phone in the future, and don't want to lose your credit with the phone company. What criteria can you use in determining how you both can reach that goal?"
- "What will happen if you don't reach an agreement?"

Brainstorming.   While some models suggest that every negotiation start with brainstorming, we recommend the technique as an option, rather than a required first step. When the technique may be useful or disputants are blocked, the mediator directs the disputants that they will use a technique to discover creative options. Before beginning, the mediator explains the rules of brainstorming.

- Disputants will think of options that could solve the problem and spend five minutes writing them down.
- The mediator will alternate in asking each disputant for an idea and record that idea.
- None of the ideas will be evaluated as they are listed.
- All ideas will be given the same respect.
- Disputants are encouraged to think about the problem in new ways.
- Building on the ideas of the other party is desirable.
- Wild and creative ideas are good, as they may lead to other ideas that are workable.

When the disputants have exhausted their supply of creative ideas, the mediator asks the disputants, "Are there ideas on the list that fit your criteria for a fair decision?" Once the list has been culled of ideas that do not meet their mutual criteria for an acceptable solution, the mediator inquires, "Are there ideas on this list that can be used or modified as part of your solution?" Through the brainstorming exercise, one divorcing couple with very young children decided that instead of moving the children between mom and dad's house, the parents would rent a condo and each live in it with the children on alternating weeks. The value of consistency for the children and enabling them to have a stable school district was most important to the parents. The decision they reached was creative and unlikely to have been selected if a judge had determined the outcome.

Linking and Unlinking.   As the negotiation proceeds, the mediator may connect agenda items together if settlement of one issue is integral or sequential to settlement of another issue. The mediator also may link issues if having more than one item on the table at the same time is advantageous. Competitive negotiators may need to trade concessions on different agenda items to feel that they are standing up to their "opponent." Cooperative negotiators may need to link issues to spur creative thinking and mutual-gains options. If disputants are bogging down in each item within a mediation about damages to an apartment, the mediator might group all of the damages together to negotiate an aggregate amount. Payments of damages might be linked to the landlord's release of a deposit.

Larger issues may need to be unpacked or unlinked when the items can stand alone and are not contingent on one another. When the principles or criteria that apply to each issue are different, unlinking may help the disputants. If disputants began a negotiation focused on aggregate damages to an apartment, the mediator separates the issues if criteria for damage to carpet are different from criteria applied to damage to landscaping.

Logrolling. Another strategy for generating options is logrolling. In *logrolling,* each party is coached on how to make concessions on some issues while the other party makes concessions on other issues. Ideally, both are conceding points in areas that have little personal cost or importance and are gaining concessions in areas that are highly important, creating a mutually beneficial arrangement. In Case 9.1, John might agree to pay half of the basic phone bill if he gets possession of the washing machine they bought together. To John, who needs a washing machine in his new apartment, paying half the phone bill is cheaper than buying a washer, so the deal meets his interests.

Role Reversal. Mediators sometimes ask disputants to engage in a type of perspective taking called *role reversal.* In a role reversal, each party is asked to state what would be fair if he or she were the other party. Parties can be asked, "What would you think about this offer if you were the other party?" "If you were the other party, what would be a fair outcome for you?" In Case 9.1, the mediator might ask John, "What would you think about the offer you just made if you were Jim?" Variations on the role reversal strategy might find the mediator asking, "What would your coworkers/friends/mother think of this agreement when they find out about it? Will they think it was fair?"

Focus on Future-Relationship Goals. Another strategy is changing the focus to the future. If past grievances are blocking creative negotiation among parties who have a continuing relationship, the mediator can change the frame of the negotiation to their future relationship. The mediator may inquire of coworkers: "What do you want your working relationship to be like in the future?" or "If you had a better working relationship, what would that look like?" Neighbors may be asked: "What would you like in a good neighbor relationship?" By building an idealized image of a good relationship, the mediator assists the parties to move toward a positive goal, rather than to wallow in past grievances.

Cost-Cutting.   If negotiations are stalling on the total cost of the agreement, the parties might brainstorm how they mutually could limit costs that arise due to the agreement. Gifford (1996) provides an example. "A management attorney who agrees to the wage demands of a certain type of worker might be concerned that in the future the union will expect similarly generous agreements for other workers. The union negotiator may reassure management that she understands that this wage agreement for certain employees stems from special circumstances, such as historical inequities, and that similar wage concessions should not be expected for other employees" (pp. 175–176). The parties might agree to drop litigation if the settlement works out, negating the need for expensive attorney fees.

Coaching.   Coaching is inherent in many techniques to assist the parties. In caucus or in session, a mediator may help the parties think about how to phrase offers, make symbolic gestures, show empathy for the other person's problems, or build contingency agreements. In caucus, the mediator might say to John, "You've told me that you're willing to pay half of the phone bill if you get the washing machine. How could you say that to Jim when we go back into session?"

Techniques for Traditional Negotiation

When one or both disputants exhibit traditional, hard negotiation behaviors, the mediator may encourage cooperative negotiation through reframing, controlling the process, and attempting some of the techniques discussed in the previous section. When cooperative negotiation flounders or disputants reach impasse about how to negotiate real, scarce resources, the mediator needs another set of techniques to assist the parties.

Traditional negotiation involves a dance with particular rules. According to Gifford (1996), the commonly understood rules for traditional bargaining are:

1. A high initial demand
2. Limited disclosure of information regarding facts and one's own preferences
3. Few and small concessions
4. Threats and arguments
5. Apparent commitment to positions during the negotiation process (p. 171)

The mediator's task during competitive bargaining is to control the process so the experience is productive and does not regress into face-threatening or degenerative discourse. Ponte and Cavenagh (1999) describe a more thoughtful approach to the dance of traditional bargaining where the mediator persists in attempting to expand the resources that are on the table for negotiation, to push for objective criteria, and to forestall early adoption of particularly negative bargaining techniques such as threats or final offers. Techniques used when mediating with traditional bargainers include:

- Create common value
- Fractionate apparent differences
- Build contingent agreements
- Bring time into the agreement
- Create a sliding scale
- Maximize relative value
- Avoid early commitment
- Discover the bargaining range

Create Common Value. Lax and Sebenius (1986) explain that most traditional bargaining focuses exclusively on *private value*—goods or money obtained through a negotiation that one party can enjoy while excluding the other from enjoying the same benefits. Negotiators, however, also can create *common value*—conditions that all parties will share and enjoy simultaneously, such as a better working environment, safer community, or not having to deal with the other party in the future. One way to moderate extreme competitive negotiation is to focus on the creation of common value during a portion of the agreement.

During a recent trip to the grocery on a cold day, a conflict was observed between a cashier and the customer service clerk. A new, cinnamon-scented pinecone product was placed near the checkstand. The checker, who found the scent overpowering, would prop open the door to let in fresh air. The customer service desk clerk would close the door because she was cold. Customers alternately complained that the scent was overpowering and that it was too cold in the store. Both workers would profit if a third party reminded them of their common goals—serving customers, having a pleasant work environment, being congenial coworkers, or keeping sales up in a flagging economy. Given the incentive to create the common value of increasing sales and good customer relationships, both parties could be encouraged to think creatively about other solutions than opening and closing the door.

Fractionate Apparent Differences. *Fractionation* is defined as breaking something down into its component parts. Fractionating and probing superficial differences can uncover fundamental commonalities. One classic example describes two individuals fighting over an orange. Both may vigorously compete for possession of the orange as their sole property, claiming they can't meet their needs without the orange. The mediator who delves into the underlying interests, however, may discover that one party wanted the orange because he was hungry and the other wanted the orange peel for a chemical experiment. Underlying the apparent differences were interests that were not mutually exclusive, if a little creativity is brought to the table.

Fractionation also is applied within a negotiable issue. In Case 9.1, the phone bill could be fractionated to a negotiation of each element of the bill: the basic charges, the long-distance charges, the long-distance access charge. By fractionating, the party who balks at paying one portion of the bill may see the fairness of paying for a basic line that he also used for an Internet connection.

Build Contingent Agreements.   When outcomes are based on the actions of others or on uncertain variables, contingent agreements can be crafted to apply to a variety of potential outcomes. *Contingent agreements* contain features that only go into effect once other conditions have been met. In Case 9.1, Jim and John could agree who will pay which amounts if the landlord cannot be persuaded to drop some of the late charges in exchange for a speedy resolution. A contingency agreement would be in place for the proportion of payment (or even how to split a reimbursement) if the landlord moderates the demands.

Agreements also can be contingent on information that will be provided by an objective outside party. Roommates in a dormitory might decide to solve their dispute by one roommate buying headphones to use with her video games to reduce noise. A contingency agreement would be negotiated in case there were no affordable headphones for her game system. Employees who both want to use the same equipment might work out a schedule of when each can use the equipment, with a contingency plan when emergency projects arise.

Bring Time into the Agreement.   If the parties agree in principle on who is responsible for debts or services, but one party can not pay the entire amount, a payment or service plan can be parceled out over time. Once an agreement in principle is reached of what will be paid, the mediator can ask, "What's the best way for both of you to make and receive those payments? Jim, are you in a position to make the entire payment right away?" If necessary, future payments or actions can be contingent on actions by the other party. John might agree to pay half of the damages to the apartment, contingent on Jim clearing the phone bill so that their credit records are not negatively affected.

Create a Sliding Scale.   When issues of relative or proportionate responsibility or fairness arise due to the parties' unequal wealth or abilities, agreements can be crafted that proportionately tax the parties according to their abilities and resources. The parties might negotiate to pay 70 and 30 percent of the costs of mediation to balance their abilities to pay. Both parties may agree that they share half of the responsibility for a debt, but one party has few resources to repay the debt. Instead of accepting a statement that one party has insufficient funds to clear his or her share of the debt now, the parties may agree that the insolvent disputant will pay a lesser amount and the party who has greater financial resources will pay more (with or without future repayment). Sliding scales balance the sacrifice each party makes.

Maximize Relative Value.   The mediator may coach the parties to think about offers that are valuable to the other party, but not overly costly to themselves. Because each party is attempting to satisfy her or his personal needs, the items that are traded in negotiation rarely are of equal value. Case 9.2 illustrates the relative value of an apology. If the insurance company had been more interested in the underlying needs of Mrs. Graham, they could have reduced their total costs.

Allen and Mohr (1998) label trades that are of low cost to one side and of higher value to the other side a *high-low exchange.* Words can be part of a high-low exchange. An apology or acknowledgment of some positive attribute of the other party may be sincere and easy to say (of low cost to the giver), but be critically important to the recipient (of high value).

Apologies can be pivotal in mediation. All apologies are not alike, however. Schneider (2000) argues that effective apologies have three components: the ritual of apology acknowledges that a past damage was created, the person apologizing appears to be regretful or shamed by the past behavior, and some vulnerability results from the apology. Disputants often need assistance in framing an apology. Sometimes, the mediator can caucus with the parties to explore their feelings of regret, explore how an apology might be offered, and suggest that the regret be expressed to the other party when the joint session resumes. Schneider concludes:

C A S E **9.2**

Mrs. Graham and the Train

An elderly woman was taking a short cut to her rural home one dark evening when she drove into a train. The train was parked across the isolated back road. The woman was not injured, but her car was damaged. On hearing of the incident, the family began to wonder if "Grandma shouldn't drive anymore and maybe we should take her keys away."

Mrs. Graham decided to sue the train company and called her attorney. Her attorney was a clever man. He researched and found an obscure law saying that it was illegal to park a train across a rural driveway. The attorney approached the train company. Negotiation ensued and the train company attorney offered to repair the woman's car. When presented with the offer by her attorney, Mrs. Graham replied, "It's not enough."

Her attorney returned to negotiation and came back with repair of the car and $2,000 compensation. Again, she replied, "It's not enough." Thinking the woman was a hard bargainer, her attorney approached the train company and said that his client needed "$10,000 compensation and repair of her car." The company finally acceded, knowing that they could receive bad publicity if the case went to court.

Proud of his work for his client, the attorney presented the $10,000 offer. Once again, she replied, "It's not enough." The attorney was stunned. Finally, he asked a question: "What is it that you need?" She replied, "I want them to write a letter apologizing for leaving the train there and saying it was their fault."

Randy Lowry of Pepperdine University tells this story.

"An apology may be just a brief moment in mediation. Yet it is often the margin of difference, however slight, that allows parties to settle. At heart, many mediations are dealing with damaged relationships. When offered with integrity and timing, an apology can indeed be a critically important moment in mediation" (p. 377). Schneider cautions that apologies when legal counsel is present are problematic, as an apology has a different meaning when transferred into a legal context than when tendered within mediation.

Avoid Early Commitment.   A firm or unreasonable early position leaves little room for creative negotiation. A take-it-or-leave-it offer is a competitive tactic to force concessions from the other party. The mediator should defuse early, unproductive offers or demands by ignoring them, reframing them, or deferring an offer until later in the session. A recalcitrant renter who is being sued for $5,000 in back rent, damages, and late fees may make an early take-it-or-leave-it statement as the first words out of his mouth during mediation: "I have only got $500 in the bank. That's all I can pay—take it or we might as well go see the judge right now." The mediator might reframe to say, "It sounds like you have some willingness to settle this issue; let's take a look at all of the details."

Discover the Bargaining Range.   When parties are negotiating money or the distribution of fixed resources, traditional bargaining often occurs. Disputants may revert to thinking of the negotiation as if they were buying a car. The dance of competitive negotiation is predictable. Each party tries to get the other to make an offer first. When the first offer is made, the other party claims it is too high/low depending on his or her perspective. An unreasonable counter offer is made. Meanwhile, each party has in mind what she or he is willing to pay and what their own bottom line is—the point at which no deal is better than a negotiated settlement.

The mediator's task is to unpack the unreasonable offers and to determine if there is a positive settlement range for both parties. A *settlement range* is the span of options where both parties might overlap and be able to come to an agreement.

In small claims court, Paul's landlord was suing for unpaid rent ($900) and late fees ($300) for a total of $1,200. Paul claimed he should not have to pay any of the rent or the late fees ($0) because the apartment had no air conditioning for most of August. In caucus, the mediator helped the landlord determine her bottom line of what was fair to settle the case. The landlord determined she could drop the late fees and take half of the rent if Paul paid it that day ($450). The mediator then met privately with Paul. Paul decided that he might lose the case in court, so he was willing to pay up to 75 percent of the rent ($600). A *positive settlement range* existed. The landlord would like to receive $1,200, but would settle for $450. Paul would like to pay nothing, but would pay up to $600. Both parties were willing to settle within the range of $450–$600 dollars.

| Landlord | $450 ——————— $1,200 |
| Paul | $0 ——————— $600 |

Knowing that a positive settlement range exists, the mediator can work with both parties (without revealing privileged information) to encourage them to bargain toward a settlement. However, if Paul was only willing to pay up to $300 and the landlord would accept nothing below $450, a *negative settlement range* exists. There is no overlap between their acceptable range of settlements. When a negative settlement range is discovered, the mediator moves the discussion to nonmonetary issues. If the bargaining between Paul and the landlord deadlocked at $300 offered and $450 needed (a negative settlement range), then the mediator may ask, "How else can the two of you close the gap in what you are willing to pay and to accept? Are there nonmonetary values that you can enter into the agreement?" Paul may agree to do one day of carpentry work for the landlord.

*B*UYING *A car almost always involves traditional bargaining. Do you think the sticker price is a realistic opening offer by a new car dealer? How can you estimate what the dealer's bargaining range is when negotiating a car purchase?*

Using the Caucus to Respond to Common Problems

We've discussed the value of caucusing, or holding private meetings, throughout the book and suggested times when it might be useful to speak to the parties privately. When the mediator deems separating the parties is appropriate, he or she pauses the session and gives a rationale for moving to private meetings. The reasons given to the disputants may include:

- "I think at this point it would be useful for me to talk to each of you separately."
- "At this point in the mediation, I typically take a few moments to speak with each of you separately to see how the session is going for you."
- "Let's change the tempo of the session. I'm going to speak with each of you individually for a few minutes."

The mediator should overview the confidentiality pledge as it applies to the caucus with both parties before beginning. When the private meeting is finished, the mediator reviews the caucus confidentiality pledge before returning to joint session or conferring with the other party. Reviewing the confidentiality pledge gives the disputants the information about whether their comments will be shared with the other party and reminds the mediator of the confidentiality standards that apply to caucusing.

The mediator can use the time while she or he is with one party to leave an assignment with the disputant who will be alone. For example, the mediator might suggest that a disputant think about what his or her real costs are, what bargaining room exists in the situation, or what would happen if the parties were not able to settle. If the session is co-mediated, one mediator may meet with each party or both mediators may meet with both parties.

While we prefer to keep the disputants in joint session as long as productive work is occurring, the mediator will need to speak with the parties separately on occasion or to *shuttle* back and forth between parties who cannot work safely or productively in the same room. Three additional uses for the caucus are to respond to disputants who do not bargain in good faith, who have hidden agendas, or who lie.

Shuttle

Shuttle mediation occurs when the parties stay in separate rooms and the mediator travels back and forth between the parties. Shuttle mediation is used in situations where the disputants are unproductive when together, it is unsafe for them to be together, or when the mediator needs to have extended private talks with each party. In caucus, the mediator probes for BATNA, WATNA, and for hidden agendas or other impediments to settlement while helping parties consider their options. In a landlord-tenant case, the mediator might ask the tenant in caucus for his opinion about the fairness of living in an apartment for a month and paying nothing for rent, even if the air conditioning didn't work. Then the mediator can move to the issue of what is a fair payment for an apartment with no air conditioning. With the landlord, the mediator might ask if the landlord thinks it is fair to require full rent when the air conditioning didn't work or what the probability is of collecting the full amount even if she wins in court. The mediator would carry the offers back and forth until an agreement is reached between the parties or the mediator decides that it is unproductive for negotiation to continue.

Not Bargaining in Good Faith

When a disputant continues to repeat an unreasonable position, uses intimidation or other coercive tactics, lies, or is otherwise uncooperative about the process of mediation, it is time to call a caucus. In caucus, the mediator would probe for the underlying reason for the tactics, check the disputant's expectations of the outcome of the dispute, and attempt to persuade the disputant to bargain in good faith. BATNA, WATNA, reframing, goal focus, and open-ended questions are among the techniques that the mediator will use with an uncooperative party. If it becomes clear that the party is unwilling or unable to bargain in good faith, the mediator may withdraw from the mediation.

Hidden Agendas

At times, the mediator knows from a disputant's comments that she or he wishes to settle the case, but observes that the disputant is unable to move from a position or to accept an outcome that seems to be advantageous. A caucus provides an opportunity for the mediator to check for hidden agendas and to ask, "What else is going on that I am not aware of?" In one case involving an unmarried, nondating couple attempting to create a visitation schedule for their baby, the mediator could not move the father to consider options. In caucus, the mediator explained what she saw happening and asked for an explanation. The father said, "Well, to tell you the truth, I'm afraid that if we create a visitation schedule, she won't take me back. I'd like to marry her." In order for the negotiations to proceed, this hidden agenda needed to be set aside or dealt with. The father decided not to talk about it, and agreed to make a visitation schedule for a period of three months, during which time he thought he could talk to her about reconciliation.

Lying or Withholding Information

Denial of responsibility is distressingly common. What begins as hard bargaining may become dishonesty if parties are unwilling to disclose key information. For example, one party in a divorce mediation may try to hide assets during the property settlement. Mediators cannot permit the disputants to go forward with an agreement based on false or concealed information. A mediator who senses that one party is lying or withholding information may confront the party in caucus and provide face-saving strategies for the party to alter her or his behavior. In caucus, the mediator can ask if the disputant wants to say anything more about their information. The mediator can ask about what seem to be apparent contradictions in their story by saying, "I'm confused about some of what you've said…" or asking, "Were you uncomfortable about that discussion?" If the disputant clarifies the information, the mediator can then help the party with a strategy to reveal the information during the session. Disputants may confess to lies during caucus and then ask the mediator not to tell the other party. Mediators cannot be complicit to lies, even to protect the confidentiality of the caucus. If a party will not provide accurate information during session and expects the mediator to act as if a known lie is the truth, the mediator should end the mediation.

Breaking Deadlocks

When disputants become firmly locked or have exhausted their ability to make offers, an *impasse* occurs. Impasse is the reason many disputes come to mediation in the first place—disputants have exhausted their own resources and need help. Mediators faced with disputant impasse must first analyze the probable cause of the impasse and then utilize techniques to break through the blockage.

Analyze the Impasse

When disputants talk their way to irreconcilable deadlock, the mediator tests the impasse against common causes, such as:

- A relationship conflict is sapping the will to negotiate the substantive issues
- Parties remain too emotional
- One or both parties misperceive or stereotype the other

- Communication efforts are inadequate or misperceived
- Negative behaviors persist
- Parties differ on what data is important or how to interpret it
- The parties' interests are mutually exclusive
- One or both parties feel coerced or feel that the proposed outcome is not fair
- The parties hold deeply rooted, different values
- Some of the standard parts of agreements are missing, such as apologies, plans for future communication between the parties, or restitution plans
- One party does not trust that the other party will follow through with the agreement

Once the probable source of the impasse is located, the mediator can select a technique to break through the impasse.

Techniques to Break through Impasse

Depending on the source of the impasse, the mediator may return to the storytelling phase to work through misperceptions or psychological issues. Specific techniques to break through impasse include:

- Return to interests
- Take a break
- Take a caucus to explore the blockage privately
- Separate the parties and shuttle mediate
- Build outside standards to judge information or solutions
- Coach the parties on their negotiation style
- Seek acknowledgments from one party for the other party's feelings or experiences
- Increase identification of commonalities
- Validate feelings
- Ask each party to paraphrase the other's comments before responding
- Separate procedural, psychological, and substantiate portions of the negotiation
- Reframe the impasse

Slaikeu (1996) recommends the *logjam* metaphor when discussing an impasse with disputants. The mediator asks, "How can we move some of these logs out of the way so the two of you can get on with your business?"

Face-Saving

One of the reasons disputants cannot manage their own conflicts is entrenchment. One or both disputants may be mired in firm positions and cannot move from their stance without believing they will appear weak. Another reason disputants cannot manage their own conflict is that they cannot transcend hurt feelings or past grievances.

Goffman introduced the concept of *face* in 1967 to describe a person's positive self-image. "*Face* is the part of your identity that you present during interaction and expect will be accepted by others. Maintaining face is part of the ever-present self-presentation goal" (Cupach & Canary, 1997, p. 110). In conflict, disputants frequently perceive moving from a hard position as a loss of face, particularly when less savory traditional negotiations tactics such as threats, blaming, and personal criticism have been evident (Cupach & Canary, 1997). The Hawaii model of mediation builds face-saving into the process by requiring pre-mediation where each party can disclose their feelings to the mediator in private and the mediator can coach the disputants on how to proceed (Ogawa, 1999). The balanced mediation model does not require face-saving work during pre-mediation, but does encourage the mediator to be sensitive to face issues.

Part of the mediator's task is to orchestrate conditions so disputants can move from their positions without losing face. Mediator tactics for face-saving include:

- Coaching parties on how to make offers without denigrating the other person
- Helping disputants create a logical rationale for change
- Coordinating apologies
- Transforming how parties perceive or talk about the actions of others
- Emphasizing the relative value of each party's gains during negotiation

Disputants will refuse outcomes that are advantageous to them economically if they are not advantageous to their self-concept. In Case 9.2, Mrs. Graham is more interested in protecting her self-image as an independent person than she is in monetary compensation.

How important is face to you? Can you remember a time when you did not manage a problem because your feelings were hurt or you were afraid that settling the issue would make you look bad? How would you recognize a threat to face felt by a disputant?

Mediator Ethics and the Negotiation Phase

What does the mediator do when the agreement reached by the disputants seems unfair to one party, is socially repugnant, is illegal, or could be harmful to externalities? Most states with codes of ethics provide the guidance that mediators should raise questions when the interests of external parties are not being included and should consider the overall fairness of the agreements disputants make. The Pennsylvania Council of Mediators (2001) instructs mediators to

---

CASE **9.3**

The Questionable Gift

Bohn started a job six months ago at a loan company that specializes in mortgage loans. His job is to process the loans brought by the independent contractors who solicit the loans from realtors selling to first-time home buyers. Bohn noticed that the independent contractors often bring items to the loan processing agents as "thank you" gifts. These gifts range from candy to coveted sporting and entertainment tickets. The other loan processing agents love the attention and the gifts and do not want the current system challenged. Bohn is certain that this practice is bribery and is not legal. Bohn raised the issue with his boss. Bohn explained how uncomfortable it was to receive the gifts and believed it put pressure on him to pass questionable loan contracts.

The boss understands Bohn's concerns, but doesn't want to change the system. They agree that Bohn will have a personal policy of not accepting gifts from the contractors and realtors, but that the policy for the rest of the loan processing agents will be up to them.

"dissociate from any agreement that the mediator perceives to be so far outside the parameters of fairness (based on learned common sense), as to be unreasonable." The Mediation Council of Illinois (2001) requires mediators to sign a written statement of nonconcurrence or, in some cases, withdraw, when the parties come to an agreement "that the mediator finds inherently unfair.... While mediators must be impartial between participants, they must not be neutral toward fairness." Mediators should consult the most current standards of practice in their state or territory to determine how issues of fairness are treated in their jurisdiction.

> *WHAT SHOULD the mediator do if Bohn and his boss in Case 9.3 decide that two competing ethical standards are appropriate for their office?*

Mediators also err during negotiation due to their own desire to be helpful. When disputants seem to be bickering or taking too long to formulate options for settlement, it is tempting for the mediator to become increasingly intrusive into the process. Negotiation and bargaining, however, are a dance. The mediator's primary virtue during this phase is patience. Permit the disputants to talk to each other and to grapple with their difficulties. Give the disputants latitude to struggle while they work toward their own solution. Be patient.

> *WHAT SHOULD mediators do if the disputants agree to outcomes that are legal, but the mediator finds personally repugnant? Does the code of conduct for mediators in your state or territory give any advice about how to handle repugnant decisions?*

Summary

Competition and cooperation are two opposing approaches to negotiation. Competitive negotiators usually take firm positions; cooperative negotiators search for mutual gains. Each approach to negotiation is associated with different tactics.

Mediators vary in their directiveness. Directiveness refers to control of the process, which is different from intruding into the outcome of the negotiation. Mediators utilizing the balanced mediation model are prohibited from intrusiveness.

Eight mediator techniques to foster cooperative bargaining include: establishing criteria, brainstorming, linking or unlinking, logrolling, role-reversal, focusing on the future relationship, cost-cutting, and coaching. Additional techniques useful with competitive disputants include: creating common value, fractionating, contingency agreements, adding time into the agreement, sliding scales, relative value maximization, avoiding early commitment, and discovering the bargaining range.

Private meetings are useful during the problem-solving and negotiation phase. Mediators may use the caucus to shuttle or to check with disputants about good faith bargaining, hidden agendas, or lying.

If an impasse occurs, mediators will analyze its cause and select a technique to unblock the logjam. Face is an important concept for mediators and a common impediment to settlement.

Mediators may use the caucus to check with disputants about unique ethical issues during the negotiation phase. In some jurisdictions, mediators have special obligations if they deem a decision unduly unfair.

CHAPTER 10

Settlement and Closure

*T*he final phase of the mediation process establishes the path the disputants will take after the mediation. Depending on how the negotiation phase unfolded, the mediator will help the parties craft an agreement or end the mediation without an agreement. This chapter provides the basics of agreement writing, differences in writing agreements and contracts, choosing the language for the agreement, and closing mediations that do not end in settlement. Regardless of how the mediation ends, it will be successful if the parties achieve a greater *understanding* of each other and their interests.

Why Write Agreements?

Agreements meet the needs of parties to have a record of the mediation. A written agreement creates a concrete document that memorializes the mediation and the behaviors that each party agrees to uphold. Future disagreements may be prevented by a written document that addresses key issues. When signed by each party, agreements can add to the disputants' sense of ownership of the decisions. The agreement also can serve to remind the disputants of their joint negotiation successes, offering physical evidence that the parties can and did agree.

Types of Agreements

Informal Nonwritten Agreements

People create informal agreements every day. These agreements are sealed with a handshake or a verbal commitment. If two friends are having lunch together and one says, "I'll pay for it," the other might say, "Okay, if I can get it next time." The friends would be unlikely to pull out a piece of paper to memorialize their commitment to the lunch plan. Generally, if there is high trust between the parties, if both parties support the decision wholeheartedly, and if the content of the agreement is straightforward, an informal, nonwritten agreement will suffice. In community disputes, for example, the parties may be satisfied with an informal, verbal agreement. As described earlier, sometimes the exchange of phone numbers is enough of an "agreement" to satisfy both parties because they can contact each other if future difficulties arise.

Informal Written Agreements

In many types of mediation, an informal written agreement, sometimes referred to as a *Memorandum of Understanding* provides enough structure and security for the disputants. An informal agreement is written by the mediator, uses the disputants' wording as much as possible, and typically is kept private between the parties involved. This chapter focuses on how to create and draft an informal written agreement.

Formal Written Agreements

In some mediations, the agreement serves as a document of record and must follow special guidelines. Child custody, court mandated, and victim-offender mediation agreements, for example, may require specific written formats. The audience for the agreements is not only the disputants, but may include judges, probation officers, or government agents. Specific training in writing formal agreements is beyond the scope of this book and should be included as part of the advanced training in each specific mediation context.

Formal Contractual Agreements

Formal contractual agreements usually are crafted by attorneys. Nonattorney mediators with specialized training may aid parties in creating drafts of formal legal documents that disputants then take to their attorneys. However, creating formal contractual agreements requires more instruction than this book is intended to provide.

Is the Agreement Legally Binding or Legally Nonbinding?

The language of agreements can be confusing for new mediators. Any agreement that is written, signed by each party, dated, and witnessed has legal implications. The issue, however, is that nonattorney mediators are not in the business of creating legally binding contracts. Instead, disputants are memorializing the mediation event and creating *legally nonbinding agreements.* The mediator's intent in creating the document is to assist the parties in reaching their own decisions.

Binding agreements are legal agreements. In most states, mediators who are not attorneys cannot represent themselves as writing legally binding contracts. Creating a binding contract could be illegal for nonattorneys under their states' unauthorized practice of law statutes. <u>*Nonbinding agreements*</u> are philosophical agreements. Nonbinding is a legal term, meaning not directly enforceable through the courts. However, nonbinding agreements created in mediation generally are upheld in court when challenged. The term "nonbinding" can be very confusing to disputants, leading them to believe they have no responsibility to be "bound" to the agreement. For this reason, we recommend that mediators refer to their written documents simply as "agreements" or as "memorandums of understanding."

Nonattorney mediators should include a statement of the mediator's intent within the agreement form (Figure 10.1 on page 166). The mediator's intent statement could read: "The mediator's intent was not to draft a legally binding contract. However, any signed agreement may have legal implications. Parties may wish to seek the advice of legal counsel before signing." We further recommend the use of the phrase "agreement writing" to distinguish from contract writing.

Novice mediators often ask if the phrasing about the mediator's intent or seeking legal counsel hinders parties from signing agreements. In our experience, the answer is no. Most people are aware that signing and dating a document in front of witnesses carries legal consequences. This consequence is not a fact that should be hidden from disputants, but is not usually a concern for them in the creation of the agreement. If asked by disputants if the agreement is legally binding, the mediator should be forthright and state, "Signing any agreement could have legal ramifications. If this is something that concerns you, I encourage you to seek legal advice before signing it."

When writing a mediated agreement, the mediator considers two questions to select the level of formality: (1) What is the purpose of this agreement? (2) Who is the audience? If the purpose of the agreement is to record an understanding between the two disputants, then nonattorney mediators are qualified to offer this service. If the purpose of the agreement is to be the first draft of what will become a legally binding document, then more training in writing such drafts is required for nonattorney mediators, and disputants should have their attorneys review the document. The second question, "Who is the audience?" also dictates the form that the agreement takes. If the only audience is the parties themselves, the wording of the agreement may be less formal (but not necessarily less specific) than if the audience is a judge or a probation officer.

ACTIVITY 10.1

Review the applicable laws and guidelines in your state about parameters in agreement writing for nonattorney mediators.

A Format for Writing Mediation Agreements

Informal written agreements are common outcomes of successful meditations. While some mediation outcomes necessitate contractual agreements (for example, child custody agreements, business partnership agreements, covenants, and so on), Memorandums of Understanding often are sufficient. Drafting the agreement with the parties at the table is beneficial as it allows the parties to be part of the agreement writing and to check the usefulness and accuracy of the agreement's wording.

Ideally, the mediator will have access to equipment that will allow all parties to have a personal copy of the agreement once it has been signed. Some mediators use laptop computers and portable printers to run several copies of agreements, and all parties will sign all copies. Others use copy machines to make sure that all parties have copies of the agreement. If such resources are not available, mediators can handwrite agreements, have the parties sign the handwritten document, then photocopy it the next day and mail it to each party. The goal is for all parties to have access to the same information at the same time.

Agreements should include the following items:

1. The title of the type of agreement ("Mediation Agreement" or "Memorandum of Understanding")
2. The first and last names of each of the parties
3. A general context statement (Examples: "Division of Property," "Termination of Roommate Agreement," "Child Custody")
4. The date that the agreement was created
5. The name of the mediator and center where the agreement was created
6. Detailed instructions or behavioral guidelines that outline the expectations for each of the parties involved
7. Statement of mediator's intent
8. Signature lines and dates for each party and mediator(s)

Figure 10.1 on page 166 illustrates the components of a mediated agreement.

MEDIATOR NOTEBOOK 10.1

The Mediated Agreement Form

Using Figure 10.1 as a model, create a form for your own written agreements.

[handwritten: Memorandum of Agr. or Understanding]

FIGURE 10.1 Sample Mediation Agreement

Rodriguez Mediation Center
Mediation Agreement

This Memorandum of Understanding between <u>Cindy Bennett and Brian Morgan,</u> dated <u>January 22, 2004,</u> serves to document the following voluntary agreement(s) in respect to their termination of their roommate status:

1. We agree that Cindy will pay 1/3 of the July 14, 2003 phone bill ($22.38) to Brian by February 1 of this year.
2. We agree that Brian will return the four CDs and the computer to Cindy when she brings over the check for the phone bill on February 1.
3. We agree to sell the couch and the loveseat though a classified ad that Brian will place and pay for and will split the money from the sales 50/50.
4. We agree that if the couch does not sell in one month, Brian will take the couch to the Salvation Army and give the donation receipt to Cindy.
5. We agree that Cindy will not call Brian's mother for any reason.
6. We agree to discuss our differences with calm voices and in private should we have any future disagreements.
7. We agree to return to mediation if we cannot work out our differences together.

We understand that it has not been the mediator's intent to draft a legal contract. However, we understand that signing this document may have legal implications. Parties may wish to seek the advice of legal counsel prior to signing this agreement.

[handwritten: can use this]

Signature: _____   Date: _____
                   Cindy Bennett

Signature: _____   Date: _____
                   Brian Morgan

Mediator: _____   Date: _____
                   Jaime Rodriguez

ACTIVITY **10.2**

Contact mediator professionals in your area to collect sample mediation forms used in their practice. Look for differences and similarities among mediation contexts, such as: The Human Rights Commission, the Better Business Bureau, Court Mediation Programs, and private mediators.

Choosing the Language of the Agreement

Great caution should be used in writing agreements so that the agreement itself does not become fodder for future disputes. How disputants are portrayed in the writing, the level of specificity, and the clarity of the agreement are critical elements in creating strong agreements. The following guidelines will make agreements more viable and fair.

Agreements Use Direct Language

The mediator should use direct and straightforward wording in the agreement. Hedge words such as, "may," "could," or "should," can lead to future disagreements. Instead, the mediator selects words like "will," "shall," and "will not." For example: "Sergio should contact Elsie if the supply shipments are to be delayed." This statement allows Sergio some latitude in contacting Elsie, as the statement is "he should" rather than "he will." If there may be a time when Sergio could wait to call Elsie, include that in the agreement: "Sergio will call Elsie if the supply shipments are delayed by more than three working days." The reworded statement allows little room for interpretation and both parties should be clear about Sergio's responsibilities.

Agreements Are Clear

The mediator ensures that all parties know what they are expected to do and when they are expected to accomplish it. An agreement that states that one party will pay the other party $500 may be acceptable or may create more problems. Clarify the specific behaviors through active questioning and discussion, and then document in the agreement as much as the disputants determine is necessary. For instance, a written statement that confirms, "Jessie will pay Margo $500," may be perfectly fine for some disputants, particularly those who have a history of cooperation and high trust for each other. However, other disputants may need more specificity: "Jessie will pay Margo a total of $500 in two installments of $250. The first cash payment will be on January 15 and the second cash payment will be on February 15. Jessie will pay by 5:00 P.M. at Margo's office on, or before, each due date."

what will happen – not what will happen what if they dont,

Agreements Generally Are Positive

Even though the agreement may be spurred by past negative behaviors by one disputant, the mediator crafts the agreement as positively as possible. A "will" statement is much more appealing than a "will not" statement. For example, "Elli will not leave her bicycle behind Mr. King's car" is not as positive as, "Elli will park her bicycle beside the garage." Occasionally however, a "will not" statement underscores the intentions of the disputants and captures their specific intent. In the sample mediation agreement (Figure 10.1), Brian was adamant that Cindy would not call his mother to tell her negative things about him as she had done in the past. Subsequently, the language of the agreement did address what Cindy would *not* do. Remember that positive framing is powerful, but that the agreement should reflect what the parties need.

Additionally, the mediator deletes indicators of bad will or destructive actions. The agreement is a plan for the future, not a rehashing of the past. The statement, "Because Robert's checks have been returned as insufficient funds in the past, he will bring cash to Jo's Appliance's when he pays the bill," will remind parties of their past disagreement. A positive statement without addressing the prior infraction will serve the parties better, such as: "We agree that Robert will make monthly cash payments on his bill at Jo's Appliances."

Agreements Are Impartial

The mediator must consider how the phrasing portrays each party. Does the language smear one party as the bad one? For example, "Taylor will not cheat on his time cards by guessing what his time was for the past week," is in essence calling Mr. Taylor a "cheat." Even if Mr. Taylor committed past misdeeds, mediated agreements are forward looking and are promises of *future* behaviors. The phrasing should address the behavior to be changed. "Mr. Taylor will record his time to the nearest five minutes on his time card each day on arriving at work and again just prior to leaving."

The mediator is as even handed as possible in the portrayal of each individual. Does each party have responsibilities in the agreement or just one side? We recommend starting the specifics of the agreements with a "We agree" preface to each line in the agreement ("We agree that…") or by stating both parties' names ("Mr. Zu and Ms. Lee agree that…"). Furthermore, agreements should try to address the behavior of both parties instead of only outlining the ways one party will change his or her behavior.

Finally, the mediator considers how power is portrayed in the agreements. Does one party have a title, and the other party not have a title? While this may be appropriate in some cases, it may be unnecessarily divisive in others.

Agreements Are Concrete

The mediator must ensure that all parties have the same interpretation of what the words in the agreement mean. The phrase, "Jeff will respect Dea" ignores the probability that parties do not hold the same interpretation of the word "respect." Parties with high conflict and low trust require more specificity and behaviorally definable language. Parties with low conflict and high trust may require less specificity and less behaviorally focused language. We recommend that new mediators emphasize concrete and behaviorally specific agreement writing. Instead of an abstract reference to respect, the mediator might reframe the agreement to focus on behaviors. The mediator would ask each party what "respect" would look like and work their behavioral definitions into the agreement. "Dea and Jeff agree to maintain a professional relationship, specifically listening quietly during meetings and waiting until the speaker is done to ask questions or make a point."

Mediators also consider the audience of the agreement. A statement such as, "Ross agrees to be respectful at work" can be open to many interpretations, and an attorney would frown at a client who would sign such a vague contract. Will Ross be in violation of the agreement if he does not show respect enough to laugh at the other disputant's jokes? When in doubt, the mediator should err on the side of asking questions that generate more specific language.

A problem may arise if one party requests higher levels of specificity than the other, such as exact dates, specific payment amounts, or precise times in the agreement, and the other party does not desire the same detail. In this situation the mediator must be aware of the needs of each party. Demanding high levels of detail may imply that one party is not trustworthy. One strategy in this situation would be for the mediator to assume the task of pressing for details so that the level of detail seems to be dictated by the mediator and the mediation process.

Language is an important consideration in creating agreements. Because language is *representative* of some idea or thing, we have many options for wording agreements. The terms, "professional," "respectful," "safe," "timely," "reasonable," "occasional," and "acceptable" are extremely abstract terms and are open to varied interpretations. Through our experiences with others, we create a similar understanding of what words mean. However, abstract terms remain highly subjective. Telling a first grader to "clean up her room," only to have the parent disagree when the daughter says it is "clean," illustrates how our own experiences with the word "clean" affect our understanding of that word.

It is incumbent on the mediator to determine the proper level of language abstraction necessary in a mediated agreement. For example, all parties may understand the term "safety" because there is a safety statement posted at the lumber mill and all employees have had safety training. However, without similar experiences with the word "safety," the expectations about what it means to be "safe" must be made more concrete during the final stages of writing the agreement.

Hayakawa (1978) compared the process of choosing the proper level of abstraction or concreteness to climbing up and down a ladder. At the top rung of the ladder is the most abstract term, such as "professional." As we climb down the ladder to the lower rungs, the description becomes more concrete. As Figure 10.2 on page 170 illustrates, when descending each step of the ladder of abstraction, words become less ambiguous. At the top of the ladder are abstract words, such as *well dressed.* At the bottom rung of the ladder are the most concrete words, such as *blue or*

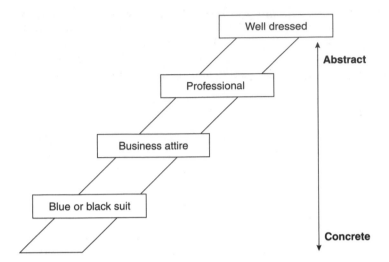

FIGURE 10.2   The Ladder of Abstraction

black suit. In each agreement, the mediator helps the parties choose a proper level of abstraction by asking questions such as: "What do you mean by business attire?" "What does respect mean to you?" "If a room is clean, what will it look like?" Generally, less abstraction is better.

Agreements Use the Parties' Words

In most situations, the mediator can use the disputants' words and write the agreement in front of the disputants. Even if the mediator is not using their exact words, their thoughts and intents are represented. Mediators ask if the wording is accurate and if the phrasing is what they want to record. Agreements are more likely to be upheld when disputants participate in wording the agreement. Including disputants in the phrasing and construction of the actual document adds to their feelings of ownership over the agreement. Agreements are only strong if the parties are willing to uphold them.

Creating Durable Agreements

Mediators want to create agreements that are durable, that will endure over time. Durable agreements help the disputants cope with unforeseen future events through contingency plans, future clauses, and reality testing.

Contingency Agreements

Even the best plans may not follow through to fruition. Mediators should ask disputants specific "What if?" questions to determine if back-up *contingency plans* should be included. In the sample agreement in Figure 10.1, Cindy and Brian plan to sell the couch and split the money. However, what if the couch does not sell? The mediator prompted the parties to consider this alternative and they decided to include a contingency plan if the couch did not sell. The disputants have a plan covering two potential futures—sale and no sale of the couch.

Future Clauses

Parties may need to consider what caused the escalation of conflict in the dispute. To avoid similar escalation in the future, the agreement should include specific communication behaviors for each to follow. On many occasions, one party may not feel comfortable talking to the other. A *future communication clause* addresses how the parties will communicate in the future. E-mail is another common area of complaint where a discussion of future interactions may be discussed. In one situation, a long-time employee was told that she was not to be promoted in an e-mail sent to the entire company. The boss regretted this action, and the employee wanted to make sure that this type of thing did not happen again. A future communication clause was added to the agreement. One question used to assist parties to discuss communication issues is: "If you had it to do all over again, what would you do differently?" The ensuing discussion may lead the parties to establishing positive future communication plans.

In addition to a communication plan, ask parties if they want to include a *future disagreement clause.* Ask disputants how they would handle a problem with the mediated agreement or other issues that may arise in the future. The mediator might inquire, "If something new comes up in the future, how do the two of you want to handle it?" Disputants may discuss how they are more likely to talk about matters with one another now that they have been through the mediation, choose to return to mediation, or establish some other method that fits their circumstances.

Reality Testing

Reality testing the specifics of agreements can be a scary proposition for the new mediator. *Reality testing* implicitly asks the disputants, "Are you sure the plan will work?" At this stage, the disputants (and mediators) probably are tired. However, rushing past reality testing may have disastrous effects. The mediator has a responsibility to the parties to aid them in crafting agreements that will last and meet their needs. The mediator must be realistic without seeming to criticize or disapprove of the ideas put forth by the disputants. In reality testing, the mediator is helping parties consider unintended consequences or unexpected situations, and testing the agreements for overall workability and reasonability.

Interests play a crucial role in reality testing. Interests become criteria for evaluating the settlement. Mediators bring the interests back into the spotlight to see if those interests are being met. For example, a tenant demanded that the landlord fix a broken window in the basement because his interest was to feel safe. Later, he agreed to postpone having the window fixed for several weeks. This agreement should raise a red flag to the mediator. Asking the tenant about his original concern for safety in light of having a broken window for a few more weeks is reality testing the agreement. The tenant may still be concerned about safety and may request that the landlord board up the window until it is fixed. By testing the reality of what it would be like to live with the broken window, the mediator reminded the tenant of his safety concerns, and a stronger agreement was the result.

Reality testing involves asking questions that address interests, but also includes prompting disputants to reflect on possible unexpected consequences of their agreements. If the agreement between neighbors is to designate space on the street for each of them to park, what happens when someone else parks on the street in the disputed parking spot? If the agreement between coworkers designates time for using the office computer, what happens if a situation requires them to alter their schedule, such as an unexpected crisis or having the computers go offline for several hours? Mediators should ask disputants about the consequences their decision will have on other people and have disputants talk about possible situations that would test the efficacy of their agreements.

Some reality testing strategies include:

1. *Placing the agreement into the future.* "This agreement will work for you now, but what about a year from now? Do you anticipate any changes in your situation?"
2. *Probing questions to flesh out possible problems.* "Have we missed any important issues that might arise?" "What if the cost of repairing the ventilation is more than you initially thought?"
3. *Considering parties not present.* "How will this change in production affect the marketing division?" "How will the children feel about this change in their morning routine?"
4. *Considering hidden costs to the parties in the agreement.* "How will agreeing to fund his trip to the London conference affect your travel budget for other personnel?" "Will agreeing to this payment schedule cause difficulties for you at home?"
5. *Making room for modifications, if needed.* "How can this agreement better meet your need for safety?"
6. *Exploring doubts.* "You seem concerned over the timeline in getting agreement from your constituencies. What exactly concerns you?"
7. *Highlighting changes of heart.* "Earlier you mentioned that seeing your children on Easter was important for you. Now you're agreeing to see them the week before. Explain how this is acceptable now."

The purpose of reality testing is to ensure that parties make informed decisions, consider options, explore implications of their choices, and create workable agreements. Do not underestimate the importance of this process in creating durable agreements.

ACTIVITY **10.3**

What could be problematic with the following agreements? Examine the language choices, the behavioral expectations, and how the agreement portrays each party. Reality test these agreements and rewrite the agreement statements into a proper agreement format.

1. Julie and Mr. McGraw, disputing neighbors, agree to the following: Julie will not throw cigarette butts into Mr. McGraw's yard. Julie's children will not enter Mr. McGraw's yard for any reason. Julie will turn off her porch light at 9:00 P.M. Julie will contact Mr. McGraw if his dog, Tiger, is in her yard.
2. Given the desire for Mr. Herra and Ms. Miller to get along at work, Mr. Herra agrees not to be belligerent to Ms. Miller during the sales meetings.
3. Jim will pay his mom back the money he owes her for the damaged car.
4. Tomas and Franklin agree to purchase a car together and share it.
5. Mr. Watson will not use the office computer when Rochelle needs it.
6. Because of past problems and misunderstandings, Charlie and Susan agree not to use the e-mail system to communicate at work.

The Writing Process

The basic steps in writing agreements are:

1. Record the general agreements during the negotiations
2. Read the general agreements, either one by one, or as a package, to determine if the agreement is what the parties want
3. Ask if there are other issues not yet addressed that need to be considered or included in the agreement
4. Rework each item in the agreement for:
   concreteness
   behavioral focus
   timelines
   contingencies
   implementation specifics
   impact on others
5. When all items in step 4 are worked through, ask about future communication and future conflict clauses
6. Read the entire agreement back to the parties and ask them if this is what they agree to do; modify as necessary
7. Have a "signing ceremony"
8. Make sure that all parties receive copies of the agreement

The physical writing of the agreement can occur in several different ways. Two methods of writing the agreement are (1) crafting each section as it is negotiated, and (2) waiting until the entire negotiation is finished. All methods involve an initial summary of the general agreement reached by the parties, followed by a reworking of the agreement for greater clarity and specificity.

Agreement Writing Methods

Some mediators choose to write agreements as each point is agreed on. After the agenda is set, the process would follow a set pattern:

1. Statement of an issue to be negotiated
2. Negotiation
3. Settlement on that one issue
4. Write agreement on that issue
5. Repeat the process on the next issue

The process would repeat steps 1 through 4 until all issues were mediated. The one-at-a-time approach would be ill-advised if there were issues that needed to be packaged or traded off.

Writing the entire agreement at the end is a second method of constructing agreements. Mediators take notes of tentative or actual agreements that the parties make during the negotiation. Once the negotiation phase is completed, the mediator summarizes his or her notes about the total agreement package and leads the parties through the agreement-refinement step. As each part of the agreement was refined and revised for specificity and workability, the mediator would record it on the agreement form.

Some mediators use a combination of both processes, depending on the issues involved and the level of cooperation between the disputants. No matter which process is used, the mediator's notes must capture the essence of the disputant's agreements.

Writing from General to Specific

The mediator begins the final agreement writing by summarizing the agreements reached by the parties. The mediator could briefly say, "The two of you have agreed to a flex-time schedule for Sarah for the period of one year. During the coming year, Sarah will work a forty-hour work week, but only twenty of that will be at the office, in four, five-hour shifts per week. Is that what the two of you agreed?" At this point, the mediator may ask if other related contingencies or issues need to be discussed. For example the mediator could ask, "Since you run a five-day-a-week business, does it matter which day Sarah will take off and does it need to be the same every week?"

As the agreement solidifies, the mediator rewords the language of the agreement as necessary for *concreteness, behavioral focus, timelines, contingencies* and other *specifics* for implementation of the agreement. Reality testing can be done as the agreement evolves. In Sarah's case, her boss preferred that she work Monday through Thursday, and Sarah agreed. Therefore the agreement included mention of the Monday through Thursday work week. On completion of all of the issues to be negotiated, the mediator can ask about the inclusion of "future communication" or "future conflict" clauses.

Final Reading and Signing

When the entire agreement has been crafted, the mediator will read the entire agreement to the parties. Ideally, parties have a draft of the agreement in front of them while it is read and discussed. The mediator and the disputants can modify the agreement, as necessary. At this point, the disputants may need to have their agreement reviewed by another party (such as their attorneys, family, constituents) prior to signing. If agreements are not signed at the drafting of the document, a signing ceremony might be scheduled.

The *signing ceremony* brings the parties back to sign the agreement. While not always necessary, the signing ceremony serves an important function. When parties are in the room together, there is an impetus to complete the agreement by signing it. When parties are at home and receive the agreement in the mail to return, agreements tend to become deprioritized. While not all agreements require signatures, the act of signing provides an extra measure of ownership over the agreement. Finally, the signing ceremony provides a chance to ensure that all parties receive copies of the agreement at the same time.

Occasionally, the signing ceremony may evolve into an extended mediation over some detail of the agreement. The mediator should have a reasonably clear schedule when parties return for a signing ceremony to allow time for any added negotiations.

To create durable agreements, parties need to leave the mediation table believing that their interests were met and that *they* created the agreement. Disputant ownership of the agreement is a primary goal for mediators when leading parties through the agreement process. On reflection, parties should consider that they achieved better results with the mediation process than they could have achieved elsewhere and that their interests were addressed in the final agreement.

Closing a Nonagreement Mediation

Sometimes mediations do not end in agreements. This is not the mark of a failed mediation. The true success of a mediation lies in how the relationship between the parties has been affected and how prepared they are for their next steps. If the parties have a greater understanding of the other or of their future options, then a mediation can be considered a success. The key here is not to become ego-involved in reaching agreements or to pressure disputants to settle. Disputants may not be able to agree, but that is not necessarily a reflection on the mediator.

The process of ending a nonsettlement mediation should be blame free. The mediator might explain, "Sometimes mediation isn't for everyone or every dispute." Take ownership as the mediator for ending the mediation. Use "I" language. The mediator could explain that he or she has exhausted his or her skills and feels that the mediation is not making any progress. Validate the parties' feelings. Explain that their effort in seeking mediation was worthwhile and review their progress. Facilitate the parties in generating options for where to go next. The mediator may need to outline why the process and goals inherent in mediation no longer match their case. Sometimes cases do not settle. The mediator must be prepared for those occasions with a strategy to provide closure for the disputants.

Summary

Agreement writing serves an important function in the mediation process. The agreement document provides evidence of the settlement and allows the disputants to have a concrete resource for reviewing the specifics of what is expected of them. When the parties have a large role in agreement creation, it increases their feelings of ownership over the outcome.

Informal nonwritten agreements occur when parties verbally agree and do not require written documentation. Informal agreements work best when parties have a history of trust in each other and a continued relationship. Informal written agreements, the focus of this chapter, serve to memorialize the mediation event. Crafting formal written agreements requires advanced training. Courts, businesses, and governmental agencies often require mediated agreements to be written in specified formats. Advanced training on this type of agreement writing is required for practitioners. Formal legal agreements, or legally binding agreements, usually are the domain of attorneys. Nonattorney mediators who embark in contract writing may be guilty of engaging in the unauthorized practice of law.

The language of an agreement should be direct, clear, and phrased positively. Mediators should take care to see that the parties are represented fairly and equitably in the agreement writing. Choosing a proper level of abstraction is necessary to make agreements as strong and clear as possible. Mediators should use the words of the disputants as much as possible.

In creating durable agreements, the mediator should reality test the specifics of the agreement to see if it is reasonable and workable. Developing contingency agreements is one way to have parties consider alternate futures.

Not all mediations will end in agreements, and mediators should be aware that this is not the mark of a failed mediation. Success is measured in improved relationships, greater understanding, and clarity on where the disputants go next. Strategies for ending mediations positively include the mediator taking some ownership for the mediation ending and helping parties to problem solve their next steps.

11 The World of the Mediator

Our task is not to fix the blame for the past, but to fix the course for the future.
—John F. Kennedy

Mediators share President Kennedy's view that it is better to focus on the future than dwell on the past. After learning the balanced mediation model presented in this book, some readers will go on to additional training and become volunteer or professional mediators. Other readers may integrate the skills of mediation into their daily lives without formally practicing mediation. Whether professional or volunteer, all mediators share a value of building better futures.

This chapter delves into the world of the mediator by discussing some common variations on the basic mediation model, examining mediation as a profession, delineating a checklist of skills for mediators, and suggesting ways to integrate the skills of mediation into everyday life.

Variations on Basic Mediation

The model of mediation presented in this book encompasses the phases and skills inherent in most models practiced in the field. While the phases may be labeled differently, and specialized skills for a specific arena of mediation may be added, the balanced mediation model should serve the novice mediator well.

While there are innumerable variations on the basic model, we will mention three that are common: co-mediation, panel models, and extended pre-mediation.

Co-Mediation Models

As we stated earlier, sometimes a team of two mediators is useful to balance power, culture, or other variables. Some professionals prefer to work in teams to balance their own strengths and weaknesses or to share the workload. Mediator trainees customarily co-mediate with experienced mediators as a part of their internship or development process.

When co-mediating, the mediators should discuss in advance how they will coordinate their work. Mediators need to address a variety of process and tactical questions:

- Will one mediator take the lead role and the other mediator a supportive role?
- Will each take the lead in a particular phase of the mediation?
- Will both take notes or just one?
- How will the co-mediators signal a desire to speak privately together or to gain the floor?
- Will the mediators discuss what to do next in the mediation in front of the parties (to model positive communication) or in private?
- How will one mediator take the lead when he or she sees a critical opportunity to transform the conflict?
- Who will take the lead in formulating the agenda?
- Who will draft the tentative agreements?

When both mediators will be active in the process, each should be included in the opening statement so the disputants become accustomed to both talking and exerting process control. Co-mediators could each deliver a portion of the mediator's opening statement or the lead mediator could include the other mediator by asking him or her a questions such as, "Is there anything else we should do before we begin?"

Many co-mediators will model positive communication with each other in front of the disputants by discussing what they should do next during the session. For example, if the lead mediator is at a loss about what question to ask next during storytelling and issue identification, he might turn to his co-mediator and say, "Natalie, I feel that we're starting to get a general picture of the circumstance that brought Jamal and Henry here today, but I'm not sure we have all the issues on the table yet. What do you think we should do next?" Natalie might respond: "Well, let's ask each of them if there are other issues that they would like to discuss before we move on to the next phase."

Panel Model

Any model that uses more than two mediators is called a *mediation panel*. Sometimes all of the panelists are highly trained professionals. More often, however, panels are used in programs where some mediators have less-intensive training. Community mediation is one arena where mediation panels are common. For example, the original community boards model from San Francisco used three volunteer mediators: two co-mediator lead specialists and one note-taking specialist. Each co-mediator on the panel could be attentive to one of the disputants at all times, because they were relieved of the need to take notes or track issues. The note-taking specialist recorded issues and commonalties and summarized when requested by the lead mediators and when the parties were ready to begin negotiating.

Panel models offer four advantages to mediation programs. First, novice mediators have a safe environment for their inaugural mediations. Second, the role of note-taking specialist is available to volunteers who choose not to pursue the mediator role. Third, the panel model provides consistency in training new mediators to use a particular model. Finally, the camaraderie of panel mediation is a recruitment asset for volunteer programs. Volunteers may enjoy the companionship of serving with others on a panel.

Extended Pre-Mediation

Professional mediators, particularly those who accept high-conflict cases, may engage in extensive pre-mediation activities. In addition to the pre-mediation functions discussed in Chapter 4, the mediator engages in the functions of the storytelling and issue-identification phase. In lengthy or multiple sessions, the mediator interviews each party to identify and work through emotional barriers to settlement, encourages disputants to accept responsibilities for their own feelings and behaviors, and extensively coaches the disputants on how to talk to each other. Some transformative mediators believe the success of the mediation depends more on the work during the extended pre-mediation than the events during the joint session.

Victim-offender mediation models typically have extended pre-mediation. After the victim and the offender are interviewed to ensure that they fit the qualifications for victim-offender mediation, a mediator meets several times with the victim and the offender privately. The mediator works through the stages, including potential outcomes, with both parties and coaches them on how to communicate with the other. Mediators may work extensively with the offender on how to show personal responsibility for his or her actions. Mediators work extensively with the victim on fear or anger management and on how to express feelings in front of the offender. Individual work with the parties can span several sessions. The mediator only will schedule a face-to-face meeting when assured that the victim and the offender can be brought together productively, without revictimizing the victim. Extensive training is provided by victim-offender programs in the skills of extended pre-mediation.

Mediation and the Internet

Online dispute resolution (ODR) evolved from a focus on interpersonal disputes in the 1990s to become an explosion of business cases in 2000 (Solovay & Reed, 2003). Through consulting businesses such as Square Trade and OnLine Resolution, individuals in different states or countries can work out disputes that cross geographic boundaries. The largest source of on-line business is the Internet auction company e-Bay, that generates over 75,000 cases a year when buyers and sellers need assistance to work out the details of their agreement.

ODR is most appropriate when both parties have regular and affordable access to the Internet, all parties (and the mediator) can read and write moderately well, disputants are prepared in advance, a private (password protected) means of discussion is available on-line, and face-to-face mediation is not an option or not desirable for other reasons (Hammond, 2003; Raines, Helie, & Rule, 2002).

To learn more about ODR, visit:

The ODR Newsletter: http://www.odrnews.com/
Public Disputes Online: http://publicdisputes.org/

Mediation as a Profession

Thirty years ago, hardly anyone knew that mediation existed and few practitioners considered themselves professional mediators. Today, mediators abound in the public and private sector. Mediation is in a stage of development where it is practiced both as a volunteer activity and a profession. The Rand Institute in 1997 estimated a 300 percent increase in the demand for court-connected mediation in the next few years (Mosten, 2001). Private citizens are encouraged to learn mediation to be of service to their community as volunteer mediators. Mediation also is a professional occupation with certification or licensure and standards of practice. Mosten's book, *Mediation Career Guide,* provides detailed information about establishing a private practice or looking for a job as a government mediator.

Standards of Professional Conduct

Throughout this book, we have presented ethical issues for mediators. Ethical issues apply to the volunteer and the professional. Both groups have responsibilities to those they serve and to the larger community. Those who practice mediation should be aware of the standards of practice in their jurisdictional area and keep informed on new developments in the field. Membership in a professional mediation association, at the state, province, or national level, is one method of staying current with the community of mediators and a changing legal environment for mediators. Professional mediators are expected to continue their education in mediation and to expand their skills and knowledge through classes, training workshops, or conference discussions.

Professional Mediator Competencies

Not all mediators feel comfortable in every setting. Some mediators have the talent and disposition to work with juveniles who have entered the criminal jus-

FIGURE 11.1   Mediator Skills Checklist

Mediators Should Have the Ability To

Analyze

- ☐ Distinguish between interests and positions
- ☒ Differentiate among types of issues and the strategies that apply to each issue
- ☐ Analyze the problem from the various perspectives
- ☐ Differentiate emotional from substantive issues
- ☐ Reframe positions into mutually solvable issues
- ☐ Identify commonalities

Communicate

- ☐ Elicit interests from others
- ☐ Convey the expectation that disputants will be cooperative
- ☐ Model cooperative behavior
- ☐ State and explain their own needs and expectations
- ☐ Check perceptions
- ☐ Listen to defuse emotions
- ☐ Listen for facts
- ☐ Paraphrase and validate emotions
- ☐ Paraphrase substantive content
- ☐ Ask "How" and "What" questions
- ☐ Make "I" statements
- ☐ Teach disputants how to make "I" statements
- ☐ Articulate BATNA (Best Alternative to a Negotiated Agreement)

- ☐ Articulate WATNA (Worst Alternative to a Negotiated Agreement)
- ☐ Summarize a disputant's needs clearly
- ☐ Write agreements in concrete, measurable language

Coordinate

- ☐ Facilitate the creation of a pool of possible solutions
- ☐ Integrate options for solutions
- ☒ Facilitate the creation of objective criteria for solutions
- ☐ Set agendas for formal negotiation

Exhibit Flexibility

- ☐ Be open to creative solutions
- ☐ Forgive and permit others to save face
- ☐ Adapt to the style of others
- ☐ Be sensitive to cultural variations among disputants
- ☐ Create closure when a mediation terminates

Control

- ☒ Redirect unnecessary competition
- ☐ Deal with difficult people
- ☐ Ignore positions
- ☐ Establish ground rules for negotiation
- ☐ Appropriately respond to negative attacks

tice system. Others are more suited to work with high-conflict divorce and child custody cases. Community-minded individuals might find a home in community mediation where they help neighbors work through their disagreements. Some are comfortable in working with highly technical business cases. Many mediators will specialize in only one context, where others will mediate in multiple contexts.

Each mediator, through guided practice and experimentation, will discover her or his strengths and preferred practice areas.

Figure 11.1 presents a checklist of skills for mediators. Obviously, it is difficult to master all of these skills during a single class or workshop. The acquisition, development, and mastery of mediator knowledge and skills is a lifelong process.

For those readers who choose to become mediators, we offer this advice: Learning new skills is a difficult task. Be diligent, but recognize that mediation is a process. Learn the techniques, but be open to intuitive insights that will help you work with the disputants. Experiment with different contexts of mediation and models. Work with a mentor or professional mediator. Watch and learn from others. Join a community of mediators and stay connected to that community. Find areas of practice that meld your personality and skills in a comfort zone that works for you. Forgive yourself when you make mistakes. Most of all, be patient with yourself as you develop your skills and be patient with the disputants you work with as they strive for their own comfort zones within negotiated agreements.

ACTIVITY 11.1

Research the mediation community in your area. What volunteer or professional groups exist? Interview a mediator regarding her or his professional memberships and continuing education strategies.

Mediation Skills in Everyday Life

Many readers of this book will never become professional mediators—both because there is not a large market for entry-level professional mediators, and because they have other career plans. The latter group may be of service to their local community through volunteer or part-time work or use their skills in other contexts. Individuals trained in mediation are invaluable group members in the team approach that abounds in the modern workplace. Bringing the skills of reframing and summarizing to any meeting can enhance a group's effectiveness.

Individuals trained in mediation also can reap personal benefits. An awareness of the causes of interpersonal conflict, behaviors that provoke defensiveness, or enhanced abilities to listen and paraphrase can provide insight into one's own interpersonal conflicts.

The Promise of Mediation

While mediation is no panacea for all of the world's ills, mediation does offer hope to individual citizens and communities—hope that difficulties can be resolved without becoming violent or winding up in court. In 2002, the EPA and timber

> **MEDIATOR NOTEBOOK 11.1**
>
> **A Lifelong Approach to Mediation Skills**
>
> Examine the checklist of skills in Figure 11.1. Evaluate your current skill in each area on the checklist. Do you feel "not at all competent," "somewhat competent," "or very competent" in each skill on the checklist? For any items listed as "not at all competent," what actions will you take to improve your skills or knowledge? Which items would be the most important to work on first and which items could be part of a multi-year plan? As this chapter suggests, acquiring skills is a lifelong process for mediators.

company Boise Cascade settled a Clean Air Act violation case worth $20 million—believed to be the first mediated settlement of the Clean Air Act—saving millions of tax dollars that might otherwise have been spent on litigation (Boise Cascade, 2002). Literally thousands of individuals and businesses have settled their disagreements with the assistance of a mediator. Mediators are drawing some communities closer together by healing neighbor relationships. Through mediation programs tied to the juvenile justice system, children are being given a second chance. Mediation is making a difference in people's lives.

Summary

This book presented information for beginning mediators. The world of the mediator includes many models of mediation. Variations on the balanced mediation model include co-mediation, panels, and extended pre-mediation.

Professional mediators are expected to uphold appropriate standards of conduct and to maintain their professional competence. Individuals who learn the skills of mediation have opportunities to exhibit their competence at work and in personal relationships.

Mediation is making a difference and improving people's lives. While we do not wish to overstate the potential of mediation, neither do we wish to underplay its possibilities. Mediation is a profession and a service activity with enormous transformative potential.

APPENDIX A

Mediation and Culture Readings

Avruch, K. (2003). Type I and Type II errors in culturally sensitive conflict resolution practices. *Conflict Resolution Quarterly, 20*(3), 351–372.

Barnes, B. L. (2002). Building conflict resolution infrastructure in the Central and South Pacific: Indigenous populations and their conflicts. *Conflict Resolution Quarterly, 19*(3), 345–362.

Brigg, M. (2003). Mediation, power, and cultural difference. *Conflict Resolution Quarterly, (20)*3, 287–306.

Diamant, N. J. (2000). Conflict and conflict resolution in China: Beyond mediation-centered approaches. *Journal of Conflict Resolution, (44)*4, 523–546.

Galaway, B., & Hudson, J. (1996). *Restorative justice: International perspectives.* New York: Criminal Justice Press.

Gudykunst, W. B., & Gao, G. (1990). Uncertainty, anxiety, and adaptation. *International Journal of Intercultural Relations, 14,* 301–317.

Honeyman, C., & Cheldelin, S. I. (2002). Have gavel, will travel: Dispute resolution's innocents abroad. *Conflict Resolution Quarterly, (19)*3, 363–372.

Irving, H. H., Benjamin, M., & San-Pedro, J. (1999). Family mediation and cultural diversity: Mediating with Latino families. *Mediation Quarterly, (16)*4, 325–339.

Ma, R. (1992). The role of unofficial intermediaries in interpersonal conflicts in the Chinese culture. *Communication Quarterly, (40)*3, 269–278.

Ogawa, N. (1999). The concept of facework: Its functions in the Hawaii model of mediation. *Mediation Quarterly, (17)*1, 5–20.

Tan, N. (2002). Community mediation in Singapore: Principles for community conflict resolution. *Conflict Resolution Quarterly, (19)*3, 289–302.

Umbreit, M. S., Coates, R. B., & Roberts, A. W. (2000). The impact of victim-offender mediation: A cross-national perspective. *Mediation Quarterly, (17)*3, 215–231.

Yarn, D. H. (2002). Transnational conflict resolution practice: A brief introduction to the context, issues, and search for best practices in exporting conflict resolution. *Conflict Resolution Quarterly, (19)*3, 303–320.

APPENDIX B

Role Plays

Role Playing a Mediation Case

Role playing is an integral part of learning. During role plays, mediators have an opportunity to explore the phases of the balanced mediation model and to develop specific skills. Role players develop an appreciation for the feelings, styles, and tactics that disputants may bring to the mediation table.

When role playing as the mediator, you should start with the opening statement and proceed through the phases. Your instructor may focus the role play on a particular phase of the mediation process, for example: opening statement through the end of the storytelling and issue-identification phase. When learning, it is important to work the phases in sequence, rather than skipping to negotiation or solutions too quickly.

When role playing as one of the parties, your job is to begin with the confidential information provided in the case and then add details that are in the spirit of the character that you are portraying. If the mediator asks you a question where the information is not provided in the case, answer the question by making up the detailed answer. For example, the Case of the Broken Saw does not specify exactly how many years the two have known each other or details of other specific purchases that have been made in the past. If the mediator should ask you, "How long have you known Mr. Hughes?" make up an answer that fits the rest of the case description. Avoid exotic answers to questions that might unnaturally skew the experience for the mediator. For example, saying as the business owner that "The result doesn't matter, because I'm going to jail for embezzlement next month anyway," is not in the spirit of the case description and is not helpful.

Mediators and character players should avoid stepping out of character to analyze the case or to critique the mediator's behaviors and choices. If the mediator is at a loss, he or she should simply pause and consider what might be a good question to ask next, summarize, consult the mediator notebook for ideas, or seek counsel from the instructor.

Case of the Broken Saw

Case Information Provided to the Mediator

Party 1: J. McGuire, framing/construction contractor
Party 2: H. Hughes, owner of H&H Hardware
Type of Dispute: Customer complaint

J. McGuire called to work out an agreement over a broken saw the contractor claims was under warranty. The disputants have had one interaction, which did not resolve the problem. Both parties have strong feelings about how each has treated the other during their last interaction.

Confidential Information for J. McGuire, the Customer

You own a small construction/framing company and purchase your tools from H&H Hardware in your small community. You believe in supporting the "Mom and Pop" businesses, rather than in the warehouse retailers, even though you know that they can't buy their stock in bulk. Subsequently, you pay a little more for your tools, but supporting your local economy and other small business owners is important to you.

One and half years ago you bought a 9 inch, ¼ horsepower circular saw ($149.99) from H&H Hardware. The kid salesman you bought it from stated that it had a full three-year warranty. You have other saws that you primarily use in your framing work, and you wanted a "back-up" saw for those occasional jobs where you had an extra person helping you work. The saw gets used about four times a month and only for minor cuts.

You were cutting a board last week, and the saw seized up and quit. When you went back to the store, you found that the original "sales kid" went away to college. After telling your story first to one young man, then the "head" of sales, you were referred to H. Hughes, the owner. By this point you were a bit grumpy and short tempered. You insisted that the store needed to fix this saw and loan you one until you got the saw fixed.

The owner told you that the warranty didn't apply because you were a professional and that the conversation with the original sales kid didn't have a bearing on the "here and now."

As a framing/construction business owner, you *know* the expected quality of your equipment. You also know that the saw was used less than what many "nonprofessionals" would use it. You feel that the hardware store not only misrepresented the saw, but has handled your complaint poorly. You vow to tell everyone you know about your experiences with the hardware store in hopes of damaging their reputation.

A friend told you about mediation, and you thought you would give it a try. You called the mediation center.

Your Positions: Have H&H Hardware fix the saw and loan you another until it is fixed (even though you don't really need it).

Your Interests: You want to have the owner recognize that you bought the saw because of your belief in supporting a small-town business. Frankly, you didn't read the warranty until the saw broke. It does specify that this warranty is for nonprofessional use only. The original sales kid couldn't have known that you were a professional. You don't want to make an enemy of the store owner. This could hurt both of your businesses.

What You Might Be Willing to Accept in the Option-Generating Stage: You would pay the cost to have the saw fixed, after H. listens to you. If you feel like the store owner is really listening to you, you would be open to other reasonable solutions.

Confidential Information for H. Hughes, the Store Owner of H&H Hardware

You have owned a small hardware store for 23 years. You have survived the influx of large companies who suffer from a questionable customer-service reputation, but generally have lower prices. Your reputation is important to you, and you are well respected in this small community.

J. McGuire owns a framing/construction company and purchases many tools and supplies from your store. About a year and a half ago, J. McGuire bought a 9 inch, ¼ horsepower circular saw ($149.99) from your store. The sales kid who sold it was a real swindler. You have an incentive program for your sales staff, and this kid, Roger, would lie to his own mother to get a sale. You were pleased when he finally left the store to go back to college a month ago. You still have some anger left over about Roger's sales tactics. There have been several repercussions to his work since he left. And now J. McGuire is another one.

In most cases you "go to bat" for customers who experience problems with their tools and have even taken a loss on some of Roger's sales, just to keep the customer happy. But J. McGuire is a different story.

J. McGuire is a professional and should have known the limitations on the warranty. The owner's manual clearly states that the saw is not intended for commercial use. You feel that regardless of the former sales kid's claims, J. voided his warranty through the professional use of this saw. In addition, you are still a little miffed at J. for being a bit grumpy with you when you last spoke. J. insisted that the store needed to fix this saw and loan another saw until the current one got fixed.

You are concerned about the negative image that J. has of your store, and you know McGuire Construction is well liked in the community. You are afraid that J. may bad-mouth the business and hurt the store's reputation. You have been in business for a long time and you *know* the quality of the tools you sell.

Honestly, you think that with the pull you have with your vendors and sales reps that you could probably get the saw repaired or replaced under warranty. You contend, however, that J. McGuire's attitude precludes you from giving any special treatment.

The mediation center called you to set up a mediation after J. contacted them.

Your Positions: J. McGuire should have known that his saw was not under warranty and shouldn't expect you to do anything.

Your Interests: You are afraid of having your reputation tarnished. You don't want to make an enemy of J., and you would like to continue having McGuire Construction's business.

What You Might Be Willing to Accept in the Option-Generating Stage: Getting the saw fixed—and absorbing that cost if necessary—if J. won't bad-mouth the company. If you feel that J. is really listening to you, you would be open to other reasonable solutions.

Case of the Ad Agency and the Intern

Case Information Provided to the Mediator

Party 1: M. Olivero, intern
Party 2: Pat Harrington, agency owner
Type of Dispute: Intern and field supervisor conflict

M. Olivero is a student who is enrolled in an internship for Harrington, Inc., an advertising agency. Olivero has just been informed that (s)he will not be receiving a high grade for an internship for which (s)he believe (s)he has worked very hard. P. Harrington claims that the work initially was high quality, but is no longer deserving of high marks. The chair of the academic department has referred the case to the campus mediation program.

Confidential Information for M. Olivero, the Intern

You are a senior who took a one-year internship at an advertising agency at Harrington, Inc. You briefly thought about going into advertising, but after this internship, you are certain that this is not the career for you. You find the people you've worked with to be flighty and phony. Pat Harrington, a nice enough person, who owns Harrington, Inc., hired you. Harrington wanted an energetic student (probably as a frugality since an intern isn't paid as much as a regular employee). The first few months at the agency were great. You were treated well by Pat and Pat's spouse, Chris (who did all of the accounting/bookkeeping). They even ordered you cards that gave you the title "Media Director."

You had never worked in advertising before and had to learn most of the job by yourself. The woman you replaced spent one afternoon showing you the "ropes" of how to buy time from radio, television, and print media sources, and she gave you a book that had the station ratings. However, the media world is a lot like buying a used car. When you call an account representative from a radio station, you "barter" for the best buy. It took you a long time to feel competent in your demanding role. You knew you were being used as an employee rather than as an intern, but you also knew that the experience was rich, so you didn't complain. After five months, you are almost to the point where you don't have to look everything up for each media placement—you've just about got it down.

Early on, you even made some changes in how the clients' accounts were billed, streamlining the process so that the agency would get money faster from clients for the media time. Because of your ingenuity, you were given more responsibility for some of the monthly billings. You felt important and respected. Then it happened: Harrington decided to merge with a local graphic artist, Teresa, and the growth of the business had a bad effect on the atmosphere at work. You are ready to leave at the end of the semester, instead of finishing the year like you had told Pat you would. You feel badly, but you just can't take it anymore.

The business went from being a three-person operation to an office of ten in just one month. While you were able to handle the responsibilities given to you before the merger, you are overwhelmed now. Before you had time to look up every little thing (or ask, because Pat was around more often), but now you find yourself either working too slowly or making mistakes because you are expected to do too much. You are really upset that your work is not the best you can do, but you are in survival mode now. It seems that the artist, Teresa, is always calling you on the carpet for some minor thing. To top it off, you know that Teresa doesn't like you and has even told you that you are incompetent. Well of course you are! You're an intern who hasn't been appropriately trained!

The semester is ending, and you are hoping to get a decent grade out of this internship. You have decided to go to graduate school next year, but know if you get a "C" on this internship you may lose your shot at a very competitive graduate school. Your last evaluation, a "D," included feedback from Teresa, and you are worried that she will have a big impact on your final grade. You already told the agency that you will be ending the internship this semester and will not stay next semester as you had originally planned. They were given two weeks notice of your intentions to vacate the position. You don't have another internship lined up, but anything has to be better than this. It's just not fair that your grade can't be based on the job you took, instead of the nightmare it turned out to be.

Your Positions: Teresa shouldn't evaluate you. You should be evaluated on the original internship job description. You want an "A" for the internship, because you did a great job without sufficient supervision.

Your Interests: (Only reveal interests after being properly validated or questioned by the mediator.) You want a good letter of reference. You want to be recognized for your hard work. You don't want the internship to hurt your chances at graduate school by getting a five credit C.

What You Might Be Willing to Accept in the Option-Generating Stage: Have Pat be the only one to evaluate you—once you feel Pat understands your "side." If you feel that Pat is really listening to you, you would be open to other reasonable solutions, including maybe staying longer.

Confidential Information for Pat Harrington, the Agency Owner

You and your spouse, Chris, have always dreamed of having a successful advertising agency. The year has been tough financially, but you have survived, barely. You have been hiring students because they aren't as expensive to pay, and they are willing to work part-time, so you don't have to pay benefits. The intern position is that of "Media Buyer." Really, the job of Media Buyer isn't that difficult, so up until now there haven't been any problems. You had the student intern that previously worked for you train M. Olivero before leaving. The training was completed in an afternoon.

M. answered your want ad at the university for an intern. You liked how M. could take a joke and keep up with the artsy characters that hang out in an ad agency. M. asks lots of questions about things you think are simple but showed great initiative by helping streamline the billing process.

This fall, business really started to pick up. You landed a big car dealership as an account and ended up working with a talented graphic artist, Teresa. You recognized that Teresa has a lot of potential, and the two of you decided to merge your clients and business. This has been a very successful venture and has taken a three-person operation (you, your spouse, and M.) to an office of ten people—bringing in that much more business!

However, you are not able to be around the office as much as you used to be. M., you felt, had learned enough of the media-buying business to go it alone. Instead, you are being told by Teresa that M. is making lots of mistakes. At first you were skeptical about the bad reports, because M. had been so "on top of it." But, sure enough, when you double-checked M. Olivero's efforts, the work was not of the high quality you had come to expect. And to top it off, M. just announced that (s)he will be leaving in two weeks instead of staying for the year, like you had originally thought. The holidays are coming up and this a terrible time to leave. You know that the announcement is meant to get back at the company for some reason. You are really hurt that you are being "dumped"—particularly during the busy season!

It's too bad, because you really like M., but you are finding that because the work is not of the high quality it once was and that you are getting bad reports from Teresa (who, you get the feeling, really dislikes M.), you will have to grade the internship a D or maybe a C–. You know that Teresa does tend to believe the worst about people, but you don't want to offend her this early in your partnership together. Additionally, you don't want to fudge on grades because you have had a good working relationship with the department at the university, and you want to keep the good interns coming.

Your Positions: M. should not be rewarded for substandard work. M. should have talked to you if there was a problem.

Your Interests: (Only reveal after being properly validated and questioned by the mediator.) You don't want to be left short-staffed during the busy season. You don't want M. to taint the relationship with the university. You want to evaluate fairly.

What You Might Be Willing to Accept in the Option-Generating Stage: Keep Teresa out of the evaluation process and re-evaluate M. in light of what was discussed here today. If you feel that M. is really listening to you and makes some concessions, you would be open to other reasonable solutions.

Case of Waves at the Surf & Turf

Case Information Provided to the Mediator

Party 1: J. Fascilla, a new waiter
Party 2: B. Truba, head waiter
Type of Dispute: Employee conflict

B. Truba contacted you regarding a dispute with a coworker. B. is the supervising waiter at Surf & Turf restaurant. J. Fascilla is also a waiter at the same restaurant. You were informed by B. Truba that both parties are willing to come to mediation. B. didn't think it was fair to tell you any more without J. there, so you do not have any additional details about the case.

Confidential Information for J. Fascilla, New Waiter

You began working at Surf & Turf restaurant about two months ago. You fudged a little bit when you were hired, saying that you had restaurant experience—when in fact you had just worked fast food in your small hometown.

Surf and Turf is a bit more upscale than your previous job; they use real linens and glassware. You have been pretty confident that you can handle it. You didn't get much training; you just watched the waitress who was leaving for a day. But, how tough can this be? You are a good worker, and get along with almost everyone. Customers like you, and your tips have been about the same as everyone else's.

The only drawback to the job is B. Truba. It seems that B. is always watching over your shoulder in order to catch you making a mistake. Yes, you will bend a few food rules—especially the ones that seem kind of dumb (like how to place a plate down in front of a customer, or keeping your thumb off of the top of a plate when you are carrying it, or not putting your pencil behind your ear next to your hair). You have had it with B's pickiness.

One day B. got really mad at you as soon as you stepped into the kitchen. Okay, (s)he saw you lick a bit of cherry sauce off of your thumb before you picked up the next plate, but you were being really careful not to touch the top of the plate. The place was packed, customers had been waiting for their food, and you just didn't have the time to run and wash your hands before serving the next platter. B. saw you and yelled loudly enough for most of the staff (and probably customers) to hear, "That's it! I have had enough of your cutting corners. You are incompetent, and I am going to recommend that you are fired." B. did tell the assistant manager what happened, and the assistant manager recommended mediation to work out this "personality" problem. B. called and you've shown up for the mediation.

You were embarrassed by the comment and furious at how B. handled the situation. But most of all, you need the job and are afraid of losing it. You are working while going to school, supporting your two-year old daughter by yourself, and this place pays well, especially considering the tips.

Your Positions: You want B. to lighten up and leave you alone. You want the stupid rules to go away. You want B. to never yell at you again.

Your Interests: (To be revealed only after being validated and questioned by the mediator.) You want to do a good job and improve your tips. You want to feel valued and competent at your job.

What You Might Be Willing to Accept in the Option-Generating Phase: More training, even with B., if B. is nice to you. Establishing rules for how B. can remind you of the procedures. If you feel that B. is really listening to you, you would be open to other reasonable solutions.

Confidential Information for B. Truba, Head Waiter

You began working at Surf & Turf restaurant about twelve years ago. You are the top waiter and get the most tips. Your customers love you, and management appreciates how competent and efficient you are. You are the best waiter around. Surf and Turf is a bit more upscale than your average restaurant; they use linens and glassware.

While you were on vacation, J. Fascilla was hired to replace Karmela—a really bad waitress. You were happy to see Karmela go, but you can't believe how incompetent the new person is. J. Fascilla is fast and personable, you'll give her/him that, but s/he bends the rules like they don't even exist. This infuriates you because you recognize that the food rules are there for good reason—preventing disease and for aesthetics.

You are in line for a promotion to assistant manager at the new Surf & Turf that is being built across town. As such, you are pretty tight with the management, and you are concerned that J.'s mistakes are going to cost the restaurant customers. You have been watching pretty closely so that you can offer the management specific examples of the problem behavior.

You have documented J. Fascilla breaking the following rules:

1. Placing a plate down in front of the customer with the meat at the back of the plate. The meat should be in the front so that the juice doesn't drip on the other food on the plate.
2. J. lets a thumb rest on the top of a plate while carrying it.
3. J. puts a pencil behind the ear, next to the hair, uses it, and then doesn't wash his/her hands before moving from the pencil to the carrying of food. (Pencils should be in a pocket, not your hair!)
4. J. will pick up the tips (money) and not wash his/her hands before handling food.

You shared these observations with J. as the events occurred. One day, you saw J. lick a bit of cherry sauce off of a thumb before picking up the next plate. That was really the last straw. You saw J. do this and then yelled at him/her in the kitchen area. You said, "That's it! I have had enough of your cutting corners. You are incompetent, and I am going to recommend that you are fired." You did tell the assistant manager what happened, and the assistant manager recommended mediation. You called and you've shown up for the mediation.

You were embarrassed by the comment and you do regret losing your temper.

Your Positions: You want J. to stop bending the rules or leave the restaurant.

Your Interests: (Only reveal after being properly validated and questioned by the mediator.) You want to show that you are good management material and that you can work out a reasonable agreement with J. You are embarrassed and sorry for yelling. You need J. to follow the rules. You take pride in your work and want the restaurant to remain higher class.

What You Might Be Willing to Accept in the Option-Generating Phase: Retraining J. yourself, if she is willing to listen. Not yelling anymore. If you feel that J. is really listening to you, you would be open to other reasonable solutions.

Case of Waves at the Surf & Turf, McCorkle and Reese, *Mediation Theory and Practice,* Boston: Allyn & Bacon. Copyright © 2005 Pearson Education Group, Inc.

Case of the Daycare Dilemma

Case Information Provided to the Mediator

Party 1: F. Wiggins, parent of two children, ages 2 and 4
Party 2: E. Nearhoof, daycare provider
Type of Dispute: Business provider and customer

F. Wiggins called your office to mediate a dispute with her daycare provider, E. Nearhoof. Currently the kids are at home and Wiggins took off one week to be with them until this dispute is settled. The caseworker contacted Nearhoof to set up the mediation time, but was unable to gather any details about the issues in the case.

Confidential Information for F. Wiggins, Working Parent of Two Children

You are a working parent with two children, Mike and Jessica, ages 2 and 4. You originally wanted to stay home while your spouse worked full-time, at least until the children got into school, but you ended up getting a great job that you just can't afford to quit. However, you do feel some guilt about not being home with your kids. Your spouse is a schoolteacher who has summers off and long vacations, but for the fall and winter your kids need to be in daycare full time. You have a neighbor, E. Nearhoof, who runs an "in-home" daycare where you take your kids.

Initially, you took them to a large daycare, but you felt that your children were getting lost in the crowd. You were thrilled when you saw your neighbor taking in kids. You like Nearhoof's child, Benny. Benny is well behaved and clean, and you think that E. is a good parent. Your kids really love being at E.'s house and seem content.

Your children are, of course, beautiful. The problem lies in that one of the other children at the daycare is intellectually gifted. Alex is almost 4 and is far ahead of children in his age group. He was talking in full sentences by 18 months and reading at 2½. He is really amazing. You think that it is pretty cool that your kids are around such a smart kid all of the time, and you think that E.'s house is very enriching. However, you feel that Alex is getting a lot more attention than your kids and that E. is "playing favorites." When you come in to pick up your kids, it seems that E. spends more time talking about Alex's achievements that day rather than your own kids' achievements. Granted, you were really interested at first and probably encouraged such talk, but now you are tired of it.

E. takes the kids down to the park (about one block away) at least three times a week. About a month ago, your oldest, Jessica, fell off of the monkey bars and cut her leg badly enough to warrant stitches. You were upset that she was climbing so high, and you told E. that you would appreciate if your kids were watched more closely. You think that you hurt E.'s feelings, but you needed to say something.

Finally, you are tired of the way that E. does business. As E. is the only adult at her home daycare, if E. is sick, there is no one else to watch the kids. S/he has been sick two times in the last six months. If E.'s son, Benny, is sick, s/he will call you and tell you not to bring your kid over (you leave for work at 7:30 A.M.). One time E. called you at 6:30 in the morning to tell you not to bring the kids over! S/he also has made it very clear that you can't bring your kids over if they are sick (running a fever or a nose that isn't running clear). But, you have noticed that Alex was there last week, and he was obviously really sick. When your kids can't be in daycare, you have to rely on the kindness of your mother-in-law, who has agreed to be a "back-up" for your daycare. However, she lives 35 miles away from your workplace, and you hate not being able to give her any warning.

The final straw came on Friday of last week. You had a very important meeting and were called in the middle of it to "come get your kids." Michael (your 2-year-old) was running a fever and had been throwing up at daycare. There were only two hours left of the workday, and you were swamped. Your spouse, a high school coach, was away at a game that day. You told E. that you couldn't come over right then, that you were in the middle of an important meeting, and that s/he would have to keep the kids. E. got a little testy about it, and you simply reminded E. that s/he made exceptions for Alex, and s/he could make an exception for your kids just this once. You abruptly said, "Goodbye," and got back to your meeting.

When you picked up your kids two hours later, E. told you that she can't be taken advantage of and that you need to be more considerate or find another daycare provider. You left, and haven't brought your kids back since.

However, you can't find another place to watch your kids, and your kids are missing E.'s house and the other kids terribly. You really want them to go back, but you want some ground rules set. That is why you have come to mediation.

Your Positions: You want the same rules for everyone. You want E. to let you know the night before if s/he can't watch your kids. You want E. to keep your kids if they aren't *that* sick.

Your Interests: (Only reveal after being properly validated and questioned by the mediator.) You really don't want to change daycare providers; your children love E. You want to be treated fairly, and you want assurances that your kids matter as much as Alex. You want to hear about what your kids do each day, because you feel badly when you miss hearing something.

What You Might Be Willing to Accept in the Option-Generating Stage: Getting a call as early as possible when your children can't go to daycare the next day, even if that means in the middle of the night. You might be okay with arranging for a third-party to pick up your kids if they are sick. You'd like daily reports about how and what your kids do each day, even if it is in the form of a three-minute chat at the end of the day. If you feel that your neighbor is really listening to you, you would be open to other reasonable solutions.

Case of the Daycare Dilemma, McCorkle and Reese, *Mediation Theory and Practice,* Boston: Allyn & Bacon. Copyright © 2005 Pearson Education Group, Inc.

Confidential Information for E. Nearhoof,
Daycare Provider

You are a single parent who has one son, Benny (age 4). You had Benny while you were still in high school and worked hard to finish your high school degree. When you finished, you found that you could only get minimum wage jobs, which would barely pay for daycare. You decided to open a daycare of your own so that you could be with your son. You love what you do, and with the few kids that you take in, you are able to make ends meet financially.

You were excited when F. Wiggins started bringing in her two kids, Mike and Jessica (ages 2 and 4). That family obviously makes a good living, and with the addition of Mike and Jessica, you now are feeling more financially secure. Besides, you have grown to love Mike and Jessica, as you do all of the kids. Jessica is quite the storyteller and is a big help around the place. Mikey (the 2-year-old) is enthralled with toy trucks and is so easy to keep happy. You really don't want the kids to go.

There is another boy, Alex (aged 4), who is intellectually gifted. He was talking in full sentences by 18 months and reading by 2½ years of age. He is a handful, and his parents are a pain. But he is a good kid, and you like the community of children who you have at your home everyday. You really are amazed at Alex's achievements—you've never seen such a bright kid.

You take all of the kids down to the park (about a block away) at least three times a week. About a month ago, Jessica (F.'s oldest child) fell off of the monkey bars and cut her leg badly enough to require stitches. You felt horrible, but the accident could have happened to anyone. You were watching the kids and were really offended when F. told you that you "needed to watch the kids more closely." This hurt your feelings, but you never said anything else about it.

You also know that F. is angry about the way you run your daycare. You do this all by yourself, with no back-up help. Twice in the last six months you had migraine headaches—so painful that you couldn't really see. You didn't want to have kids around because you were afraid that you couldn't watch them carefully. So you called each parent and told him or her as soon as you thought everyone would be up, around 6:00 A.M. Also, you called everyone once a couple of months ago when your son was sick. You had been up all night with him at the hospital. He had a respiratory infection and you were scared when his breathing became shallow. You called everyone from the hospital around 6:30 A.M. The only parent who was really grumpy with you was F.—in fact, you didn't even get to tell the entire story before F. had to hang up.

You have a pretty strict policy regarding parents bringing sick kids to daycare. If they are running a fever or have other infection symptoms, you insist that they pick up their kids. Alex was sick last week, and you tried to call his folks to pick him up. But they were not at their work numbers. Alex's dad was away at a conference, and Alex's mom wasn't answering her cell phone (she's a real estate agent). You were really upset with her because you didn't want Alex there, and you let her know when she did show up that she needed to be available at all times. You don't think that this problem will happen again with Alex.

Last Friday, Michael started to run a fever and was vomiting. You called F. around 3:00 P.M. to come and get him because he was sick. F. said s/he was in the middle of an important meeting and couldn't come and get him until 5:00. F. then told you that you seem to make a lot of exceptions for Alex, and the least you could do was keep Mikey for two more hours, then she abruptly said "Goodbye," and hung up. You couldn't get past her secretary when you called back.

When F. picked up the kids at 5:00 P.M., you told her that you couldn't be taken advantage of and that you didn't want Mikey to infect the other kids. If s/he didn't like those rules, s/he needed to find another provider. F. has kept Jessica and Michael out of your house now for over a week.

Your Positions: Kids should not be at daycare when they are sick. Parents need to be able to pick them up when called. Parents should have a back-up plan when they can't pick up their kids or you can't provide care.

Your Interests: (Only reveal after being properly validated and questioned by the mediator.) Looking back on the whole situation, you wish that you and F. could work something out. You miss her kids and frankly are scared about making ends meet without them. You agreed to come to mediation so that you could set this matter straight. You want to be fair to everyone, but not be taken advantage of.

What You Might Be Willing to Accept in the Option-Generating Stage: Calling parents as soon as you know you won't be able to watch their kids. Having a "sick room" for emergencies. If you feel you've been heard and understood, you might be open to other reasonable solutions.

Case of Wood.com

Case Information Provided to the Mediator

Party 1: J. R. Keyes, programmer for Wood.com
Party 2: P. D. Moneymaker, chief financial officer for Wood.com
Type of Dispute: Employee conflict over scarce resources

The "Wood.com" company is a new start-up computer company that has been doing so well that they have moved their staff of twenty into a virtually new building. Some problems with the move have arisen that the company president (an 18-year-old computer whiz) has been unable to resolve.

The building is a new, two-story, steel and glass building near the river. One side of the building faces the river, and another side faces the new bridge across the St. Martin River.

Confidential Information for J. R. Keyes, Programmer for Wood.com

The "Wood.com" company is a new start-up computer company that has been doing so well that they have moved their staff of twenty into a virtually new building. Some problems with the move have arisen that the company president (an 18-year-old computer whiz) has been unable to resolve.

The building is a new, two-story, steel and glass building near the river. One side of the building faces the river and another side faces the new bridge across the St. Martin River.

You are one of the best programmers at the Wood.com company. The company manages the Internet sale of wood furniture from 100 manufacturers throughout the world. You personally created and maintain the Web site that has won several awards and attracted over 200,000 hits per day. The company really can't succeed without someone of your talents.

When the company moved into the new building, you assumed that you would get the second best office in the building, after the president. You were really amazed when P. D. Moneymaker, the company "accountant" wanted the same office. You and P. D. have been fighting over the office and the president finally sent you to mediation to work things out.

It is important to you to have an office that says you are successful and respected. Of course, it needs to have fast computer modem access too. Anybody who is important will have a view of the river. You spend so much time in your office at the computer, that a view is really nice. The office you want has access to the nice bathroom in the executive suites. You hardly ever leave the office and have very little interaction with the others in the company—except by e-mail. You're not too sure what everybody else does, except the other programmers that you work with.

Your Positions: You should get the nice office by the river because you spend much more time at the company and you are so important to the business. There are plenty of nice offices on the other side of the hall for P. D. to occupy.

Your Interests: (Only reveal after being properly validated and questioned by the mediator.) You want recognition for the work that you do. You want other people to know that you are important. You want the company to succeed.

What You Might Be Willing to Accept in the Option-Generating Phase: An office across the hall if you get some recognition in the company in some other way. You are open to other suggestions that meet your needs.

Case of Wood.com, McCorkle and Reese, *Mediation Theory and Practice*, Boston: Allyn & Bacon.
Copyright © 2005 Pearson Education Group, Inc.

Supporting Document for Both Parties

First Floor

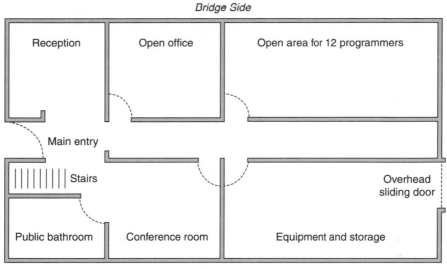

Second Floor

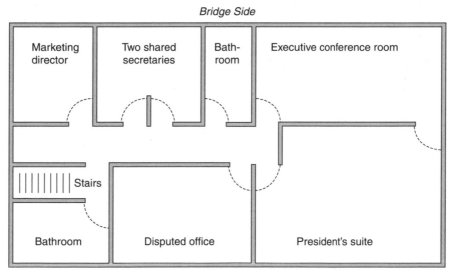

Confidential Information for P. D. Moneymaker, C.F.O. of Wood.com

The "Wood.com" company is a new start-up computer company that has been doing so well that they have moved their staff of twenty into a virtually new building. Some problems with the move have arisen that the company president (an 18-year-old computer whiz) has been unable to resolve.

The building is a new, two-story, steel and glass building near the river. One side of the building faces the river, and another side faces the new bridge across the St. Martin River.

In the old office building, you were in the office next to the president and were accustomed to just stepping across the hall for decisions regarding credit lines for companies, investment options, and what strategies to use with banks to acquire your start-up operating capital. As the chief financial officer, you are responsible for the entire fiscal and monetary strategy for the company, including recommending salaries and perks to top-performing employees. It is crucial that you be positioned to have a lot of face-to-face contact with the other key decision makers—the president and the marketing director. There is a suite of offices in the nicest part of the building facing the river that the president selected for the executive team. You don't understand why J. R., a programmer, wants to intrude into the executive suite. If you don't have constant access to the president and aren't successful in getting the needed continuous financing for the company, there won't be a company.

Most of the employees don't know what a thin line the company is walking on. You advised the president against the move into the new building, but were over-ruled. You have to admit, albeit grudgingly, that the area will help with the company's image and prestige. Sometimes it's really hard to work with the computer-whiz kids; they don't seem to have a very firm grasp of reality—everything is just a big video game to them. You can imagine what the bankers would think if they came and saw J. R. playing video games and eating pizza in the office next to the president.

Your Positions: You should get the nice office by the river because you are the chief financial officer and you deserve it. J. R. is merely a programmer.

Your Interests: (Only reveal after being properly validated and questioned by the mediator.) The image of Wood.com is important to you and you really want the company to succeed. You need the best office because you need access to the president, and you occasionally have important people meet you in the building.

What You Might Be Willing to Accept in the Option-Generating Phase: J. R. being in the executive area, but not in a place of high visibility. If J. R. is in the executive suite, J. R. needs to dress and act more professionally. There is a very small budget for building alterations. You might be willing to spend some of the money to meet J. R.'s needs, but only if J. R. is going to be reasonable.

Case of Wood.com, McCorkle and Reese, *Mediation Theory and Practice,* Boston: Allyn & Bacon. Copyright © 2005 Pearson Education Group, Inc.

REFERENCES

Allen, E. L., & Mohr, D. D. (1998). *Affordable justice: How to settle any dispute including divorce, out of court.* Encinitas, CA: West Coast.

Alliance for Education in Dispute Resolution. (2002). ADA mediation standards. [adopted 2000] http://ilr.cornell.edu/alliance/ada_mediation_standards.htm.

Australian Conflict Resolution Network. (2002). *Conflict kit.* http://www.crnhq.org/freechecklist.html.

Administrative Office of the U.S. Courts. (1999). http://www.uscourts.gov/press_release/98.case.html.

Antes, J. R., Hudson, D. T., Jorgensen, E. O., & Moen, J. K. (1999). Is a stage model of mediation necessary? *Mediation Quarterly, 16*(3), 287–301.

Arkansas Alternative Dispute Resolution Commission. (2002). Requirements for the Conduct of Mediation and Mediators.

Bagshaw, D. (1999). Developing family mediation standards: An Australian experience. *Mediation Quarterly, 16*(4), 389–406.

Bailey, J. D. (2000). *An exploration of empowerment in divorce mediation.* Unpublished doctoral dissertation, University of Houston.

Ballis Lal, B. (1995). Symbolic interaction theories. *American Behavioral Scientist, 38*(3), 421–441.

Barker, L. L., Johnson, P. M., & Watson, K. W. (1991). The role of listening in managing interpersonal and group conflict. In D. Borisoff & M. Purdy (Eds.), *Listening in everyday life: A personal and professional approach* (pp. 139–162). Lanham, NY: University Press.

Beck, C. J. A. (1999). *Family mediation myths and facts.* Unpublished doctoral dissertation, University of Arizona.

Beer, J. E., & Stief, E. (1997). *The mediator's handbook* (3rd ed.). Gabriola Island, B.C., Canada: New Society.

Binder, D. A., Bergman, P., & Price, S. C. (1996). Lawyers as counselors. In E. W. Trachte-Huber & S. K. Huber (Eds.), *Alternative dispute resolution: Strategies for law and business* (pp. 41–48). Cincinnati, OH: Anderson.

Boise Cascade, EPA settle air quality dispute. (2002, March 14). *The Idaho Statesman,* p. B1.

Borisoff, D., & Merrill, L. (1991). Gender issues and listening. In D. Borisoff & M. Purdy (Eds.), *Listening in everyday life: A personal and professional approach* (pp. 59–85). Lanham, NY: University Press of America.

Borisoff, D., & Victor, D. A. (1989). *Conflict management: A communication skills approach.* Englewood Cliffs, NJ: Prentice Hall.

Bradley, S., & Smith, M. (2000). Community mediation: Reflections on a quarter century of practice. *Mediation Quarterly, 17*(4).

Branham, S. (1999). Using facilitation and mediation to manage a Brownfields project. *EPA Pilots News, 2*(2). http://www.instrm.org/bfnews/v2i2/6facil.htm.

Bush, R. A. B., & Folger, J. P. (1994). *The promise of mediation: Responding to conflict through empowerment and recognition.* San Francisco: Jossey-Bass.

Cloke, K. (2001). *Mediating dangerously: The frontiers of conflict resolution.* San Francisco: Jossey-Bass.

Cohen, C. F. (1999, August). When managers mediate. *Dispute Resolution Journal,* 65–69.

Cohen, O., Dattner, N., & Luxenburg, A. (1999). The limits of the mediator's neutrality. *Mediation Quarterly, 16*(4), 341–348.

Cohen, R. (1995). *Students resolving conflict: Peer mediation in schools.* Glenview, IL: GoodYear Books.

Cooks, L. M., & Hale, C. L. (1992). A feminist approach to the empowerment of women mediators. *Discourse & Society, 3*(3), 277–300.

Cooley, J. W. (2001). *Defining the ethical limits of acceptable deception in mediation.* http://www.mediate.com/articles/cooley1.cfm.

Cupach, W. R., & Canary, D. J. (1997). *Competence in interpersonal conflict.* Prospect Heights, IL: Waveland.

Domenici, K., & Littlejohn, S. W. (2001). *Mediation: Empowerment in conflict management* (2nd ed.). Prospect Heights, IL: Waveland.

Donohue, W. A., Diez, M. E., & Weider-Hatfield, D. W. (1984). Skills for successful bargainers: A valence theory of competent mediation. In R. N. Bostrom (Ed.), *Competence in communication.* Beverly Hills: Sage.

Fisher, R., & Brown, S. (1988). *Getting together: Building relationships as we negotiate.* Boston: Penguin.

Fisher, R., & Ury, W. (1981). *Getting to yes.* New York: Houghton Mifflin.

Folger, J. P., Poole, M. S., & Stutman, R. K. (2001). *Working through conflict* (4th ed.). New York: Longman.

Galton, E. R. (1996). Mediation checklist. In E. W. Trachte-Huber & S. K. Huber (Eds.), *Alternative dispute resolution: Strategies for law and business* (pp. 369–375). Cincinnati: Anderson.

Galtung, J. (1969). Violence, peace and peace research. *Journal of Peace Research, 6*(2), 167–191.

Garcia, A. C. (2000). Negotiating negotiation: The collaborative production of resolution in small claims mediation hearings. *Discourse & Society, 11*(3), 315–343.

Gewurz, I. G. (2001). (Re)designing mediation to address the nuances of power. *Conflict Resolution Quarterly, 19*(2), 135–162.

Gibb, J. R. (1961). Defensive communication. *Journal of Communication, 11,* 141–148.

Gifford, D. G. (1996). A context-based theory of strategy selection in legal negotiation. In E. W. Trachte-Huber & S. K. Huber (Eds.), *Alternative dispute resolution: Strategies for law and business* (pp. 170–177). Cincinnati: Anderson.

Girard, K., & Koch, S. J. (1996). *Conflict resolution in the schools: A manual for educators.* San Francisco: Jossey-Bass.

Girdner, L. K. (1990). Mediation triage: Screening for spousal abuse in divorce mediation. *Mediation Quarterly, 7*(4), 363–376.

Global Arbitration Mediation Association, Inc. (2000). *History of alternate dispute resolution.* www.gama.com.

Hammond, A. M. G. (2003). How do you write "Yes"?: A study on the effectiveness of online dispute resolution. *Conflict Resolution Quarterly, 20*(3), 261–286.

Hatfield, J. T., Cacioppo, J. T., & Rapson, R. L. (1993). *Emotional Contagion: Studies in Emotion and Social Interaction.* Boston: Cambridge University Press.

Hayakawa, S. I. (1978). *Language in thought and action.* New York: Harcourt Brace Jovanovich.

Haynes, J. M. (1994). *The fundamentals of family mediation.* Albany: State University of New York Press.

Hebein, R. (1999). The prevention and cure of campus disputes. In S. M. Richardson (Ed.), *Promoting civility: A teaching challenge* (pp. 87–95). New Directions for Teaching and Learning, vol. 77. San Francisco: Jossey-Bass.

Heider, F. (1958). *The psychology of interpersonal relations.* New York: Wiley.

Irving, H. H., & Benjamin, M. (1995). *Family mediation: Contemporary issues.* London: Sage.

Isenhart, M. W., & Spangle, M. (2000). *Collaborative approaches to resolving conflict.* Thousand Oaks, CA: Sage.

Johnston, M. K., Weaver, J. B., Watson, K. W., & Barker, L. B. (2000). Listening styles: Biological or psychological differences? *International Journal of Listening, 14,* 32–46.

Judicial Council of Virginia. (2001). *Standards of ethics and professional responsibility for certified mediators.* [adopted 2000] http://www.courts.state.va.us/soe/soe.htm.

Kansas Supreme Court Dispute Resolution Advisory Council. (2002). *Model Local Court Dispute Resolution Procedures.* http:www.grapevine.net/~mediation/discussiondraft.html.

Keltner, J. W. (1987). *Mediation: Toward a civilized system of dispute resolution.* Annandale, VA: Speech Communication Association.

Kheel, T. W. (1999). *The keys to conflict resolution: Proven method of resolving disputes voluntarily.* New York: Four Walls Eight Windows.

Kosmoski, G., & Pollock, D. R. (2000). *Managing difficult, frustrating, and hostile conversations.* Thousand Oaks, CA: Corwin Press.

Kritek, P. B. (1994). *Negotiating at an uneven table: Developing moral courage in resolving conflicts.* San Francisco: Jossey-Bass.

Lax, D. A., & Sebenius, J. K. (1986). *The manager as negotiator: Bargaining for cooperative and competitive gain.* New York: The Free Press.

Leitch, M. L. (1987). The politics of compromise: A feminist perspective on mediation. *Mediation Quarterly, 14/15,* 163–176.

Lovenheim, P. (1989). *Mediate, don't litigate: How to resolve disputes quickly, privately, and inexpensively without going to court.* New York: McGraw-Hill.

Lulofs, R. S., & Cahn, D. D. (2000). *Conflict from theory to action* (2nd ed.). Boston: Allyn and Bacon.

Ma, R. (1992). The role of unofficial intermediaries in interpersonal conflicts in the Chinese culture. *Communication Quarterly, 40*(3), 269–278.

Mayer, B. (2000). *The dynamics of conflict resolution: A practitioner's guide.* San Francisco: Jossey-Bass.

McCorkle, S. (2001). *Critical questions about the ethical practice of mediation.* Western States Communication Association Workshop, Coeur d'Alene, ID.

McCorkle, S., & Mills, J. L. (1992). Rowboat in a hurricane: Metaphors of interpersonal conflict management. *Communication Reports, 5*(2), 57–66.

Mediation Council of Illinois. (2001). *Standards of practice for mediators.* http://www.mediate.com/articles.illstds.cfm.

Mediation Center of Kentucky. (2003). *Requirements for certified mediators.* [adopted 2000] http://www.mediationcenterofkentucky.com/standards.pdf.

Merry, S. E. (1990). The discourses of mediation and the power of naming. *Yale Journal of Law and the Humanities, 2,* 1–36.

Moore, C. W. (2003). *The mediation process: Practical strategies for resolving conflict* (3rd ed.). San Francisco: Jossey-Bass.

Mosten, F. S. (2001). *Mediation career guide: A strategic approach to building a successful practice.* San Francisco: Jossey-Bass.

Murray, J. S. (1996). Understanding competing theories of negotiation. In E. W. Trachte-Huber & S. K. Huber (Eds.), *Alternative dispute resolution: Strategies for law and business* (pp. 149–151). Cincinnati, OH: Anderson.

National Center for State Courts. (2003). http://www.wcsc.ndi.us/IS. HTML.

National Conference of Commissioners on Uniform State Laws. (2001). *Uniform Mediation Act.* Draft.

Nichols, M. P. (1995). *The lost art of listening: How learning to listen can improve relationships.* New York: Gilford.

NoLo. (2001). *The six stages of mediation.* NoLo's Legal Encyclopedia. http://www.nolo.com/encyclopedia/articles/cm/CM41.html.

Ogawa, N. (1999). The concept of facework: Its function in the Hawaii model of mediation. *Mediation Quarterly, 17*(1), 5–20.

Oregon Mediation Association. (2001). *Standards of practice.* [adopted 2000] http://www.to-agree.com/omastds.htm.

Peace, N. E. (2002). *Report on the ACR task force on the unauthorized practice of law.* http://www. acresoltion.org/research.nsf/key/UPL-Aug02.

Pennsylvania Council of Mediators. (2001). *Pennsylvania council of mediators ethics.* [adopted 1998] http://www.mediate.com/articles/pennethics.cfm.

Pepperdine University Institute for Dispute Resolution. (1995). *Advanced mediation practice: An interactive training program.* Malibu, CA: Pepperdine University School of Law.

Permanent Court of Arbitration. (2003). http://www.pca-cpa.org.

Phillips, B. (1999). Reformulating dispute narratives through active listening. *Mediation Quarterly, 17*(2), 161–180.

Picard, C. A. (1998). *Mediating interpersonal and small group conflict.* Ottowa, Canada: The Golden Dog Press.

Ponte, L. M., & Cavenagh, T. D. (1999). *Alternative dispute resolution in business.* Cincinnati: West Educational Publishing.

Pope, S. G., & Bush, R. A. (2000). Understanding conflict and human capacity: The role of premises in mediation training. *Family and Conciliation Courts Review, 38*(1), 27–40.

Raines, S. S., Helie, J., & Rule, C. (2002). *When and how should disputes be mediated online?* Association for Conflict Resolution Annual Conference, San Diego.

Ridge, A. (1993). A perspective of listening skills. In A. D. Wolvin & C. G. Coakley (Eds.), *Perspectives on listening* (pp. 1–14). Norwood, NJ: Ablex.

Roberts, M. (1997). *Mediation in family disputes: Principles of practice* (2nd ed.). Aldershot, England: Arena.

Saposnek, D. T. (1998). *Mediation child custody disputes: A strategic approach* (rev ed.). San Francisco: Jossey-Bass.

Schneider, C. D. (2000). What it means to be sorry: The power of apology in mediation. *Mediation Quarterly, 17*(3), 265–280.

Shailor, J. G. (1994). *Empowerment in dispute mediation: A critical analysis of communication.* Westport, CN: Praeger.

Simkin, W. E., & Fidandis, N. A. (1996). Mediation and the dynamics of collective bargaining. In E. W. Trachte-Huber & S. K. Huber (Eds.), *Alternative dispute resolution: Strategies for law and business* (pp. 847–854). Cincinnati: Anderson.

Singer, L. R. (1990). *Settling disputes: Conflict resolution in business, families, and the legal system.* Boulder, CO: Westview Press.

Singer, L. (2001). Best practices when training mediators. In R. M. Schoenhaus (Ed.), *Conflict management training: Advancing best practices* (pp. 22–24). Washington D.C.: United States Institute of Peace.

Slaikeu, K. A. (1996). *When push comes to shove: A practical guide to mediating disputes.* San Francisco: Jossey-Bass.

Sockalingam, S. & Williams, E. (2002). *Culture, conflict, consensus: Culturally competent mediation.* Association for Conflict Resolution Annual Conference, San Diego.

Solovay, N., & Reed, C. K. (2003). *The internet and dispute resolution: Untangling the web.* New York: Law Journal Review.

Standards for private and public mediators in the state of Hawaii. (2002). [adopted 1986] http://www.state.hi.us/jud/adrstds.htm.

Stephenson, M. O., & Pops, G. M. (1991). Public administrators and conflict resolution: Democratic theory, administrative capacity, and the case of negotiated rule-making. In M. K. Mills (Ed.), *Alternative dispute resolution in the public sector* (pp. 13–26). Chicago: Nelson-Hall.

Stienstra, D. (2003). *The Alternative Dispute Resolution Act of 1998: Seeds of change in the Federal District Courts.* National Center for State Courts. http://www.ncsc.ndi.us/IS.HTML.

Susskind, L. E., & Field, P. T. (1996). *Dealing with an angry public: The mutual gains approach to resolving disputes.* New York: The Free Press.

Texas Association of Mediators. (2001). *Standards of practice for mediators.* http://www.txmediator.org/codeof.htm.

Thomas, K. W., & Kilmann, R. (1977). Developing a forced-choice measure of conflict-handling behavior: The MODE instrument. *Educational and Psychological Measurement, 37*(2), 390–395.

Trachte-Huber, E. W., & Huber, S. K. (1996). *Alternative dispute resolution: Strategies for law and business.* Cincinnati: Anderson.

Umbreit, M. S., Coates, R. B., & Roberts, A. W. (2000). The impact of victim-offender mediation: A cross-national perspective. *Mediation Quarterly, 17*(3), 215–229.

United States Institute of Peace. (2001). *Conflict management training: Advanced best practices.* (R. M. Schoenhaus, Trans.). Washington, DC: Author.

Ury, W. L., Brett, J. M., & Goldberg, S. B. (1988). *Getting disputes resolved.* San Francisco: Jossey-Bass.

Van Slyke, E. J. (1999). *Listening to conflict: Finding constructive solutions to workplace disputes.* New York: American Management Association.

Van Winkle, K. M. (1997, Spring). Alternative dispute resolution: Approaches for public policy. *LBJ Journal of Public Affairs, 9,* 17–28.

Warters, B. (2000). *Campus Mediation Centers List.* www.mtds.wayne.edu/CMC.htm.

Warters, W. C. (2000). *Mediation in the campus community: Designing and managing effective programs.* San Francisco: Jossey-Bass.

West, R. L., & Turner, L. H. (2000). *Introducing communication theory: Analysis and application.* New York: McGraw Hill.

Wildau, S. T. (1987). Transitions: Moving parties between stages. *Mediation Quarterly, 16,* 3–13.

Wilmot, W. W., & Hocker, J. L. (2001). *Interpersonal conflict* (6th ed.). New York: McGraw Hill.

Wolvin, A. D., & Coakley, C. G. (1993). A listening taxonomy. In A. D. Wolvin & C. G. Coakley (Eds.), *Perspectives on listening* (pp. 15–22). Norwood, NJ: Ablex.

INDEX